How to Write and Sell
Your First Nonfiction Book

How to Write and Sell

Your First Nonfiction Book

Oscar Collier
with
Frances Spatz Leighton

St. Martin's Press
New York

Design by Amelia R. Mayone

Library of Congress Cataloging-in-Publication Data

Collier, Oscar.
    How to write and sell your first nonfiction book / Oscar Collier
with Frances Spatz Leighton.
        p.   cm.
    Includes bibliographical references.
    ISBN 0-312-03846-1
    1. Authorship.   I. Leighton, Frances Spatz.   II. Title.
    PN147.C755   1990
    808'.02—dc20   89-24190
                                                            CIP

First Edition
10 9 8 7 6 5 4 3 2 1

Contents

A Note to the Reader   **vii**

Part I: The World of Nonfiction Books and Authors

1. Write a Nonfiction Book and
Gain Satisfaction, Authority, and Cash   **3**

2. The World of Nonfiction
Books—Where Do You Fit In?   **18**

3. Should You Go It Alone or Get a Coauthor?   **31**

Part II: The Book Presentation Package: Key to a Contract

4. Targeting Your Audience—
The Vital First Step   **45**

5. Writing a Nonfiction Book Proposal   **53**

6. Assembling Bio and Exhibits to Add
Flash and Bulk to Your Presentation   **80**

Part III: **The Road to Publication**

    7. Money Talk—Agent Talk   **97**

    8. How to Target Publishers and
       Get Their Attention   **110**

    9. Understanding a Book Publisher's Contract   **120**

Part IV: **Gathering Your Material and Actually Writing It**

    10. The Art of the Interview   **137**

    11. The Art of Research—Search and Seize   **150**

    12. The Many Faces of the Biography   **166**

    13. Getting Down to the Actual Writing   **186**

    14. How to Deal with Editors and Copy Editors   **207**

    15. Writing the Whole Manuscript on
        Speculation—With Notes on Self-Publishing   **220**

Part V: **Helping Your Book Succeed**

    16. Publicity: Gravy Train or Treadmill?   **233**

    17. Keeping Your Book Alive   **250**

    18. Can This Be You Entering the
        World of the Writer?   **259**

    Checklist: What Makes a Good
    Nonfiction Book   **263**

    Acknowledgments   **265**

    Suggested Reading and Reference   **266**

    Index   **272**

A Note to the Reader

This book is a collaboration between a literary agent and a professional writer. Because my coauthor's career has included writing many kinds of nonfiction books, including some major best-sellers, we have drawn extensively from her actual experiences of coping with writers' problems—some amusing—and even have included a sample of one of her book presentations that went to a publisher and became a successful book.

And I have drawn on many incidents and anecdotes from my own career in book publishing—not only as an agent, but also as a book salesman, publicist, editor, and publisher. The richness of our joint experiences, however, has been generously supplemented by interviews with writers, editors, publishers, literary agents, and by research in books, magazines, and newspapers. And I would particularly like to thank George Sullivan for permission to include one of his excellent book proposals.

Throughout this book the "I" refers to me, the longtime literary agent. But much of the actual writing is by my experienced coauthor, Frances Spatz Leighton, whose talents include the skill of writing in the voices of her numerous coauthors.

Of the chapters you are about to read, each of us wrote half. Then my chapters were enhanced as they went through Fran's typewriter, and hers were edited and sometimes enriched by me.

We hope that this introduction to the world of nonfiction books will help take the fear out of your own first trip across this exotic landscape of nonfiction book publishing. May your first experience be a happy one!

—Oscar Collier
Seaman, Ohio

Part I

The World of
Nonfiction
Books and Authors

1

Write a Nonfiction Book and Gain Satisfaction, Authority, and Cash

If you want to write a nonfiction book, there is an excellent chance that you can sell it to a publisher. How do I know? Because the reading public's appetite for information, unusual experiences, and entertainment is truly enormous. Let me give you some proof.

THERE'S A MARKET OUT THERE

Each year 40,000 new nonfiction books are published in the United States—40,000 new book titles!

Think about that number for a while. Say it aloud. *Forty* thousand. Forty *thousand*. If you decided to read all the non-fiction books published in the United States in a single year, even if you were a speed reader and read a whole book each day, and you started when you were ten years old, you would be 120 before you finished. That's the size of the market. And in such a big market there's room for new writers—room for you.

NONFICTION VS. FICTION WRITING

It's much easier to get started writing nonfiction books than novels. The reason? Only an eighth as much fiction is published each year—only 5,000 new titles. And you have another big advantage as a nonfiction writer. You don't have to write a nonfiction book to sell it. Many would-be writers don't know that most nonfiction books are sold *before* they are written, from a brief presentation only. By contrast, most works of fiction, and practically all first novels, are sold only after they are finished, complete manuscripts. So in addition to having an eight-to-one sales advantage, you as writer of a nonfiction book will have to do much less work on speculation before being able to test your book idea on publishers.

And you have still another advantage: You don't have to be a great writer to sell a nonfiction book. Fiction sales depend almost entirely on the *skill* of the writer. Nonfiction sales depend, instead, on the *authority* of the writer, or on how interesting or exclusive your *subject matter* is. So if you are an expert on a subject, have desirable and interesting information, or can offer a new viewpoint on an old subject, there is a good chance that people will want to read your nonfiction book. They are hungry to share what you know and can tell them.

But best of all, your readers will judge your book on how interested they are in your subject, not on how well you write about it.

THIS BOOK IS AN EXAMPLE

Take a businesslike look at the book you're reading right now. It is one kind of nonfiction book. Two experts have teamed up and are sharing with you, the reader, their specialized information. I'm not a professional writer. I'm a literary agent, former book editor and book publisher who has helped bring more than a thousand books into being, and most of them were nonfiction.

Aspiring writers have come to me and told me that they

have ideas for books and have asked me how to present their material to book publishers and get their books published. I know what makes book presentations sell because I've bought them as editor and publisher and sold them as agent. Because of my experience, I decided there was a need for my expert information and that I could put it in book form.

WE'LL HELP YOU WRITE AS WELL AS SELL

Since this is a book on how to *write* a nonfiction book as well as sell it, I have asked a highly skilled and successful professional writer to work with me as a collaborator. My coauthor, Frances Spatz Leighton, has helped more than thirty people, as a hands-on-the-typewriter coauthor, actually write their unique experiences, or package their professional expertise, as published books.

And some of the books she coauthored have been major best-sellers. They made money in book form—and also as magazine condensations and excerpts, newspaper serializations, quotations in textbooks, TV movies and miniseries, paperback reprints, and foreign editions published in many languages.

Between us, the writers we have worked with have ranged from maids to movie stars, from secretaries to psychiatrists, from cooks to cabinet ministers—literally from A, an amnesia victim, to Z, a zookeeper. And all had fascinating nonfiction books to write and sell.

YOU CAN DO IT, TOO

We can tell you that regardless of your previous experience and background, if you want to sell and write a nonfiction book, we can help you. And we will not only share our own experiences, but also share with you many instructive success stories of other first-time authors.

We can help you choose a winning subject. We can tell you how to put a professional gloss on your work if you choose to write it yourself. If you prefer teamwork and don't mind

5

sharing the money your book earns, we can show you how to find and work with a professional coauthor.

Most important of all, we can tell you how to present and sell your nonfiction book in ways that will maximize its chances with a publisher, *before you write it.*

FACE YOUR DOUBTS—
THEN MEET TWO FIRST-TIME AUTHORS

Yeah, yeah, I can hear you saying: Sure, a literary agent and a famous writer can write and sell a book. But what about *me?* Let's face your doubts and difficulties right now.

- Can you really write a manuscript of 250 to 400 double-spaced, typewritten pages—60,000 to 100,000 words?

- Can you conquer your own uncertainty, then face the skepticism of spouse, family, friends, business or professional associates?

- Dare you expose your ideas, thoughts, experiences, knowledge to the unfeeling scrutiny of agents, editors, publishers, critics, booksellers, librarians, and the reading public?

I can feel for you, for I have witnessed the misgivings of other writers, even highly experienced ones.

A REPORTER WONDERS IF HE CAN WRITE A BOOK

I'll never forget the anguished phone call I received from Fred Sparks, a Pulitzer prize-winning reporter. As his agent, I had sold an outline-presentation of his first nonfiction book. It was to be an account of the first year of the marriage of Jacqueline Kennedy and Aristotle Onassis—*The $20,000,000 Honeymoon: Jackie and Ari's First Year.*

We had a publisher, Bernard Geis Associates, who enthusiastically agreed to pay a good advance against royalties, and had already paid half of the advance on signing the contract, even though not a single word of the book itself had been written.

Now Fred Sparks had a deadline of just six months to produce a finished manuscript on his timely subject, so he sat down to write. But there was a problem he hadn't thought of before.

"Oscar, I just realized I can't write a book. I reread the contract. It has to be *sixty thousand* words. I never wrote anything longer than three thousand words in my life. I'm a newspaperman, not an author. We'll have to return the money to Bernard Geis."

Horrified at the thought of returning money to a publisher, I quickly replied, "Fred, have you ever written a *series* of newspaper pieces? I know you have. You just sold a three-part series all over the world."

"Why, yes, many of them, around two thousand to three thousand words for each part. But even for a five-part series, that's around ten thousand to fifteen thousand words at most."

"Fred, a book is just a twenty-part series. You call the parts chapters. Instead of writing five three-thousand-word installments, you write twenty of them. That's sixty thousand words."

"You mean if I write a twenty-part series that's a book? Sure I can do that. Why didn't anybody tell me? Good-bye. I'm going to work."

And he did. The book he wrote not only succeeded in hardcover, but got a profitable paperback reprint deal from Dell Books, and an excerpt sold to *Ladies' Home Journal* for a nice piece of change. It was serialized in many newspapers and condensed in the *National Enquirer*. In one form or another, it was published in many countries all over the world, with each sale making additional money.

A SECRETARY WRITES A BOOK

Okay, that's clever, you say. But he was already a professional writer, used to meeting deadlines and turning out

7

copy. *You* never wrote anything longer than a school report or letter in your life. And even then you found it hard to stretch your thoughts out to fill enough pages.

Let's look at another example. Joan Wiener was a young secretary who worked for me when I was president of a small book publishing firm in New York. When she wasn't at work, she saw rock musicians and was interested in yoga. She was a vegetarian, and many of her young friends were too. She was a very sincere person who wanted only to do work that she believed would contribute positively to life on earth.

After a couple of years she quit to get married, and I sold the publishing company and began to work as a consultant for American Express on travel books.

One day I got a phone call from Joan. "I'm pregnant, and I'm working as a temporary secretary. I want to do something worthwhile. How can I get out of this trap?"

Because Joan was an interesting and lively person, I invited some American Express executives to have lunch with her, to see if together we could help her—possibly with a job at American Express.

The lunch was a sparkling experience, and the executives were fascinated. But afterward one approached me and, speaking for the others as well, said, "She is too original, too sincere and idealistic to make it in a large company. She should go into business for herself."

When I called Joan and gave her their message, she replied, "That's fine. But in business doing what? I don't have any skills except typing, taking dictation, and filing."

"You're a pretty good vegetarian cook. I know you feed your husband and a crew of young friends all the time. Why not write a vegetarian cookbook for today's young people? You're different from the vegetarians of the past."

"Oscar, you know it's hard for me to write even a letter on my own. How can I write a whole book?"

"Joan, don't you think you could write *one* recipe? All you have to do is write a list of ingredients, give directions how you use them to make a dish, and say how many it will serve."

"Sure, I can do that. In fact, I have a few recipes already."

"A cookbook is just a collection of a hundred or more recipes. If you can write one, you can write a hundred—and you'll have a cookbook."

Joan wrote a dozen sample recipes, a short introduction telling whom the book was for, and assembled a table of contents. I made a large multiple submission of her presentation to twenty publishers at once, and Alan Rinzler, then a senior editor at Holt, Rinehart and Winston, offered her a contract.

With the help of her friends, she wrote the book, Holt published it and sold more than 20,000 hardcover and paperback copies. Ballantine Books reprinted *Victory Through Vegetables* in a mass-market paperback edition that sold many more copies. Publishers in Holland and Mexico brought out foreign editions. Joan, who now writes under the name of Joan Bordow, was launched into a career and now has written ten books, all on subjects she considers worthwhile—motherhood, nutrition, sewing, coping with grief after the death of a child, baking, and other subjects.

WHAT IS A NONFICTION BOOK?

The point of these stories is that most nonfiction books are simply collections of information, organized in a handy way. You don't sit down and write 60,000 words at a gulp. You break your book idea into parts and chapters. And you write each part, a sentence, a paragraph, a page at a time. Eventually the sentences, paragraphs, and pages accumulate into a chapter and the chapters into a book. A chapter, incidentally, is simply a segment of a book that makes a particular point or advances a step in your argument, theme, or set of instructions.

Fred Sparks collected, with heroic legwork, all the facts he could about how Aristotle Onassis spent money on his new wife during their first year of marriage. How many jewels did he give her? How much did each cost? How many residences did he have for her and himself? What did it cost to use them? How did they travel—by yacht, by air, by limousine?

How much did each mile cost? The result of the accumulated facts was a surprising and entertaining book-length story of something very unusual—a one-year honeymoon that cost $20,000,000 by his best estimates, together with the story of how he got his information.

Joan Wiener Bordow collected and adapted recipes for the kind of vegetarian cookery young people of her age were interested in. She tested, perfected, and wrote up her recipes in her own words one recipe at a time. And her book succeeded because it was launched during a time when there was a flood of interest in vegetarian cooking with its high-fiber, health-enhancing, and weight-controlling qualities.

GETTING STARTED

There's no big mystery about how to get started on your first book. There are several ways. You can start by collecting information—at libraries or elsewhere. You can start by writing down bit by bit what you already know. You can just make loose notes or write a series of essays. If you choose, you can start by interviewing others on the subject of your choice. If it's a book of remembrance, you can start by going through your diaries and souvenirs.

Don't let the idea of a book intimidate you. You don't need to know everything there is to know about a subject. You are going to draw a line around just a particular aspect of it and make that part of it your own. You don't want to boggle the mind of the reader. No, you just want to make a little corner of the subject come to life in the reader's mind as no one else ever has before.

And if the information you have collected one way or another is useful, inspiring, unusual, timely, persuasive, entertaining, or exclusive, a publisher will be interested. And if readers like your writing style, they will praise you and tell their friends to buy your book. But even if you merely write it adequately, if the information is in demand, they will buy it anyway—and you will have gained *satisfaction, authority,* and *cash.*

MOTIVATION FOR WRITING THAT BOOK

So now let's talk about motivation and meet a few writers I know to see how they were motivated. You might find you have much in common with one or another of them.

WRITING FOR THE SATISFACTION OF SELF-EXPRESSION

Let's imagine that your name is John R. Coleman. Your friends call you Jack. You have many friends. You're an administrator. You're at the top of your profession. You are responsible for a great deal of money. You have even written, in collaboration with other experts, some technical works on your specialty. But you are restless. You want to get away and try, even if briefly, something new, fresh, and most of all, different.

You are fifty and divorced. Your children are grown up or in college. You can arrange, because you are in the academic world, a sabbatical period—a few months off. What will you do?

Well, the name is real and so was his dilemma. His heart's desire was so far removed from his lofty position—what would people think?

John R. "Jack" Coleman, president of Haverford College, labor economist, chairman of the Federal Reserve Bank of Philadelphia with nominal responsibility for two billion dollars, and collaborator on academic books by such significant figures as Nobel prize-winner Paul A. Samuelson and George P. Schultz, later Secretary of State, admitted it to himself. "I want to try my hand at manual work."

It wasn't a sudden yen. In fact, he later confessed that "every time in recent years I looked ahead to some time out, my thoughts turned to seeking and holding blue-collar jobs. The idea of breaking out of what I normally do and taking up different roles for a while was so compelling that I would have felt cheated had I done anything else."

So in the spring, without letting anyone except his son know what he was planning, Jack Coleman drove away from

Haverford, Pennsylvania, for a few months and looked for a job doing physical labor. He was not consciously doing research for a book—he was embarking on a grand adventure. He took along only a car, $200 in traveler's checks, clothes, a few cooking utensils, and books. To get home in an emergency, he had a gasoline credit card.

For the next eight weeks, as he later detailed in fine plain prose in his book *Blue Collar Journal*, he worked as a ditch digger, restaurant worker, and finally as a garbage man. And each night, no matter how tired he was, or how uneventful a day seemed, he wrote about it in his diary.

At the end of the eight weeks he immediately took a vacation and spent a month turning his diary into the beginning of a book manuscript while everything was fresh in his mind.

Then armed with his partial manuscript and a front-page article about his experiences in *The New York Times*, he came to New York to seek a literary agent to market his book. Arriving in Manhattan, he simply looked in the phone book and found the name of an agent nearby that appealed to him.

So it happened that I was startled that same summer to see walking into my office a man with the raw sunburn and red neck of a manual laborer—but dressed in an elegant pin-striped suit. Coleman recognized my surprise at his appearance and immediately introduced himself.

"I'm Jack Coleman, president of Haverford College. I'm writing a book and I thought an agent might be able to help me find a publisher."

Still a little skeptical—it's not every day that someone claiming to be president of a famous college walks unannounced into an agent's office and says he needs help—I invited him to sit down, and after looking over his partial manuscript and hearing his story, I agreed that he had a good project going.

Working with Gene Young, then a senior editor at Lippincott, he finished his manuscript, and it was published to a good deal of acclaim. More than 10,000 copies were sold, and it was a selection of Religious Book Club. It has been quoted in more than twenty textbooks. The Jozak Company made a

TV movie based on the book, *The Secret Life of John Chapman*, and when it was aired on CBS network TV, it outpulled the second episode of *Camelot* and a major football game. The movie has been shown twice more on TV. Articles about or by John R. Coleman have appeared in *Time, Newsweek, People, Philadelphia, New York*, and numerous other magazines and newspapers, in addition to generous book review coverage of his book and his network and local radio and TV appearances to discuss his experiences.

The book changed his life. It gave him the satisfaction of realizing a dream and, for the first time, of writing in a style he liked. And when I last saw him, he was departing for a sort of permanent blue-collar job—as chef of an inn that he, his son, and his daughter-in-law have bought in Chester, Vermont: The Inn at Long Last.

WRITING A BOOK TO GAIN OR CONSOLIDATE AUTHORITY

Satisfaction in life can be a powerful motivation. But to others, gaining authority in their chosen field is a more important reason to write a nonfiction book. Consider the experience of Pamela McCorduck. Before writing her first nonfiction book, Pamela was teaching English at a university in Pittsburgh and having problems with tenure because she wanted to write about science instead of the humanities. After her first nonfiction book, *Machines Who Think: A Personal Inquiry into the History and Prospect of Artificial Intelligence*, was published by W. H. Freeman, she was able to quit her job, move to New York, and armed with the book's reviews, make half again as much in her first year of free-lancing by writing articles for *Cosmopolitan, Redbook, Science Digest*, and other publications as she had made as a professor.

As a result of the book, she can, if she wishes, lecture on her subject—the history of artificial intelligence—every month for $2,500 to $3,000 a lecture, plus expenses. And she was invited to teach in the English Department of Columbia University—the name of the course is "Science Writing."

Her first nonfiction book has sold 25,000 copies in hard-cover, and sales are continuing at the rate of about 2,000 copies a year. It was also published in German, Japanese, and Hebrew. By writing the first history of this subject, Pamela founded a new branch of the history of science. And she has followed her first success with two additional acclaimed books. She is now an established authority.

In order to achieve this success, Pamela McCorduck had to finance her initial research herself, and she struggled long and hard to find a publisher. But some writers need cash right away.

WRITING FOR MONEY

The writer whose story I'll tell now had a truly desperate need for cash. Because of the nature of his story, he has asked me not to use his real name, so I'll call him John Dough. John Dough had a job working for a large company in the Midwest. He gained some writing experience working on the house organ of his company. He was married and had several children to support. But John Dough became a gambler and, finally, a compulsive gambler—and constantly lost money, as most compulsive gamblers do.

As his need for money to gamble with became deeper, he began to write bad checks for small sums, then move on to new places. Finally he was wanted on bad check charges in twenty states, and the FBI had a warrant out for his arrest.

John Dough was a desperate man on the run, and he came up with a desperate plan to get some money, pay his debts, and return to his family a free man.

He would write a dramatic, soul-chilling book about his experiences as a compulsive gambler, sell it, and use the proceeds to make good his many bad checks.

He went to a small city near New York, took a job as an orderly in a hospital, and worked eight hours a day, then wrote for eight hours more. After fourteen rewritings he had 222 pages. "They had to be perfect," he said.

But when he finished his manuscript, he had a breakdown the final night he was working—and had to spend ten days in the hospital paralyzed, all his muscles frozen. Though the hospital diagnosed this as a serious disease, he believes it was a psychological complaint. At the end of the ten days he was able to move again, and with the aid of a professor at a nearby university who had befriended him, he got his clothes and sneaked out of the hospital in the middle of the night, medical bills unpaid.

He hitched rides to New York, arrived at ten in the evening, manuscript in hand, and slept on the subways until morning.

As he had heard that literary agents would probably be on Madison Avenue, he made his way there, and looking up an address in the phone book, went to the nearest one, James Seligmann.

"I looked terrible," he recalled. "I had lost weight, my clothes were dirty. But I told Seligmann when I visited him in the morning that he had to sell my manuscript by that very afternoon. He said it couldn't be done—that it might take four or five months to sell even a very good manuscript, and he had never heard of me before. But finally he became curious, and I told him my story.

"He decided to have a reader, whom I later learned was his wife, read the manuscript overnight, and the next morning he told me the reader liked it, and he would call an editor who owed him a favor, and try to get quick consideration. I found a job washing dishes and slept in empty buildings.

"On the third day we sold it to the editor, and the editor wanted to take me to lunch. He told me to meet him at Sardi's, a famous theatrical restaurant. I said we had better meet elsewhere, my clothes weren't fit for a restaurant. So the editor met me on a street corner, took me to his apartment, lent me some clothes, and we had lunch at Sardi's."

John Dough put together a list of his bad checks, and an attorney for his publisher contacted the people who held them and offered to pay them off. Most accepted, but a few said they would keep the checks, as they were small amounts, for John Dough's autograph. After the checks were paid off,

15

$250 was left of the advance royalties. But a small movie sale, for $5,000, was money enough to tide him over until the book was published.

After publication he went on "The Tonight Show," "The David Frost Show," "The Merv Griffin Show," and other major TV programs to publicize the book. It was praised in *Book World*—the reviewer said it was reminiscent of Dostoyevski—and Ring Lardner, Jr., gave it a good review in *The New York Times*. The book was reprinted in paperback by Bantam.

John Dough never looked back and has gone on to write book after book, under his own name, and to ghost-write books for many others. He makes from $60,000 to $70,000 a year and gradually has ceased gambling. But he still writes for cash, and likes to get his money from a publisher quickly.

"The main thing is to be able to sit down and do it—to be able to bear the inactivity, staring at the wall, and writing it down on the page. It takes a lot of self-discipline," is his writing advice to you.

A GRAB BAG OF SUCCESS STORIES

In selecting the preceding three stories to show three reasons to write—for satisfaction, to gain authority, and to make money—I purposely skipped writers who had super successes with their first book.

But maybe you should keep that kind of potential in mind too. It can be inspiring, and maybe you can become one of them. Just consider the case of David Reuben, M.D. His first book, *Everything You Always Wanted to Know About Sex but Were Afraid to Ask*, was a Number 1 best-seller and sold two million in hardcover and eight million in paperback in the United States alone, and three and a half million hardcover and ten million paperback in forty foreign countries. And believe me that kind of sales generates tremendous royalties!

Barry Goldwater, a first-time U.S. senator from Arizona, who squeaked through his first election as conservative Republican on Eisenhower's coattails, wrote *The Conscience of a Conservative*. The book sold five million copies, and transformed Goldwater into the Republican candidate for president of the United States.

Harry Browne went from conducting financial seminars locally in California to best-seller author with his first book, *How You Can Profit from the Coming Devaluation*, and then rewrote it as his third book which became the Number 1 bestseller, *How You Can Profit from a Monetary Crisis*, making a tidy profit himself in the process.

Helen Gurley Brown has parlayed her initial best-seller, *Sex and the Single Woman*, into a career as writer and later as the acclaimed editor of *Cosmopolitan*.

Elizabeth Ray went from being a Congressional secretary to author of a 1.85 million-copies seller about her experiences, *The Washington Fringe Benefit*.

And that list is just of a few authors I've had professional contact with!

So let's go on, and in the next chapter examine the world of nonfiction trade books. You might want to visit it, as author of a first nonfiction book—or go to live there permanently, as a professional author.

2

The World of Nonfiction Books— Where Do You Fit In?

Let's set the scene:

You are a photographer. You approach a famous athlete, and he allows you to photograph him in the very actions that have made him a champion. In time, you have a wonderful collection of stop-action photos that explain graphically exactly how to perform like a champion in a popular sport. So what do you do with these wonderful pictures?

One approach would be to make a book of them. So you approach a publisher. The publisher says, "These are beautiful photographs. But they are not of much use unless there is a text with them. We don't publish *photo books*, but we do publish books about *sports*."

Soon the publisher has found a well-known writer on the sport your athlete subject is famous for. The writer writes a text, the famous athlete agrees to lend his name to the book, and your photos are used. The result: *Tennis* by Pancho Gonzales, with text by Gladys Heldman, and photos by you. And what kind of book is it finally, in the estimation of reviewers? A how-to book, a book that teaches tennis by showing how a world champion makes each motion of the game in pictures and words.

The book became easy to sell once it was described as a how-to book. How do you, a beginner at writing a nonfiction book, describe your book idea to a publisher in terms that he will understand and see as a commercial opportunity? To do this, you need to learn something about the categories that agents, publishers, booksellers, and librarians use to describe all nonfiction books.

At first glance there would seem to be as many kinds of nonfiction books as there are subjects to write about. Even a cursory survey I made of large bookstores in the ten-block section of New York's Fifth Avenue that boasts Barnes & Noble, B. Dalton Booksellers, and Doubleday Book Shops revealed a multiplicity of categories. I jotted them down from the labels on the walls and tables of these large, major bookstores and found myself with a list of eighty-one categories in all:

anthropology
antiques
art
art techniques
astrology
astronomy
Asia, Africa, Mideast
automobile
aviation
beauty
belles lettres
Bibles
biography
boating and sailing
business
business and professional
careers/résumés
child development

computers
consumer reference
cooking
current affairs
dance
dictionaries
diet and health
diets
Eastern philosophy
economics
education
electronics
engineering
English reference
exams and reviews
exercise
family
fashion

film
games and puzzles
gardening
gay studies
health
history, military
history, U.S.
history, world
house and home
how-to
humor
inspiration
investing
Judaica
law
literature
management
mathematics
medical
music
natural history
nature
occult

opera
performing arts
personal finance
pets
photography
physics
pictorial
political science
psychology
real estate
reference
religion
sales
science
secretarial
sex education
sociology
sports
television
travel
women's health
writing reference

Another approach to classifying nonfiction books is to look at lists of the kinds of books that book publishers say they want to publish. Two such leading reference books are *Literary Market Place*, published annually by R. R. Bowker Company and *Writer's Market*, published annually by Writer's Digest Books. Each of these lists about one hundred categories, but each has different entries in their hundred categories, so there is no agreement there.

A directory of literary agents, *Literary Agents of North America*, also has about one hundred categories of nonfiction books that agents say they want to secure from writers—but this, again, is a different list from those in the above directories or the bookstore category list.

So while one list will be from "agriculture" to "world

affairs," another might be from "accounting" to "women's studies."

Looking at nonfiction books like a librarian establishing a new small public library, it is possible to pare the list down to about thirty subjects.

Or if you want a really large list of categories, you can use the numbering system of libraries from 000 to 999—a thousand categories in all, divided into ten main super categories.

After studying these hundreds of possible categories of nonfiction books, Fran and I have created, for the purpose of this book, our own list of the different sorts of nonfiction works—seventeen in all—aimed at helping you write and sell *your* particular nonfiction book.

We'll get to that shortly. But first let's talk about you. You and your attitude.

Let me tell you a little story—a true story—from the standpoint of the publisher. Simon & Schuster had placed under contract a well-thought-out and worthwhile book with a message. But the message concerned today's educational system. And who, outside of the field, had ever heard of its author, Professor Allen Bloom?

And so they decided a 10,000 copy first printing would be more than adequate to fill the demand. They were wrong. Dead wrong. Happily so. The book sold 466,000 copies in 1987 and became the tenth best-selling book of the total year.

And what was the name of the book? *The Closing of the American Mind*. And its message? In a nutshell, that America is today in crisis, socially and politically, because of the educational system. That young people have lost their place—their feeling of belonging and the ability to make new goals.

What is the message in that story for you? The message is that you never know what will skyrocket. The message is also this: Write on a subject dear to you—or better yet, just a small segment of that subject that permits a more intimate view.

Of course we can speak in generalities. I am asked by beginning writers, "What kind of nonfiction book is most popular?"

21

I tell them the most popular at this time are biographies, how-to, and self-help books.

But again at this moment it is not important for you to try to fasten onto something that is popular. Almost any kind of book can become a good seller. With an open mind, look over the variety of books that you could write. What catches your eye? Your imagination?

Dwell a moment on each of the seventeen categories in our list. Check the ones that intrigue you so you can delve into them later. If it's some form of biography you like, there will be a whole chapter on the subject.

THE COLLIER-LEIGHTON GUIDE LIST OF NONFICTION BOOK CATEGORIES

1. How-To and Self-Help

How-To books are books of instruction, and Self-Help books are books about how to improve your mind and feel better about yourself.

For example, books on gardening, cooking, sales, real estate, investing, exercise, home management, pets, photography, beauty, and many other subjects usually turn out to be how-to books—books that offer instruction.

A young man named Gregg Sandreuter made enough money to finance his college education by assembling a crew and painting houses in the summer. Then he put his knowledge into a how-to book, *The Painter's Handbook*, which I helped him sell to Rodale Press.

Fran Leighton got her start as a book writer with a cookbook. She had written a Sunday supplement article about the eating habits and recipes of the presidential family—the Eisenhowers—and a publisher—Putnam's—asked the supplement if she could get enough material to expand it into a book. She wrote *White House Chef* and later expanded it into *A Treasury of White House Cooking*. Both attracted wide attention, were syndicated in newspapers, and became book club choices as well as going into paperback. Her collaborator in both books was a former White House chef.

Now for the self-help book we turn to the inner person. Books on popular psychology, religion, inspiration are aimed at improving the inner person. One of the most famous self-help books of all time is *How to Win Friends and Influence People*, in which Dale Carnegie attempts to change the reader's thinking so that he influences people by use of flattery rather than criticism.

But it is not uncommon that the categories of self-help and how-to overlap, say if you are writing a book about how to meet and marry the man of your choice. You are dealing with the mind and showing how to change one's thinking—what publishers call self-help—and you are giving instruction on where to find that man and reel him in.

2. Biography, Autobiography, and Memoirs

Biographies in all their forms—straight biographies, memoirs, and autobiographies—are the most popular form of nonfiction reading at this time. As I write this, I notice that five books of this category are currently on *The New York Times* best-seller list: *Richard Burton* by Melvyn Bragg; *Gracie* by George Burns; a modern military biography, *A Bright Shining Lie*, by Neil Sheehan; *Child Star* by Shirley Temple Black; and a physicist's memoir, *What Do You Care What Other People Think?* by Richard F. Feynman with Ralph Leighton. A chapter is devoted to this popular form of nonfiction writing.

3. History

Every period of history has its fans who will shell out large amounts of money to add books to their collections. However, it's very quirky, and fashions in historical periods come and go. The career of Bruce Catton illustrates the point perfectly. In 1949 Catton, a newspaperman, wrote his first book—the nonfiction title *War Lords of Washington*, but people were tired of hearing about World War II.

Dismayed, he turned again to nonfiction and wrote about the subject he knew best and really cared about—the Civil War. It was hard to find a publisher. The consensus was that nobody wanted to read about the Civil War either unless it was *Gone With the Wind*. And that was fiction.

Still Catton persisted and eventually Doubleday brought out *Mr. Lincoln's Army* in 1951. It was successful enough to encourage him to write another civil war book—*Glory Road*. But the triumph came in 1953 when his *A Stillness at Appomattox* was published and received the Pulitzer prize for history.

For beginning historians, writing in the history field is a difficult task. I have seen professional historians eat them alive with jealous, vicious reviews. In one case I was sure the book would have been a best-seller had it not been for the brutal attack. It appears safer for new historians to write contemporary history if they wish to avoid locking horns with established professionals. A sound example of a contemporary history that succeeded is *Parting the Waters* by Taylor Branch, about the rise of the American Civil Rights movement.

4. Contemporary Scene, Reportage

If you want to survey the contemporary scene and show what is happening, this category is for you. Fran Leighton and Ken Hoyt did a reporting job with an emphasis on humor when they surveyed the National Press Club and the Washington press corps and wrote *Drunk Before Noon*. It was Ken's first book, though he had written countless articles.

A more serious work of reportage on the contemporary scene is *Vietnam on Trial, Westmoreland vs. CBS* by Bob Brewin and Sydney Shaw. These reporters were able to use the information revealed in testimony and depositions connected with this famous trial to make many new points about skullduggery during the Vietnam war.

5. Science and Technical

If you can write clearly about complicated subjects, you can be very successful writing technical books on such sub-

24

jects as computers, electronics, aviation, and other marvels of modern life. Or you can make scientific problems more understandable. Stephen M. Hawking, though a seriously disabled invalid, is the scientist who wrote *A Brief History of Time*, concerning the effort to create a unified theory of the universe.

6. Pictorial, Art, Architecture, Communication, and Criticism

This large category covers collections of both photos and works of art; books on architecture; books on movies, TV, video, radio, and advertising; and books of criticism of the various subjects included in this category. A famous broad-sweeping book of this type is Marshall McLuhan's *The Medium Is the Message*. A narrower one is *The Films of Stanley Kubrick* by Norman Kagan. Typically, many such books are heavily illustrated—except for works of pure critical analysis.

7. Social Science, Issues, Social History

These are the social study and opinion books. Black studies. Urban studies. If you are writing a book that shows women had more to do with politics than they are credited for, it is a social history book and an issue book.

The Closing of the American Mind, which we talked about earlier in this chapter, is an issue book. The issue is education in the United States.

8. Nature and Sports

These books are about activities that are generally done in the outdoors or stadiums. If you enjoy or are an outstanding participant in some phase of nature or sports, write either a how-to book or a memoir about it—it will still be found in the sports division of the bookstore. For a fan of some sport or team, writing a book is a great way to meet your heroes and be treated with respect, rather than as a nuisance. Chandler Sterling, a retired Episcopal bishop, was just a fan of hockey until he wrote *The Ice House Gang* and became, briefly, a sports writer celebrity.

9. Travel, Exploration, and Geography

As far back as Marco Polo and even earlier, readers have loved to read about the adventures of travelers and explorers and the fascinating geography they described along the way.

Exploration is still going on. There is much wild country in Alaska, China, Australia, South America. The landing on the moon was exploration. There will be much more exploration in space. There is much exploration going on under the sea.

One of the most exciting recent exploration books concerns the South Pole and was written by Robert Swan, a noted British explorer. Swan retraced the steps of Robert Falcon Scott, competitor to Roald Amundsen. Swan and his group walked to the South Pole without dogs; they hauled heavy sledges laden with tents and food supplies.

A whole series of books was once written on how to see European countries on five dollars a day. That's no longer possible, but you can still write books on seeing the world without going into bankruptcy. Perhaps a book on backpacking in Chile or in China. It would combine how-to with travel adventures.

10. Health, Medicine, Fitness, Nutrition

If you don't have a big name, a book can give you one, as it did Jim Fixx, whose passion was running. Or you can collaborate with a big sports or medical or nutritional figure to set forth his advice on achieving good health and fitness.

An offbeat health book, *Love, Medicine & Miracles*, gave author Bernie S. Siegel, a surgeon, 387,000 readers in 1987 and made it one of the top fifteen books of the year. What was it about? Miraculous cancer cures that Dr. Siegal had seen in his practice in Connecticut.

11. Games and Puzzles

The real trick here is to get there first or early in the popularity of a new game craze. If you write the first book on three-dimensional chess or new computer games, you have a better chance of success than if you write the fourteenth.

Some people have the knack of making up new games and puzzles. There are built-in readerships for books of crossword puzzles. If you can't make up your own, you can collect puzzles of a certain type and, of course, pay for permission to use them. Crossword puzzles dealing with specific subjects are a great challenge—authors, birds, animals.

You can also do a history of a game, as Maxine Brady did with *The Monopoly Book*. It sold 125,000 copies.

Edgar Kaplan distilled his expertise as a bridge champion into a book with the broad sweeping title of *Contract Bridge Complete*.

12. Humor

If you have a skewed look at life, write it. Every decade has its own laugh masters. James Thurber of the '50s. Erma Bombeck and Art Buchwald of the '70s and '80s.

The next humorous view in the bookstores may be yours. If people laugh when you wish they wouldn't, maybe someday you will be glad they did. Start writing the way you're talking. Then study it and enhance it.

Humor comes in several ways—from overstatement or exaggeration or from understatement in which you might be bleeding profusely but say, "I think I need a Band-Aid." Humor comes from the unexpected. You are caught off guard and you laugh. And from enjoying other people's misfortunes.

Humor books frequently make the best-seller list, both story-line books and collections of jokes. If you can't write humor but love the field, try collecting other people's jokes and classify them by category. Zebra Books published a whole series called *Gross Jokes*, and some of them made the list.

13. Occult and Paranormal

So popular is this genre that bookstores have sprung up that sell only "New Age Books"—everything dealing with the occult and paranormal, with some Eastern religion and philosophy included. When I visited such a bookstore, I was a little taken aback at how many titles in it were ones I had been involved with: *It's All in the Stars,* an astrology book by Zolar—I almost ghost-wrote parts of it by some heavy editing; *The Medicine Wheel* by Sun Bear, a native American, and *Integral Yoga Hatha,* a book of meditation and health, by Swami Satchidananda and an array of others I had bought as an editor or sold as an agent.

Of course, adventures with flying saucers and interterrestrials like Whitley Strieber's *Communion* and Shirley MacLaine's paranormal books on her past lives were also present.

I had an interesting conversation with the owner of the New Age bookstore in which he tried to explain the exploding interest in the occult and inexplicable. "In the previous age," he said, "revelations came mostly to hermits and ecclesiastics, scholars and mystics. But in the new age *everybody* can have these revelations—such as learning of past lives through channeling."

14. Business, Money, Finance

Millions of people buy a book when they are convinced there is something in it for them—either help in making money or keeping what they have. If you are a successful financial consultant or write a financial newsletter, you might be qualified to tackle a book on the stock market or the buying of precious metals.

If you are an accountant, you might try for a book on minimizing other people's taxes, as H. & R. Block did. And as a real estate broker you might have a new angle on making a fortune in buying and selling or developing real estate property.

If you are a large or small cog in a big company, look around you—it was the president of Avis who came up with *Up the Organization,* about getting ahead, and certainly showed that business books do not have to be grim.

Another business book became a part of the English language—*The Peter Principle.* In it, Laurence J. Peter, with the help of coauthor Raymond Hull, employs wit in analyzing time management.

15. Sex and Relationships

The public has a voracious appetite for books on a formerly taboo subject—sex. American society is peppered with every approach to sex. The questions are still there to be answered—Is it better to live together before marrying? Better never to marry? Or to live in a commune sharing several mates?

Since the advent of AIDS, books on sex have become hard to sell—so maybe a book on relationships would be a better bet if you are interested in this category.

In 1988 an Episcopal bishop, the Right Reverend John S. Spong, reconsidered the whole problem of marriage and divorce in his book, *Living in Sin: A Bishop Rethinks Human Sexuality*. The controversial book calls for churches to perform rites to bless homosexual unions, using vows such as, "In the name of God, I, George, take you, Stan, to be my companion. . . ." The bishop also calls for churches to bless divorces and even to bless "betrothals," otherwise known as trial marriages, as well as semipermanent relationships.

16. Reference

Many professors are capable of writing reference books on their specialities. So are other experts.

A reference book is usually a collection of like things which help people find information they are looking for in a hurry.

You can do a collection, by subject, of stories that are suitable for a speaker to use in introducing his topic.

You can write a reference book which is a dictionary of new slang terms and then update it every few years.

You can do an encyclopedia of hobbies. Or medicines. Or carpentry.

17. Hobbies, Collectibles

If you can name it, someone collects it. Weather vanes. Mexican folk art. Match covers. Chess sets. Coin and gem collections. Collectors are fascinated by their own and other people's collections. You can write a book about any phase of the collector's life. The travel to quaint and offbeat places—where to look for treasures. The mounting of the collection. The protection and storage of it.

And then there is that old standby, the most popular hobby of all—stamp collecting. President Franklin D. Roosevelt was an avid stamp collector and often spent his evenings at the White House at his desk puttering around with his stamps or just admiring them.

Most books about hobbies and collectibles are really how-to books of a very special sort. If you are an expert on roses, other rose fanciers will want to read your book on your successes and failures. The trick in writing this category is to choose a subject that has a large enough audience to support the sales.

There you have it—seventeen categories that include most kinds of nonfiction trade books. Probably you already have picked your subject. Now you can mention its category when presenting your book idea to a publisher or agent.

THE VIEW FROM THE PUBLISHING HOUSE

What does a publisher want in a nonfiction book? He wants one he can sell and that is not too different from ones he has sold before. It's as simple as that—*a new angle.*

What will the new angle do? It will make the reader feel amused for having shared your skewed viewpoint. Or it may make the reader feel better able to cope with his problems of health, emotional exhaustion, money, or lifestyle.

Even though you have now seen how enormous the field of nonfiction writing is, you have also seen that there is still room for you.

3

Should You Go It Alone or Get a Coauthor?

WRITING IN SINGLE HARNESS

It is easier to write a book by yourself if you have already assembled a mass of material. For example, if you are a professor, you have lecture notes. If you are a consultant, you have your analyses of the business problems of your clients. If you're a research doctor, you have your medical journal articles already published, and your problem is simply to expand on your material and make it more understandable to the average reader.

And the same goes for whatever field you are in—if that is the same field in which you wish to write your first book. If you are a newspaper reporter, you may already have written a series of articles but decided the subject warrants more space than a newspaper can give it.

Even if the subject you have chosen is not your occupation, you may be in good shape to go it alone in writing it. Say you traveled frequently for your work or on vacations. If you kept a journal or diary of your adventures, you may have a nugget for a travel book. So before you decide you need help from a coauthor, look at what you have and see if the seed of a book is not already there just waiting to be expanded.

Or the book may be writing itself in your head. Then most likely you don't need to collaborate—at least on your first draft. Your notes may be minimal, but each night when you go to bed, you find yourself writing a chapter mentally. In that case, for God's sake, jump up and put it down on typewriter, word processor, or by hand before it gets away. First thoughts are often best.

Actually, most first-time authors write their book manuscripts all by themselves. It could be that you have much to say on a subject and you want it said exactly the way you have in mind. Even though you are an amateur and have never written more than a letter before, why not give it a try? There is no substitute for enthusiasm in achieving success.

Writing classes can open one's mind to possible ways of writing something, but they cannot make a writer out of someone who is not interested in becoming one and willing to work. Those who can write and express themselves know it, and the fact that you are reading this book means you know that you basically can do it, but just need some help and instruction along the way.

Dr. Rory Foster, a Wisconsin veterinarian, determined to deliver his message himself. It was that not enough attention was being paid to injured wildlife. Dr. Foster established a free clinic for the care of injured wild creatures, and it was a success. Then, armed with a good title, *Dr. Wildlife*, all by himself he wrote a book telling the stories of the animals which had become a part of his life. It was successfully published by Franklin Watts, condensed by the *Reader's Digest*, and reprinted in paperback by Ballantine.

The inspiration can come from many sources. The question now is, "Can you go it alone?" The examples you read in Chapter 1 were of authors who did—Joan Bordow, a secretary; Fred Sparks, a newspaperman; John Coleman, a university president; Pamela McCorduck, an English instructor; and "John Dough," a compulsive gambler. All felt they could write their book by themselves—and they did.

WHAT DO YOU NEED TO GO IT ALONE?

1. Confidence—even though it may slip now and then. You have a healthy ego that says, "Others can do it, and so can I." In fact, you really hate it when other people try to do your work for you or help you too much. It doesn't hurt to be a perfectionist and a stickler for detail. And you like to have charge of your own life.

2. You have time to work on your manuscript—or you make time by good scheduling or dropping other activities because your book is more important to you.

3. You are accustomed to doing a certain amount of work each day—you don't treat the project lightly or walk away from it because you've run into problems or you're "not in the mood."

4. You are a self-starter. You don't need someone to say, "Come sit down—it's time for you to do your writing." You don't need someone to read what you've done each day or give you praise to keep you going.

5. You believe that your subject is important enough to do what you must do for your particular book—research, interviews, planning, thought. You may search for days for just the proper joke or quote or descriptive word. You don't just look for shortcuts, though you may take a few.

6. You have a working knowledge of English. You can write a sentence, a paragraph. If you feel the need, you are willing to find someone who can help you with the mechanics of structure and grammar.

7. You can work alone in a room—can bear loneliness.

8. And most important of all, you have a need and desire to communicate. You really want to give your message to others or make people react with laughter or action.

WRITING IN DOUBLE HARNESS

But on the other hand, if you are a very sociable person who is unaccustomed to work for even short periods in isolation, or if you are so unsure of yourself that you must bounce every idea off someone else, or you honestly cannot express your ideas in written form, you need a collaborator.

The world will never know the complete truth about various books. Looking at any particular book, there is no way to tell how many people contributed to it. A single byline does not mean it was not a collaboration. It is possible to become a famous writer without being able to write.

Politicians, movie stars, sports celebrities cannot be expected to excel equally as writers. They have a great deal of help with their books, and all too frequently they do not give due credit to the actual writer. Authors of textbooks, usually professors, often use their students or assistants to help write their books, sometimes with credit, sometimes without.

If your writing is used, without credit to you, you are a "ghost." Some writers like this—they write books on one subject under their own names, and make additional money writing other people's books under the other person's name. Such a part-time ghostwriter avoids confusing his readers, who think of him as an expert of his regular subject matter published under his own name.

My coauthor has been called a ghost, but she is not. On almost any book she has written, you will find her name on the cover along with that of her collaborator. Her bylines have been amusingly varied—"as told to," "with," "in collaboration with," and even "edited by." In only one case do you have to look inside to find Fran's part in writing the book. That was *White House Chef.* No one asked her and she did not speak up or even know she would not appear on the cover. Inside on the title page it says, "As told to Frances Spatz Leighton." She didn't have an agent in those early days. An agent would have protected her.

Don't be afraid of collaboration. It can be fun. It opens a new world. You may learn much more that way. You may make a friend for life.

Writing is a lonely pursuit. Fran jokes that she likes everything about writing a book except the *writing!* That's a joke with an edge of truth. Fran loves the interviewing, the search for information at libraries, the frantic phone calls on the trail of some obscure fact. She loves it all. But then comes the lonely part. The fun is over and she must sit down at the type-writer—all alone.

But having a collaborator makes it much less lonely. She can call her coauthor and read him something or get his or her opinion.

That's the good part—collaboration takes some of the loneliness away. But the bad part is that if you are stuck with a bad-tempered or difficult coauthor, you may pray and long to be alone.

Generally, Fran has been lucky in her choice of co-authors, though I have seen collaborations fail in a burst of temper. But it doesn't have to be that way. The truth is you can usually tell by seeing someone several times whether that person is going to be difficult or has an emotional problem.

My advice to you is this: If you know a person is difficult, don't collaborate unless there is big money involved. Only then is it worth the headache you are going to have. Or you can insist on a certain payment from that person in advance—a payment that cannot be returned.

Remember, money is not the paramount thing you are after. You want to be sure that there will be a book at the end of the trail if you expend a lot of energy.

Now let's talk about normal collaborations and normal collaborators. I have given you the down side first so you will pay attention and know that taking a collaborator is a very serious step—comparable to a marriage of talents for the du-ration of a writing project.

First comes the question of the role you will play with a collaborator. Let's look at the different situations and arrangements.

THREE KINDS OF COLLABORATIONS

1. Working with an Expert

Let's say that you, the writer, are fascinated by a subject and want to write about it, but you would have to spend years to get the proper expertise. You love the subject but are not knowledgeable enough.

That's the first kind of collaboration. You are the writer, and the other person is the expert. He has spent a lifetime on archaeological digs, and he thinks he has seen Noah's ark. Or he's going to give you his adventures among the headhunters. Or he'll tell how he discovered an ancient tomb and the bad luck that befell all those who entered and breathed the air. Or he's the world's top expert on postage stamp designs. Even if he's a movie star wanting to tell about his tangled love life, he's still the expert—the *expert* on his life.

Sometimes a byline of "as told to" is necessary for credibility because the public would not believe the person telling the story could have the expertise or skill with language to write it.

It's logical that a lawyer, say, or professor would have the ability to write a book with only a little help. But, for example, when the maid-seamstress of the White House told her story to Fran Leighton, it was only honest and proper that the byline read by Lillian Rogers Parks as told to Frances Spatz Leighton. Lillian had great basic material and became a fine public speaker in the course of promoting the book, but the second byline added credibility to the writing. Nor did the joint byline keep the book from being bought by Hollywood and made into a prize-winning miniseries—*Backstairs at the White House.*

As for the mechanics of the collaboration, Leighton studied Lillian's diaries and notes about her life as a maid to First Families. Then Leighton asked the right questions, did independent research to make sure no mistakes were made and that points were logical. Backup research is very important, as you will see in Chapter 11, "The Art of Research—Search and Seize."

2. Ghostwriting

You might call this the "invisible collaboration." A movie star, say, wants to write about her fifteen great loves and three marriages but doesn't want anyone to know she needed help.

She is willing to make a deal—she will give you a chunk of cash to write her book or she will give you a percentage of the book's earnings. And your position is simply that of a ghost-writer.

If the money offered is enough to make it tempting, try at least to talk the person into allowing you to put your name on the acknowledgments page. It can merely say she is "grateful for the help and guidance of my friend, ⎯⎯⎯ ⎯⎯⎯." Or, "I must give thanks to the person who stood by me during the long writing ordeal, ⎯⎯⎯." At least you have proof that you know the famous person and have had some kind of involvement with the book.

3. *The Collaboration of Equals*

This is the collaboration in which neither of you is expert on the subject or both of you are. Both of you are going to share the research and writing on a particular subject. You are equals. You must be very businesslike and divide the responsibility. Maybe you are better at interviewing people and he is better at library research. You will write it all, or each of you will write half of the chapters.

Make lists of things he is going to research. Spell it all out, or later he may say, "Well, I don't think that's important. If you want to research it, be my guest."

And you will say, "If I had known you weren't going to pull your weight, I wouldn't have agreed to this."

I know of one man who got mixed up with a collaborator who had a drinking problem. Eventually, he had to hire a researcher to get the library material in a hurry while he himself did all the writing and all the interviews needed. He paid the researcher himself.

The overburdened writer could have asked the fellow to rewrite the letter of agreement and take a smaller cut of the book, but he didn't think of it. Or was afraid to. But, at least eventually, the coauthor agreed to share the cost of the research out of the moneys earned from the book.

The trouble is at first it all seems such fun. The talking part is fun. It's the work that spoils it—spoils the sheer joy of showing how creative you can be. *Somebody's* got to put the pages together. So you need a game plan. A division of labor. And a stable coauthor.

HOW DO YOU KNOW YOU CAN GET ALONG?

When you are considering collaboration, don't commit yourself until you get the feel of the person. Invite him or her to your house. Then get yourself invited to his house. Say you want to come over just to get acquainted and see if you are on the same mental beam. Or meet a few times at restaurants or libraries.

See how much he drinks or what kind of drugs he's on. Don't be afraid to ask in a friendly fashion if he has a drinking or drug problem—if you suspect that—saying right out that you want to be sure he won't be on a toot when you need him. If he says he only drinks or takes a joint or sniffs between projects or when he is bored, you'd better keep looking for a coauthor.

The point is you have to rely on your vibes to tell you whether you are going to have problems with his drinking, drugs, or his general disposition—flightiness or temper. Does he seem reasonable and willing to argue points without flaring up?

If the other person is the expert, you need to be around him long enough to see how he will cooperate. Are you convinced he will share his expertise? Sometimes the expert clamps down and makes it difficult for you to squeeze the material out of him. It is as if he felt you were stealing it rather than writing it up in a book in which his name comes first. You don't have to be bosom buddies. You just need to know you can get along.

And you need to know if he is going to devote time and energy to your project. Ask if he has a regular job and what the hours are. Ask if he thinks he has time for your book and how much time he expects to devote to the project. If he says he can work on it only on Sundays, or from 8:00 P.M. to midnight, and *you* will have to come to his place only at those hours, think hard about whether that can work out.

THE SEARCH FOR THE COLLABORATOR

Where do you find your coauthor? The person you want for his expertise and because his byline would help sell the book probably belongs to a club whose members are interested in that subject—archaeology, sky-diving, writing. Go there and get acquainted with the executive secretary. Get the membership names.

Go to the library. Scan books on the subject to see who the experts are and whom the experts mention as their authority.

Get acquainted with librarians. Some of them are well aware of the top names in the field in which you are interested. Look up periodical literature to find the names of experts who have written articles in a popular vein. This might indicate they'd like to cooperate with you on a longer writing project—a book.

If you are the expert in search of a writer, the local newspaper may be your starting point. If you want to write in a scientific field, talk to the science editor. He may be interested in working with you, or he may know a good free-lance writer who is looking for a project.

Check the style of magazine writers—there are magazines in almost every field. If someone appeals to you, you might write a letter to that person in care of the newspaper or magazine and ask him to call collect, if it is long-distance. Tell him, frankly, you are looking for a collaborator on a book in the field of such and such. But don't give your exact angle.

If you want to write a memoir of your own life and adventures, go to the library and see the styles of various writers. Fran has gotten a surprising number of letters from people who have read her books of other people's memoirs, asking for her help with their own narratives of personal experience.

Okay, you have your coauthor, you like him or her. You

think it will work. But don't jump the gun and start writing yet.

Robert Frost said it right—"Good fences make good neighbors." If you are going to collaborate or have anything to do with another human being, get the agreement in writing. That will provide your fences.

That's what Fran Leighton does, and she has never had legal problems with her coauthors. In fact, most of them became lifetime friends, and some collaborated again on second books.

Let's say that you are going to help someone write his memoir, as Fran does. Here are eight points to include in the letter of agreement—just tailor it to your needs.

THE LETTER OF AGREEMENT

1. It starts out: This is to confirm that you and your coauthor (put the full names in) agree to write a book. That your coauthor will supply the material and that you will be responsible for the final draft.

2. That both of you will share the earnings from every source—hardcover, paperback, TV, movie, foreign rights, and all other earnings. (I find that 50-50 is the best division, but if you are merely editing someone else's writing, 25 percent would be fair).

3. Legal responsibility. That the coauthor is responsible for the truth of the material and will hold you harmless in any court action growing out of it. That he has the right to show the manuscript to his lawyer and that he himself will initial every page.

4. Byline. The letter should tell what the byline will be. Since it is the coauthor's story, his name should come before yours. Then agree on what your own position should be. There are various ways to handle it. The one that gives you the most prestige or credit is a simple "By José James and (your name)." That is also a good way to handle a how-to book. But there are other ways that may appeal more to your

coauthor. The byline can say "with" or "as told to" or "in collaboration with." If your coauthor hates to admit he needs help in writing, it can say "edited by." The byline has nothing to do with the sharing of money, which is settled in the second point of the letter of agreement.

5. Disagreements. It is wise to state in the agreement how controversies concerning points in the manuscript or style will be settled. If the authors cannot resolve the controversy, they agree to follow the suggestion of a publisher. And if the publisher has no opinion, then they will agree to take the decision of the agent, who is the business end of the book and has its best interest at heart.

If there is no agent, they must then decide on some person who can be the judge. Someone with writing or editing experience. (This is just one reason it is often wise to have an agent, and is one of the most important points in the agreement.)

6. Agents. The agreement should say whether a literary agent will be used and name the agent if possible. If no literary agent is used, say that the publisher will handle the division of money and send separate checks to each of you.

7. Time limit. If the manuscript has not been placed with a publisher within a certain time—say six months or one year—the subject is released from the agreement. He has all rights to get his material back and is free to write with someone else, but he is not free to use your version of the book without some compensation to be agreed upon. (It is possible that the book, using part of your material, can still be sold if it has a third author who can give it some additional ingredient or dimension.)

8. Expenses. The cost of photocopying, courier and postage fees, secretarial service for the final draft will be equally shared by the authors. (Stipulate which will put out the cash and how and when it will be reimbursed.) Frances keeps an expense list and gives it to her agent—me—to send to the coauthor.

After you have your agreement—and both of you have

signed it before a witness or notary public—you can then speak freely to your coauthor without being afraid that your material will be stolen by that person. You are protected.

So, whether you decide to go it alone or to work writing in double harness, you now have a vision of what you might accomplish by going ahead with your book project. Next you need to know where you go from here.

Part II

———◆———

The Book Presentation Package:
Key to a Contract

4

Targeting Your Audience—
The Vital First Step

I'll bet you think that if you write a non-fiction book that is interesting, fact filled, and with touches of great writing, a publisher is sure to buy it. Wrong.

You have forgotten the first basic rule. Find out who wants it.

Now and again I have had to relay the sad news that the publishers I offered the project to all say there is not a big enough market for it. Sometimes I am also able to pass along the good news that the publisher was so impressed with the author's writing style and potential that he said he would be interested in seeing the author's next project if it is on a different subject.

Let me give an example. You have always been fascinated by the subject of leprosy—how it transformed people, how they were ostracized, how it was finally brought under control. So you have written a well-thought-out book proposal, and you have even included two chapters to show how fascinating the subject is. But twenty publishers have turned it down because they don't think there is enough readership, and there are already books on the subject.

So what can you, the writer, do when planning your next project? You are going to look at it from the publisher's viewpoint for a moment.

The bottom line here is that you are dealing with business people. They must have a soul, yes, or they would not be interested in such creative and ethereal things as books—they'd be selling shoes or diapers. But faced with red ink, their souls tend to shrivel. So *you* must do some thinking—checking. Tailoring.

Your editor and publisher will be thinking about the audience for your book—the market—even harder than you, and they won't offer to publish your book unless they can visualize a large enough audience that will buy it for the book to make a profit. By thinking this through yourself and estimating the market yourself and including the information in your presentation, you can help sell it, because you know better than anyone else what you hope to accomplish. And you'll *know* you have a sufficient audience.

WHO ARE YOUR POTENTIAL READERS?

Let's make a list of people who might read your book, and important facts about them from the standpoint of the publisher. This exercise will help you in your writing as well. You will want to write down:

- where they live

- how old or young they are

- their income, their buying habits

- their sex—men, women, or both

- how much education they have

- their social class, taste, prejudices, ethnic group

- what kind of publications they read

- radio and TV programs they watch

- what organizations they belong to

- where they buy books—from bookstores, super-
  markets, through the mail, or do they borrow
  them from libraries?

- their preference—hardcover books, trade paperbacks, or mass market paperbacks

- the opinion leaders they respect and follow and
  whether you can reach and influence these opinion leaders

- the possibility that your book can be used as a
  giveaway or promotion for organizations or busi-
  nesses.

BE REALISTIC IN YOUR ESTIMATES

When I was an editor, nothing turned me off quicker
than reading a presentation that stated the author's book was
suitable for every man, woman, and child in the U.S.A., and
therefore the book had a potential sale of more than 200 million. Or, if only one in twenty bought the book, 10 million. I
couldn't help but think that even the biggest-selling books,
like dictionaries, rarely reached such sales, because of competition of similar books.

For most people, a book is not a necessity but rather a
luxury item—an adornment for the home or a form of
recreation.

The truth is that book buyers are a tiny minority of the
population. A first book that sells a million copies is a rarity, a
delightful surprise for author and publisher, and its success is
like winning the sweepstakes—possible but unlikely, unless
the author is already famous on the scale of Donald Trump or
Liz Taylor.

A publisher would much rather be sure of a 10,000-copy
sale than blindly hope for a 50,000-copy sale, when contracting for a first nonfiction book.

So projecting a truly likely market in a thoughtful way is

what will impress a publisher, and the list you have made is your first step.

WRITE YOUR BOOK FOR YOUR AUDIENCE

After you have determined what kinds of people are most likely to buy your book, think about how you can best communicate with them. What is their vocabulary? Who are their heroes? What are they afraid of? What do they hope for? In short, can you become their spokesman, leader, and friend? What information do they need? How will they use it—to escape boredom, make more money, attain a better life, improve their health, become an insider, advance in their profession, learn more about the rich and famous, or what?

You, as the author, must be able to promise them something they want—and make good on your promise *by communicating in language and style they understand and respect.*

RESEARCH YOUR COMPETITION

One of the easiest ways to judge the potential audience for your book idea is to determine the success of similar books. By looking through *Subject Guide to Books in Print* for the past five or six years, you can find out what other books have been published on your subject or on allied and comparable subjects. If there has been a recent best-seller on the subject or if one is considered the bible in that field, you'd better back away.

Why spend your time on a book that a publisher won't want? However, if the so-called bible of a particular trade or profession is outdated or too expensive for most to afford, then you have a chance to succeed with "The New . . ." or "The Simplified . . . ."

For example, when I was a publisher—president of Fleet—I originated an idea for a book inspired by my own need. Because of my Christian upbringing in a small Texas town, I was lacking in knowledge of important Jewish holidays, which are a significant part of life in New York, where my business was located.

What was needed, not just for me but for schoolchildren and armchair travelers, was a book about religious holidays of all faiths. Incidentally, such books come under the category of Juvenile Reference, but they are often just as widely read by adults.

A search of the library showed that Macmillan had published a book on the subject ten years before and that it was still in print—in its twelfth printing. That showed there was still interest and that such a book could be very successful.

But of course, our book would have to be considerably different. The old book had black-and-white illustrations, so we would have color. And the approach to the holiday stories could be different.

I was able to put together a team of experts. The coauthors were a scholarly Episcopalian minister, the Reverend Howard V. Harper, and a very astute librarian, Lavinia Dobler. An editor with a Jewish background, Marcia Freedman, helped the authors plan the book. Finally, I choose an illustrator who was a practicing Catholic, Josephine Little, and she received a credit line on the cover for her art work.

The book that resulted, *Customs and Holidays Around the World*, sold for years. It was publicized by excellent reviews in library and school publications.

There are two important things I must say before we leave this topic. First, if I had found that there was even one *recently* published, good-quality book on the subject of holidays around the world, I would not have invested my company's money on a subject that was already oversupplied.

Second, the books you compare to your projected book need not be identical. If you are writing a biography of a sports star, don't just compare it with another bio of that same star and try to find out how many copies it sold. You can compare your project to other bios about comparably famous sports stars. It is good if you can find other biographies in the same sport as yours because, as research will show you, there is quite a difference in bookselling power between sports. For years baseball far outdrew football, for example.

TOTE UP THE POTENTIAL AUDIENCE

If are writing a book aimed at construction engineers, you can probably find out how many engineers are employed in the nation. You can find out how many schools of engineering exist, and what libraries have engineering books in their collections. Remember that only a small part of the potential audience will actually buy your book, no matter how excellent, useful, and revolutionary it is. But knowing the target population is a good beginning.

Then think about those who employ engineers—will they buy it too? Think about students of engineering. Will they need the book? How many of them are there? Will it become a textbook, or "recommended reading" for students?

Will it be useful for foreign engineers as well, or just American engineers? Are engineers able to buy high-priced books, or do they resist high prices? You can find out by interviewing several and asking them what books they have in their libraries and how many books they have bought in the past one or two years.

Will their wives, parents, and friends buy the book as a gift for them?

Are there book clubs that sell book to engineers? If so, list them for your publisher—that means extra sales.

Are there special magazines and newsletters that most engineers read? Is your book the kind of work that might be reviewed in these publications? How big is the circulation?

Are there companies that might buy and give away your book to engineers who are their customers, as a goodwill gesture or as a door-opener for their salesmen? If so, the publisher will hear the cash register ring as he thinks of your book—particularly if you have already talked with a company that has expressed interest in distributing such a book. Try to get a note from the company head that you can send your publisher to show the need for the book and interest in it.

Some stores sell appropriate books along with their products—hobby books in a hobby shop, carpentry books in a hardware store, gardening books in a nursery. Will your book fit into such a store?

If, after checking out all the possible sources of sales for your projected book, you must conclude it appeals to a relatively small audience, be honest with the publisher. But point out that your limited audience may be willing to pay a high price for your highly specialized, necessary, or useful book or unique art book so that you both will be able to profit anyway. In some cases the argument will work.

SHOW YOUR AWARENESS ABOUT FORMAT

Do your potential buyers like books that have lots of charts, graphs, and tables in them? If you are writing a financial book, the answer is probably yes. So plan accordingly and be sure to tell the publisher how many such illustrations you plan to use—perhaps provide a sample.

Is your audience mostly young TV viewers? Tell the publisher so in your proposal and say that that is why you are planning a short, lively book rather than a long tome.

A popular biography of a movie star will probably be better written with short paragraphs in a gossipy style. A serious history of medieval farm implements would have longer paragraphs, with footnotes, bibliography, introduction by a famous scholar, and a chronology. Tell the publisher the style of writing you plan. He is not a mind reader, and he needs to know this detail as part of his study of your book's potential audience.

At the library look at quite a few books published by the publishers you plan to approach. You want to see *their* style. Most publishers have their own way of doing things, their own book look. Some like unusual page sizes. Some stick to good old 6 × 9 inches—that has spelled gold for them in the past. And straight type—no illustrations or perhaps just one insert of several pages of black-and-white photos. Others may have several inserts of many pages of photos.

Now you've gotten a handle on your publisher and you've gotten a handle on your audience, which is waiting impatiently out there for the publication of your book. With your help, the publisher will be better able to estimate the market. You have not left it to chance. Armed with all you know, you are ready for the next chapter.

5

Writing a Nonfiction Book Proposal

If you have something timely or lively, any publisher will listen to you. And if it is hot, it is no time to be modest. You must exude confidence, authority, excitement. All these should be felt by the publisher when he reads your book proposal.

If you don't have an agent and you believe your subject is truly deserving of immediate consideration, it is not out of line to call the publisher you have in mind and ask to speak to a senior editor. If you get through to him or her, or if you leave a message with his assistant and he calls back, then say you are calling because of the urgency of your project. State the subject of the book and ask if he wants you to follow up with a letter or memo detailing your project.

Almost certainly he will—it costs little to take a look. Publishers do not make contracts on the telephone. They need something in writing to study and pass around to different members of their publishing team. And your book proposal can be in one of the two forms I mentioned above: a memo or a letter.

Whether your proposal is for a book that is simply a good

idea or about famous people and superstars, secrecy can be very important. Exclusiveness is lost if the news of the book leaks out too far in advance. With a biography there can be danger of a lawsuit to stop the book. You may remember that Frank Sinatra tried to stop Kitty Kelley's book about him, *His Way: The Unauthorized Biography of Frank Sinatra*, and the legal wrangling wasted a lot of time.

Before going into detail about how to write a nonfiction book proposal, my coauthor and I have included two actual proposals, both for books that succeeded and sold a lot of copies. By reading these and studying how they present their subjects, you can get two clear ideas of ways of presenting two different kinds of books, and after each proposal we will examine the good qualities of the proposal that you may want to imitate.

The first proposal was indeed a hot property—the memoir of the House of Representatives doorkeeper, William "Fishbait" Miller. He was not a superstar himself, but he had intimate knowledge of political superstars of Capitol Hill, some of whom became presidents. My coauthor, Frances Spatz Leighton, was approached by Fishbait's agent, Ruth Brod, and agreed to become Miller's "as told to."

Her first step was to gather enough exclusive nuggets of information from Fishbait Miller to write the book proposal, which she then put in the form of *a selling memo*. This is a hard-sell presentation of her book idea. Even though it is addressed to the literary agent, it is designed to be shown by the agent to publishers. If you don't have an agent, such a memo could be addressed to "Dear Editor," and sent to a publishing house.

Memo to Ruth Brod:

Re: Memoir of "Fishbait" Miller, famous Doorkeeper of the House of Representatives
From: Frances Spatz Leighton
This will be an exciting but balanced book by
the man who spent forty-two years of his life on Cap-

54

itol Hill, in intimate relationship with the power structure of the Congress. In a unique way his life was a combination of mother hen to the high and mighty of Congress, and errand boy—even hatchet man.

He took orders. He gave orders. He nursed legislators through their various hours of need. And for this he was paid some $40,000 a year. As Speaker John McCormack said, when calling for Fishbait, "The Doorkeeper does more work accidentally and achieves more accidentally than the Clerk of the House and the Sergeant at Arms combined."

There is no doubt about it, William "Fishbait" Miller wielded more power than even most congressmen until he was toppled in a power struggle after hanging on for twenty eight years as House Doorkeeper. Fish himself was acknowledged to be the most colorful man on the Hill, and I think his own words and recollections will bear this out. But the thrust of the book is what he saw and heard and learned and experienced in dealing with and ministering to the needs and whims of the body politic.

I want to make clear that his power did not come just from the fact that he could hire and fire the several hundred people who came under his supervision, but that when he arrived with a message for a congressman, it had the power of the leadership behind it. Fish was the trusted man. Fish was in those smoke-filled rooms, listening and ready to carry out orders.

He was privy to what Congress thought and said about various presidents when the presidents were trying to make their mark with the American public. History tends to throw bouquets at presidents past, like Kennedy and Truman. But Fish remembers how certain congressmen were calling Kennedy a "crybaby" and how Truman kept driving the Senate Majority Leader, Scott Lucas, so hard to get an impossible slate of bills passed that Lucas landed in the hospital with exhaustion. "Pigheaded" was the kindest phrase some congressmen could think of for Truman.

Truman and Fishbait had a very special relationship, and when Truman was leaving the White House, he called for Fish to come to the White House. What Truman said during that unique private talk at the White House will be revealed for the first time in this book.

So will the inside stories of how various landmark and some amusing bills were passed, how lobbyists operate on Capitol Hill, what happened when various members of royalty and heads of state came to address joint meetings of Congress. It was Fishbait's duty, incidentally, to escort all such dignitaries between the two bodies of Congress. And also to hold the Bible when a vice president was being sworn in.

He saw much. He kept the secrets of Congress. And now that he is finally telling inside stories and truths never revealed before, he will still delete a name if the man is still alive and could be hurt by the revelation. But, in any event, it will be clear that Fish feels warmth and compassion toward that teeming, scheming, scuffling, and struggling body of men and women known as the Congress.

Who drank? Who didn't? What of Wilbur Mills? Who were the great womanizers?

Who lived like kings on Capitol Hill?

Who were the practical jokers? Who were sadistic? Who said words so cruel he caused a congressional colleague to fall dead as he left the floor of the House?

Who were called "the Five Sisters" for their religious ardor? And speaking of sisters, how angelic are congresswomen?

All will be answered in this ultimate look at life as it is lived on Capitol Hill, as seen through the eyes of the famous Doorkeeper. Millions watched him on TV, intoning, "Mistah Speakah, the President of the United States." I can see the book jacket with the Capitol dome behind Fishbait's head, and the single word: "FISHBAIT."

His material is fantastic. Inside stories on the men who run the country—past and present. Touching stories like that of a particular congressman who went around dropping coins so that little kids would find them. Sad stories like what happens to Hill marriages. Incidentally, Fish used to ride Wilbur Mills's kids down Capitol halls on his mail delivery truck, long ago.

No one knows what goes on and what has gone on behind those doors like the man who has been part clown, part confidant, acting out a role of utter helpfulness and subservience. It was not a painful role. He loved the game, played it to the hilt, even once standing by while a particular congressman finished eating a popsicle at the back of the House chamber, then handed the stick to Fish, who tiptoed out to get rid of it.

Fishbait knew six presidents before they were presidents—Harry S Truman, Dwight D. Eisenhower, John F. Kennedy, Lyndon B. Johnson, Richard Nixon, and Gerald Ford. He has stories of them in all phases of their careers. (They all called him Fishbait.)

Take Kennedy. People forget that he was first a congressman, in search of fun and in search of a wife, not necessarily in the same direction. Intimate material on Kennedy as senator and president is just starting to come out—*Dog Days at the White House*, my book with Traphes Bryant, which is about to be published, and Ben Bradlee's *Conversations with Kennedy*, which just has been. Fishbait will fill in a bit more with the congressional days as well as a few from the White House days.

Historians will be especially interested in Fishbait's stories of what went on at the Democratic Presidential Convention at which JFK was robbed of his chance to be vice president. And what went on at the subsequent convention when he won the top spot. And where Lyndon Johnson fitted in. And how Rayburn and his henchmen used every trick to maintain control. Fishbait makes no bones about it. He was there to do the bidding of the power structure. He helped execute the tricks and gladly. Rayburn was his mentor and god.

I should mention that from the Convention of 1940 on, nine conventions in all, including 1972, Fishbait attended every Democratic convention in some official capacity—first as Assistant Sergeant at Arms, later as Doorkeeper at the Convention.

Conventions as seen by Fish could make a book, but we will settle for one smashing chapter on the subject to make room for other things, such as how bills are waylaid. Or used as brickbats. The trick on Capitol Hill is to act innocent but proceed to your goal in any way possible, sweeping the bodies under the rug.

Which is not to say there aren't some great and ethical men running the country. But, says Fishbait, "A congressman has to step lively not to get his tail in a legislative trap."

As I mentioned before, Sam Rayburn was the man Fishbait Miller felt closest to. It could be said that Rayburn's attitude toward women set Women's Lib back ten years. But Rayburn was to be pitied in his vain effort to understand that species. After one slight brush with marriage, Rayburn decided he'd better stick to politics. Which is not to say he didn't have sex. As you'll see in the book.

Not so delicate as Rayburn was another congressman—a very rich one—who specialized in having two pretties in bed with him at the same time. Once he thought he had nicely shipped off his wife with a kiss and a wave but she returned to the hotel where they were staying and walked in on a rare scene. It was a great charade. In spite of nudity and a little "lewdity," all persons involved, including the girls, carried off the situation with great dignity and politeness, discussing everything but what was going on. And no, the wife did not divorce him. The publisher can help decide where names can be used and where not.

It is not too unusual that sex is used on Capitol Hill to get damaging material on a congressman from one of his female aides. In one case a pretty aide on a congressman's committee was "friendly" both with the congressman and one of his male aides. In this case the male aide was playing along with a certain columnist to get a story involving the congressman's financial records. The male aide made a date with the young lady and enlisted her help in "nailing the bastard so he won't dare run again."

But the girl was coy and said she'd need a little time to get the files. She went to the congressman (we'll see what the publisher says about naming him) and told him what was going on. He said, "Well, let's give him another date and this time let's have a recording machine in your purse." It went on from there to a great confrontation scene in the congressman's office that taught the aide a bit on loyalty. If he was ever able to get another job, that is.

There was one congressman who had to have sex three or four times a day or he was miserable. He was known for a time as the Hill's own male nympho, and his office looked like the dressing room of a beauty contest. A few congressmen were gay.

One congresswoman worked out her sexual frustration with a male delivery man who showed up every day at the same hour. It was said that even in this enlightened age, she believed she would not get pregnant if she conducted the affair standing up.

The chapter on security on the Hill is a very strong one. All about the shootings and tragedies and near tragedies that have occurred, the security measures that have been suggested, and those that have been inaugurated. All the adventures Fish has had in protecting the governing body.

The public has no way of knowing what goes on behind scenes when the President announces he is going to Capitol Hill to deliver a message. Hearing Fish give a blow-by-blow description of the rushed meetings and planning and involvement of person after person becomes as funny as a comic opera. And topping off the humor is the contrast of the excitement and high tension of the Hill people with the boredom of the president (especially Nixon), who just wanted to get it over with as fast as possible, "and get the hell out."

Very funny, too, is what happens at a joint session when a female guest of honor has to go to the little girl's room. One story he tells, about the wife of a foreign head of state being in agony to get to the rest room while all the protocol of escorting her there was being worked out by Fish, will have readers falling out of their chairs.

I think the health regime of the various members can be hilarious. One had to have his spoon of honey every day. Another went around chewing sliced raw sweet potatoes, which he made the girls in his office bring in for him.

Then there are the many stories of congressmen bringing in ghastly food from their home states and forcing their colleagues to eat it while cameras clicked. In World War II a Louisiana Congressman decreed that Congress set a good example by eating muskrat and sending the beef "to the boys overseas." The House Chef served the stuff up, and many legislators ate with gusto while the movie cameras whirred. But afterward some of them were so sick they could hardly make it to the men's room.

Fishbait, whose real name is William Mosley Miller, was on the Hill forty-two years, twenty-eight as Doorkeeper, until deposed by the current Congress. He seems to have memories of everyone important who passed through the doors of Congress. He was behind scenes participating in historic moments, such as FDR's herculean effort to make it seem he was walking to deliver his State of the Union speeches. Fish was there as the architect's office set up the elaborate ramps and screen of shrubbery to hide FDR's legs. He describes exactly how the "walking" trick was handled by FDR and his son, James Roosevelt.

Incidentally, James came back later as a congressman to Capitol Hill and Fish noted that he still hadn't broken himself of one bad habit. He would chew his tongue. FDR, Jr., came to the Hill, too, as an elected congressman, and he didn't chew his tongue. But he had another bad habit. He kept putting things off and didn't do his homework. And that, says Fish, made him a dum-dum congressman.

Fishbait frequently traveled with congressmen running for reelection, and he is going to give his own primer on how to get votes. He will show how and why some made it and others didn't. He will also tell how various congressmen and -women have reacted to defeat. When Mrs. Farrington lost out to John Anthony Burns as delegate from Alaska, she was so bitter she wouldn't even offer Burns the courtesy of a chair in her office or let him use her telephone, when he came to Washington ahead of time to attend orientation meetings. Fish had to take pity on him and let him use a corner of his office. As a result they became good friends.

Friendship almost cost Fish his life on another occasion, and if it hadn't been that his wife, Mable (cq), decided she deserved a little of his time too, Fish would not be here to write his memoir today. He was scheduled to go on that ill-fated trip to Alaska. Mable insisted he go with her to Atlanta instead, so Begich took a man from his office instead of Fish. All disappeared with their plane—including Hale Boggs.

There are many acts of kindness that go on unnoticed on Capitol Hill, and Fish will throw some bouquets around, where credit is due. But he will also tell of the acts of unkindness, selfishness, and pettiness. He will tell how far miserly congressmen can go in saving every penny for themselves and reaching out for more.

And then there are the feuds. Almost every congressman is a "high school senior class president or behaves like one." And a few have been "prom queens." It isn't too easy to know who hates whom because some men pretend to love the guy they are trying to knife, in a polite, congressional way, and some congressmen pretend to be feuding for political reasons while being real drinking buddies after hours.

What various members of Congress said about various presidents also comes along in here. And speaking of presidents reminds us that most of the ones Fish knew are now dead, and he was an important helper at their funerals. When JFK died, Fish made countless trips to the White House because of various problems. And Fish helped Lady Bird at LBJ's memorial service. She said she hoped her grandchildren would get the benefit of Fish's knowledge of the Capitol. Well, maybe they still will, if they grow up and read his book.

Lady Bird's husband called Miller his buddy, his trusted friend, as did the five other presidents he had known in depth. But Fish feels closest to Jerry Ford for one reason—both were deserted by fathers who left home and never came back. Fish, incidentally, is the father of a daughter (now married) who went to National Cathedral girl's school with LBJ's daughters, Luci and Lynda Bird.

Among other details you should know is that Fish ruled a three-million-dollar empire on Capitol Hill and his salary was only a trifle less than a congressman's. He is not a poor man. His retirement pay, I believe, is still something like $40,000, give or take a thou.

Somewhere in the book there must be some of the anecdotes about House pages and other employees who came under his supervision. He kept some kids from becoming juvenile delinquents. He was supervisor of 357 employees—doormen, document room workers, telephone clerks, snack room attendants, custodians, and even shoeshine boys.

His file of photographs taken through the years is worth a fortune in itself, but everything is going to Ole Miss, his favorite university, after we are done with the book. We have pictures of Fish with presidents and kings and Hollywood beauties like Ginger Rogers—both kissing and not kissing—with Mae West, with Lassie, with midgets of the circus and giants, and with cute pigtailed Oriental children on the steps of the Capitol reading, of all things, a "Know Your Congress" book. We have Fish playing baseball with the Hill club—the House Democrats—and James Roosevelt is at bat. Fish is catcher. The name of the opposition team was The Republicans. We have Fish with Mickey Mouse and with Shirley Chisholm, and we have him with Ford in the

House Chamber when Ford was about to speak. At work and play with Rayburn, Truman, other Hill stars. At conventions. You name it, we have it.

The most important function of this book, I think, will be that it gives little vignettes and sidelights about famous people. Churchill and his gold toothpick. Estes Kefauver and his lousy memory. Bella Abzug and how she cursed him out and tried to get around him when he would not permit her to wear her hat on the floor of the House. He was the only person who could get her to part with her hat, and that is a long and funny anecdote, replete with four-letter words. Clare Boothe Luce and how her attitude toward him changed after the tragic death of her daughter. That, too, starts out as a very funny story with Clare detesting him. Lyndon Johnson cussing Fish out in Texas. As a matter of fact, Fish has been cussed out by some very important people.

I think, however, the reader will not be cussing him but will be sometimes deeply touched, sometimes amused, sometimes surprised, and it is hoped, glad to be treated to this peephole view of the Capitol. I am happy to say Fish is one of the few persons I have worked with who does not mind telling all the dumb and sometimes inadvertent mistakes he has made.

Which makes him a bigger man. And certainly a more lovable one.

I know that certain publishers have been after you about this book, and one called me whom I referred to you. As soon as you know which publisher is best for this particular material, I would like to talk with the editor who will be assigned to it. Then we can decide on how important chronology is in the book and how important division of chapters by subject matter. Or shall we have a combination?

We span forty-two years, remember, so this is an important point. Also, shall the emphasis be on the lighter side or the heavier side of legislative battles and power politics? I opt for the lighter side even of power politics.

All the best,

Frances Spatz Leighton

P.S. I'm sorry that I could not be more explicit in giving actual anecdotes in this memo, but at this stage we are afraid of having our material stolen. When I did the memo for Mary Gallagher's best-selling book, *My Life with Jacqueline Kennedy* that is exactly what happened. The memo was pirated. Published coast to coast.

I haven't touched the surface yet on things that will be included in the memoir. What congressmen have done when in their cups is certainly a very important part of the story—when soused, one of them would drive his car on the sidewalk. Fishbait has material on the plans that were being made for Nixon's impeachment trial. He personally was getting tickets printed for it when Nixon threw in the sponge.

What did this memo accomplish? What does it have that catches the attention of publishers? For one thing, it titillates the reader with the promise of secrets to be revealed about our famous legislators, and it gives a few examples. Almost everybody loves to hear a few tales told out of school. For another thing, it promises humor and gives amusing insights into the lives of political figures who were household words at the time—everything from their health regimes to their sex lives.

Because the material in the memo was so powerful, Fran did not need to add the elements publishers would usually insist on—table of contents, sample chapter, and a description of how various chapters will be handled. The memo sold the book, which became a best-seller and a Literary Guild choice. It was also syndicated in newspapers and went into paperback, where it again was a great financial success. The title leaned heavily on Miller's job: *Fishbait—the Memoirs of the Congressional Doorkeeper.*

In contrast to Fran's hard-sell proposal, the following presentation by George Sullivan has a low-key, soft sell that persuades by presenting interesting facts about his subject in a well-organized way. He does go into detail about many of the chapters that will be in his book, weaving his "sell" into the description of the actual content. When he presented this, the subject was very timely—America was in the midst of an energy crisis. This proposal is a fine model to follow for many kinds of more factual, how-to, or reportorial books. George Sullivan is the successful author of more than one hundred books.

George Sullivan
[address and phone number]

Wind Power for Your Home

Spiraling power costs, the craving for a pollution-free environment, and dwindling supplies of fossil fuels have skyrocketed interest in wind-generated energy. The National Oceanic and Atmospheric Administration recently announced the number of requests for information about wind energy has almost doubled in the past eighteen months. According to NOAA, approximately one hundred utility companies throughout the United States are testing or planning to use wind energy conversion systems, including Pacific Gas and Electric Company and Southern California Edison Company.

The Federal government recently installed three windmills on a hill near Goldendale, Washington, to generate electricity for the Bonneville Power Administration. Alcoa, Bendix, Boeing, General Electric, Hamilton Standard, Kaman Aerospace, Westinghouse, and United Technologies are among the firms that are now heavily committed to research and development in the wind energy field.

This new book, the first of its type, explains the practical value of the wind's energy to the average home owner, spelling out how a wind energy conversion system can be used to light lights, power appliances, provide heat, and pump water.

The book's opening chapter explains the physics of a wind energy conversion system, or WECS. (They're not called "windmills" because wind-electric systems have more to them than blades that spin in the breeze.)

All wind energy conversion systems obtain their energy by slowing down the wind that passes through them. The energy the wind loses is gained by the spinning blades of the system, and this rotational movement is, in turn, used to move a coil of wires in a magnetic field. Out comes electric current. Diagrams are used to show the operation of a typical wind energy system, and different types of systems are pictured.

"Siting" is the title of another early chapter. In choosing a location for a wind machine, one must determine the site where the airflow is the strongest and most consistent. According to manufacturers of wind energy systems, the greatest cause of dissatisfaction among owners is that their machines fail to produce as much power as expected. This problem can often be avoided by proper siting.

The chapter explains how to "prospect" for the fastest, least turbulent wind speed on a given piece of property. The "cube law" is explained in detail. It states: "The wind's energy is proportional to the cube of the wind's speed." In other words, when the wind's speed doubles, the wind power increases eight times. That's why finding the best possible location for the wind system pays rich dividends in terms of power production. National and local siting maps are presented in this chapter. Wind measuring instruments, such as the totalizing anemometer, are explained and pictured.

"Once you know how much wind is available to you," says the text, "you have to decide how much electric power you want or need to produce." A chapter of the book is devoted to determining one's electricity needs. Specifically, the chapter tells how to figure one's *average* kilowatt-hour consumption and *peak* kilowatt-hour consumption. Both of these statistics are critical in buying a system of proper size.

Three chapters of the book are devoted to the basic components that make up a wind energy conversion system. These are the rotor/generator assembly, the tower, and the electrical equipment.

Rotor/Generator Assembly—

The rotor is the bladed device that converts the energy derived from the wind into rotary motion. The generator converts the rotary motion into electric energy.

Dealers and distributors of rotor/generator assemblies are listed in this section. The product line offered by each is described in terms of generating capacity (expressed in kilowatts) and the lowest wind speed (in miles per hour) at which this occurs. Rotor diameter for each assembly is also given. Prices are listed. Each type of assembly is either pictured or diagramed.

How does one choose an efficient and well-designed system and not a turkey from the dozens available? This chapter tells. The Department of Energy has conducted tests of most residential-sized wind energy conversion systems to determine the efficiency of each under real-life operating conditions. The chapter discloses how to obtain the results of these tests.

Getting a good warranty is also vital, the chapter says. Coverage should include not only the mechanical integrity of the system, but its performance as well. Sample warranties are presented.

Towers—

Vibration, rigidity, and wind buffeting resistance are among the factors that should be appraised in purchasing a tower. This section discusses each of these topics.

How much should the tower cost? Should it be self-supporting or guyed? These questions are answered in depth. Standard methods of mounting the rotor/generator assembly atop the tower are assessed.

Electrical Equipment—

From a standpoint of the generation of electricity, wind energy conversion systems are of two basic types—the "stand-alone" system and the "grid-connected" system. This section examines both types in detail, surveying the advantages and disadvantages of each.

The stand-alone system is self-contained and uses heavy-duty batteries to store excess power during periods of high winds for later use when the winds diminish. Battery "banks," the text declares, are usually of sufficient size to provide three to five days' storage capacity. A backup generator is required for emergencies. Costs involved in installing such a system are evaluated. Typical battery storage rooms are pictured. Battery maintenance is discussed.

Other power-storage methods, while largely

theoretical, are mentioned. These include hydrogen storage, flywheel storage, and compressed air storage.

Batteries provide only direct current, the text points out, which won't work in most appliance motors and can ruin stereos and TV sets. These require alternating current. The solution: The system must contain an inverter to turn d.c. into a.c. Different kinds of inverters are surveyed.

"Stand alone systems," says the text, "make the most sense in rural or isolated locations where the costs of bringing in commercial electric power are high. But in areas where commercial power already exists or is available at relatively low cost, a grid-connected system is recommended." The last-named is explained in detail. A synchronous inverter that interfaces with the local commercial power system and matches the home owner's energy output with the local line voltage and frequency is what is required. When the wind energy system is producing more power than the home owner requires, the synchronous inverter feeds the excess into the utility grid. In those instances where the system is not producing sufficient power for the home, the inverter draws what's needed for the utility. Various types of synchronous inverters are appraised.

These chapters feature several case histories, comprehensive interviews with individuals who operate successful wind energy conversion systems. These include a Cape Cod couple whose wind system works so well that they're able to run their electric meter backward, selling power to the local utility, and a Puget Sound family whose wind system, mounted atop a 20-foot tower 50 feet from their house, cost not much more than $1,000.

Another chapter of the book is devoted to wind systems that are used exclusively for pumping water.

"Pinwheels on stilts," they have been called. The various components required for such a system are explained. These include: a multibladed rotor mounted atop a tower; a tail vane (to keep the blade facing into the wind); a shaft connected to a set of gears and a cam that move a connecting rod up and down; the rod, which, in turn, operates the pump. A storage tank is also required. A typical system is diagramed. Various systems are pictured.

One of the book's final chapters is titled "Wind Electric Conversion Systems You Can Build Yourself." It gives detailed instructions and carefully drawn plans for constructing a wind energy system that is capable of producing electricity for a variety of light-duty tasks. It costs $350 to build the unit. Construction is depicted by means of step-by-step photographs. Plans and designs for the construction of wind systems are available from a wide range of sources, and these are listed. For instance, VITA (Volunteers in Technical Assistance) offers a 40-page booklet titled "Low Cost Windmill for Developing Nations." It presents complete plans for building a wind machine capable of providing power for a wide range of uses.

The concluding chapter of the book discusses federal energy tax credits available to owners of wind energy systems.

The text explains the two aspects of residential energy credit:

- Credit for energy conservation which, as of January 1, 1980, amounted to 15 percent of the first $2,000 spent on components to conserve energy.

- Credit for renewable energy-source expenditures, which, as of the same date, amounted to 30 percent of the first $2,000 spent.

The chapter also explains the energy conservation items for which one can take credit. These include:

- Insulation—fiberglass, cellulose, etc.—for ceilings, walls, floors, roofs, and water heaters.

- Storm or thermal windows or doors for the outside of your residence.

- Caulking or weather stripping for windows or doors for the outside of your residence.

- A furnace replacement burner that reduces the amount of fuel used.

- A device for modifying flue openings to make a heating system more efficient.

- An electrical or mechanical furnace ignition system that replaces a gas pilot light.

- A thermostat with an automatic setback.

- A meter that shows the cost of energy used.

Local tax breaks are also detailed. In Colorado, for example, the state offers an added 30 percent tax credit on top of the federal credit of 40 percent, which makes it possible to recoup 70 percent of the cost of a wind energy system in one year. Congress has also passed legislation, the text points out, making businessmen eligible for tax credits for wind energy expenditures. This chapter also examines the provisions of the Public Utility Regulatory Policies Act of 1978 (PURPA) that mandate that public utilities must purchase energy from qualified "small producers" at rates that are "just and reasonable."

The book's appendix provides sources for additional information, offering listings in these categories:

- Manufacturers and distributors of wind energy conversion systems in the United States and Canada.

- Manufacturers of anemometers and other weather instruments.

- Manufacturers and distributors of towers and mounting hardware.

- Private organizations (such as the American Wind Energy Association) that provide information and advice.

- Books and periodicals devoted to wind energy, including more than a dozen government publications.

Wind Power for Your Home is the first complete and practical guide to explain in detail how electric power may be derived from the wind. Previously published books on the subject have been either historical or highly technical. These include *Wind Catchers* (Stephen Greene Press, 1976, 226 pages, $12.95), a history of windmill progress in America beginning with Colonial times, and *Power from the Wind* (Van Nostrand, 1948, 224 pages, $9.95), which concerns the installation of the Smith-Putnam turbine near Rutland, Vermont, in 1941.

Wind Power for Your Home is 50,000 words in length and contains 100 photographs and drawings, these to be supplied by the author. Based largely on the author's interviews with wind system manufacturers, owners of wind systems, and government officials, both federal and local, the book is being prepared for delivery in the summer of 1983 for publication the following year.

George Sullivan has written a good-sized shelf of nonfiction books as a full-time free-lance author. Two of his recent books have concerned the field of alternate energy. They are *The Complete Book of Solar Energy* (G. P. Putnam's) and *Wood Burning Stoves* (Cornerstone Library, Simon & Schuster).

Mr. Sullivan was born in Lowell, Massachusetts, and brought up in Springfield. After three years of service as a Navy journalist, he attended Fordham University. Following graduation from Fordham, he worked in public relations in New York City before becoming a free-lance writer.

He lives in New York City with his wife. He is a member of PEN, the American Society of Journalists and Authors, and the Authors Guild.

Note how explicit and complete George Sullivan's book proposal is. Starting with his name and address at the top, it then gives a useful and descriptive title. Page 1 starts with an opening lead, and proves that the subject is a good one, and immediately relates it to the potential buyer. Then it goes into a description of the chapters, citing many facts and specifics. Throughout it emphasizes the usefulness of the book to the book buyer. It briefly describes other books on the subject and contrasts his approach to theirs. He cites two books he himself has written on similar subjects, showing his chief qualification. He tells how long the book will be, how many illustrations it will have, and when he is prepared to deliver it. And he winds up with a succinct yet powerful brief author biography. Simon & Schuster published *Wind Power for Your Home* and sold more than 200,000 copies.

These two professional writers didn't need to submit sample chapters with their book proposals—they could show many already published books as samples of their work. But you, as a first-time author, are in a different situation.

ABOUT SAMPLE CHAPTERS

It is especially important to have sample chapters if you haven't published much on the topic of your book. If you have published a considerable amount, photocopies of your articles may suffice. Also, sample chapters are especially important if you are planning to handle your material in an unusual way or the subject is very technical. The publisher has to be convinced that the average reader can understand your material and that it will hold reader attention.

If you thought your memo alone was sufficient and the publisher asks for a sample chapter, don't panic. Writing it is not that hard. And the fact that the publisher has asked for it means that he's already halfway sold.

What is a chapter? It is one phase of your subject. It's like an article. It has a strong or intriguing beginning. It has a middle section that expounds on the point you have raised. And it has an ending that shows how that particular action turned out and hints at what happens next—a bit of a tease.

As illustration of what I mean, let's take author Norman Mailer in his book *Marilyn,* and at random pick Chapter 7 entitled "The Jewish Princess."

It begins with the "orgy of publicity" surrounding the wedding of Marilyn Monroe and playwright Arthur Miller.

The body of the chapter maps the rapid deterioration of the marriage and the problems Miller has with Marilyn during the filming of *The Misfits*. The filming also becomes a horror story for costar Clark Gable.

The chapter ends with what happens as a result of all the tension—Gable's heart attack the day after shooting finished, and his death eleven days later.

There you have a good chapter. One that has a strong beginning, a middle, and an end that ties up a segment of the story. It is a chapter that can stand alone. We'll go more into the subject of sample chapters later.

As I have indicated, publishers are not shy about asking for a sample chapter or two if they are having trouble making up their minds on whether to make a bid for the book, based on your memo. They may need to know you can give simple directions in weaving, for instance, or making a collage. They may need to know how you plan to hook the reader. In that case send the first chapter, which sets the tone and gives the general feeling of the book.

It must be an exciting chapter—an important chapter—but perhaps not the most important or the one giving away the deepest secret or most startling inside information.

The problem is that the publisher may not take the book.

Though most publishers are ethical and do not leak information, you cannot be sure. You must protect yourself as best you can. Never have anything damaging even in a memo. If you must put it in, check it with your lawyer to be sure you can't be sued. And remember the word "alleged." It may be the most important word in your memo in keeping you out of trouble. "He alleges." "He claims that So-and-so sired a baby." Be as careful in your memo as you would be in your manuscript.

HELP WITH YOUR PROPOSAL

You have seen examples of proposals that have sold books. Now let's go from cases to general advice. Here is a slightly revised version of a six-page guide I send to clients who ask for help in writing their book proposals

HOW TO WRITE A NONFICTION BOOK PROPOSAL

The presentation of a book to an agent or publisher is a practical document, not a sample of the author's good writing style. It should be from twelve to twenty five pages long. It should tell all the facts about the project in a concise, straightforward way.

It should include such elements as the subject and why the subject is interesting, the need for the book, sample anecdotes to show the kind of material available, the market for the book, the author's qualifications, the author's plan of how to present his subject, and such other information as he wishes to present.

It can be accompanied by a "Tentative Table of Contents," and the author's bio or résumé (in the case of coauthors, bios or résumés of each author), and ideally, should have some sample of the author's published or unpublished work attached to prove that he can write effectively. If possible, it should include a "working title," that is, a title that is simple, memorable, convenient, and indicative of the book's content. The working title and the final title are often very different, so it is not necessary to agonize over a good working title. If no other working title can be thought of, then it might be called "untitled nonfiction book project about (subject of book)."

The purpose of the presentation, which can either be a memorandum or a letter with attachments, is to supply complete information necessary for a publisher to use in making a decision about whether or not to make an offer for the book. Therefore, also included should be an estimate of the amount of time needed to write the book, and an estimate of the probable length, stated either in number of words or number of double-spaced manuscript pages (not book pages), and an indication of the kind of illustrations the author can supply, if any.

The presentation will be seen not only by an editor or editor in chief, but by the sales department, the publicity department, and in some cases by executives of the company. Therefore, it must be plain enough and broad enough in its content and appeal to be of interest to anyone who sees it. It must be able to speak for itself without the author being there to explain it or prove any of its points. This aspect should be kept in mind, even when the author has already been in direct contact with several members of a publishing house.

Publishers do not expect an author to be modest or reticent about his qualifications or achievements. And a passionate belief in the importance of the subject is not a handicap. Nor is a well-buttressed statement that the author feels himself to be the most qualified person to do the book.

The author's bio should include any information or experience that is even remotely related to his qualifications. Authors with very extensive qualifications can sometimes rely on published material about themselves, such as their *Who's Who* bio, or an article or review that discusses their backgrounds very thoroughly. If this method is used, a copy of the printed material should be attached, not merely referred or alluded to.

It is not necessary or preferred to bind a presentation. Simply place a typewritten title page on top, and a paper clip or staple is quite sufficient to hold the pages together. The presentation need not be typeset or even elegantly typed. But it must be typed well enough so that it can be Xeroxed with a clear copy resulting. If you still desire to fancy it up a bit, a plain or colored file folder is an appropriate cover with a label attached, identifying its title and author.

That is the background information you need. Now for the actual letter or memo you need to send to your literary agent or the publisher, telling him or her about your book.

Outline

Form: Either a letter or a memo

1. An introductory statement that you are going to write a book, with tentative title and a description of the subject and scope of the book. This can vary from a sentence or two to a page or more, but brevity is preferable. It is like the lead paragraph in a newspaper story, except that it can be longer.

2. An indication of the public's appetite for (or need for) your book and proof of the importance of the book's subject to a definite audience. You can point to other material published or available about the subject, in newspapers, magazines, on radio, TV, in movies. You can mention other books related to the subject and why yours is different and still needed. You can give a brief history of the story, together with a statement of the broadness of the appeal of the subject, and a definition of the market for your book—what groups of persons it will appeal to, reviewers who might find it of interest, the sort of publicity you expect. You might mention groups and clubs you think will give autograph parties.

3. Some sample anecdotes to indicate the kind of interesting information and the approach the author will use. A few surprising facts or shockers the book will contain.

4. A statement of your qualifications to write the book: the length of your association with the story, other related

works of yours on the subject—even office reports or technical papers. Personal contacts that will help the book, the extent of this network of information and sources. The amount of research already done.

Then say that further material will be found in the biography that is enclosed. [Help with your bio is in the next chapter, Chapter 6, "Assembling Bio and Exhibits to Add Flash and Bulk to Your Presentation."]

5. A brief description of the author's plan for the book's organization, referring the reader to the attached "Table of Contents" for details.

6. The approximate length of your projected book, expressed either in estimated number of words or number of double-spaced manuscript pages. Give a description of the illustrations the author will supply, if any.

7. A statement of the approximate length of time, in months, it will take you to write the book from the time of signing the contract. If a substantial advance is required, mention why. It can be you are the only person in the world who has this information, or mention various large advances you have received in the past. Or explain that it will be an expensive book to write because of travel, necessity to acquire research materials, or whatever. It is usually better (unless there is rigid need for a minimum amount of money) not to specify exactly the amount of advance required.

8. Any miscellaneous comments, such as need for speed in getting a decision, if required, need for speed of publication, if required. It might be that the book will tie in with a world event, such as the Olympics. Or it may be you have an offer from another publishing house but are not happy with it. Do not mention the name of the publisher making the offer and only say so if it is true. You stand a chance of killing a new offer if the new publisher does not want to compete to make a high bid. Remember, the advance is only the first part of your book earnings. Actually, if you have an agent, it is wise to let him explain your monetary needs or existing bid from another publisher.

9. Tentative Table of Contents. The chapter titles can de-

scribe the content of chapters or tease the imagination. It is wise to include a paragraph or more of description of the contents of each chapter.

10. Author's bio or résumé, plus any exhibits of interest, any samples already written. In the next chapter we'll talk about how to put together an impressive but honest bio.

6

Assembling Bio and Exhibits
to Add Flash and Bulk
to Your Presentation

When I have told first-time authors I need their bio for the publisher, some have recoiled in horror and insisted they have no background worth speaking of and probably now the publisher won't want their book. Nonsense. The publisher can make a good thing of it if you say that you left school in the fourth grade to support your mother, worked in the potato fields, and that you educated yourself in libraries and in night school. Actually, I'm impressed myself!

TAILORING YOUR "AUTHOR'S BIOGRAPHY" TO YOUR PROJECT

From long practice of interviewing writers, I have learned that almost all of them have qualifications to write their books—even though often they have never thought about writing their qualifications down.

For example, most writers have some formal education—often college degrees and specialized training. Or, if they don't, they learned the fascinating facts they plan to include in their books through equally fascinating life experiences. So don't hold back these obvious qualifications—your complete education, whatever it is and in whatever field, your special training, and your related life experiences.

Perhaps you have done some kind of writing previously— for a newspaper, for a house organ of a business, for a magazine, for an academic journal, press releases, ad copy, brochures for organizations, legal briefs, movie or video scripts, for school publications, long letters home while traveling, in a diary or journal, school and college term papers, thesis and dissertations, newsletters for organizations, business reports.

Tell it. Don't embroider it. Just tell it.

As an editor and publisher, I was reassured by *any* kind of writing experience—naturally, the more the better. So don't neglect to tell your previous writing experience, however meager or unrelated. If your work has been published extensively in newspapers or magazines, don't just say so— give a list of your credits even if it is a long one, attached to your author's biography, and include both in your book presentation package.

Your job experience, or professional life, may be very impressive to a publisher. At the very least, it shows you have been able to get a certain number of things done in your life. So list your most important jobs and titles, and summarize the rest.

Any connection you have with your subject should be featured—"Have collected material on wind-surfing for fifteen years, and have three file drawers full of research materials." "Have practiced woodworking for several years and won three awards." "Have attended more than fifty professional meetings of stamp dealers and know personally the main stamp collectors of the U.S.A." "Have corresponded with the world's leading experts on the history of Hawaii for the past seven years." "Have done seven lengthy interviews with patients who recovered from Hodgkin's disease, and am prepared to contact others to complete the research."

Any awards you have won in connection with your subject are of particular interest. Don't be shy in mentioning fifth place in a competition—you are a writer now and don't have to be number one in a competition. Sophia Loren won only second place in a beauty contest—and still went on to become a superstar.

Organizations you belong to are of interest to a publisher, so list any that are important in themselves or related to your subject.

If you are listed in directories, include the information.

If you have lectured or made speeches or been chairman of meetings, that's interesting—you can promote your book with the public.

If you have appeared on TV, been interviewed on the radio or in print—even in organization newsletters or company publications—it's worth including.

Have you traveled extensively? Do you read and speak foreign languages? Then say so.

Have you ever been elected to office? That shows initiative and leadership.

After you have assembled all the information about yourself, write it up, very completely, in a three- or four-page narrative.

Then, and only then, condense it a little if you like, say to a page, or a page and a half, but keep the flavor—those amusing or interesting facts about yourself and your project. It can be much longer than the average author's bio that you see on a book jacket. The publishing house has copywriters who translate your bio to the snappy copy on the book jacket, condensing these salient points.

Here is the author's bio of Patricia Penton Leimbach, as it appeared on the jacket of her first book, *A Thread of Blue Denim: A Farm Woman's Celebration of Country Living:*

> Pat Leimbach lives with her full-time farming husband and three sons at End-O' Way Farm, Vermilion, Ohio. Her column, "The Country Wife," has long been a popular feature of the Elyria *Chronicle-Telegram,* and she is *Farm Journal's* "favorite female contributor.

"Fifteen minutes with Pat Leimbach reveals more of the real American farmer than fifteen days with a farm magazine or fifteen years with *The New York Times.*"

—*Farm Journal*

Pretty neat, isn't it? When you read it, it's hard to guess how much material the publisher originally had to work with.

Attached to your bio, you should include any articles about yourself, your listing in *Who's Who* or other directories, or other published biographical material about yourself. Perhaps you have a press release used for your lectures or speeches.

If your qualifications are very powerful and you are nationally known, it might be best to state them briefly. Here is the author's bio from *Justice: The Memoirs of an Attorney General,* by Richard Kleindienst:

Richard Kleindienst is an attorney in Tucson. He graduated magna cum laude from Harvard in 1947, and Harvard Law School in 1950. He was deputy attorney general from 1969 to 1972, and attorney general in 1972 and 1973. He lives in Tucson with his wife, Margaret, and has four children.

The qualifications of an expert, who is not a national figure, usually are given in more detail to prove his credentials to the general public. Here is the author's bio of Alan S. Donnahoe, author of *Basic Business Statistics for Managers:*

Alan S. Donnahoe served as Chief Executive Officer of Media General in its first twenty years as a public company, during which it grew from a very small company, with only $14 million in total assets, to Fortune 500 status as the seventh largest newspaper company in the country. Today, in addition to long experience on other boards, he continues as vice chairman and director of Media General.

During his career he has dealt with thousands of corporate reports, created one of the finest management information systems ever devised, and developed what may be one of the outstanding market research programs in the United States. Under his direction, Media General created its Financial Services Division, with a variety of publications and one of the most comprehensive databases available on more than 4,000 companies in the United States.

Now you have your proposal. You have your bio. That's good but it's not enough. Let's take a harder look at sample chapters and find out how publishers feel about them, and then let's add a little flash.

MORE ON SAMPLE CHAPTERS

Some editors are like shoppers in a cheese store. They want to taste a sample before they buy the whole package. Yes, the display is good and it is very tempting, but they still want to hold off with that decision.

Some publishers are inflexible in their demand for sample chapters before they will put a book under contract. When I presented the proposal for my first book, *How to Write and Sell Your First Novel,* written in collaboration with Fran Leighton, I did not include a sample chapter.

Carol Cartaino, then editor in chief of Writer's Digest Books, said she liked it, but that she would also have to see at least one sample chapter—it was company policy. Carol knew me well; we had worked together for a time in the same company. But that made no difference. Company rules rule. Keep that in mind and don't feel hurt if you are told that exceptions cannot be made for you. In this case, even though Carol knew my abilities, others in her firm did not.

ADVICE ON SAMPLE CHAPTERS

Writing sample chapters presents certain problems. If you haven't completed your research and need financing from a publisher to ferret out the most crucial or hidden part of it—perhaps going halfway across the country to a little-known archive to get it—you may have to write a chapter about one of the less important aspects of your subject.

And which chapter should you write? The first chapter might not always be suitable. If you are writing a book about a dangerous exploration, Chapter 1 may be devoted to how the decision came about—the decision to undertake the exploration and the preparations for it. But this chapter is not the gist of your book—the long story of the difficulties you overcame and what you found when you finally arrived.

In that case, write a chapter that narrates an incident in which you are in deep trouble—a cliff-hanger of a chapter. That's what Peter and Barbara Jenkins did in a book I have in my library, *A Walk Across America*. They literally are about to fall off a cliff when the book opens.

A second way to handle the problem is to change your book a bit. Instead of telling how the great adventure came about and the preparations for it, do what John Kirk, editor in chief of Bison Books, recommends for informational books. Write a first chapter that is "an overview of the whole book," as he calls it. It summarizes what the book will cover.

For books on issues, he believes a first chapter that strongly states your thesis is most effective—and you can then devote the rest of the book to proving your point.

Such first chapters fit the formula, "Tell them what you're going to tell them, tell them, then tell them what you told them."

Another approach is to select a chapter that is a fascinating case study from the middle of the book. For our book on the novel, referred to earlier, I wrote a chapter showing the development and unique virtues of an author who started writing novels late in his life—Arthur Gladstone—but who went on to write almost fifty published novels.

It was not terribly hard to write but, as Fran likes to say, "No writing is easy." In preparation for the chapter I could not rely just on memory. I had to do new research and carry on a long telephone interview with my subject, even though I had selected Gladstone because I already knew a good deal about his life and work—my literary agency had represented him. I also selected him because I knew that his writing methods exemplified certain important points I wanted to make in the book.

WHAT DO EDITORS LOOK FOR IN SAMPLE CHAPTERS?

George Witte, an editor at St. Martin's Press, likes to see a good-sized sample—even up to 100 pages of a 300-page manuscript from an unpublished author. He says he hopes the writer will show in this material "that he is able to write, has a spark in his writing." He wants to be sure "the writer has done a good chunk of his research" and can write with "a voice of authority." In some cases, however, such as when the author has journalistic credits, Witte does sign up books without sample material.

On the other hand, *Katherine Schowalter,* an editor for John Wiley & Sons, usually doesn't want much, or even any, sample material. To her, the presentation itself, with perhaps an Introduction, is enough. What she wants, she says, is to be convinced by the presentation that the audience is there.

She wants your presentation to show her that you have thought out your book, researched your subject, and examined the competition to determine if there is indeed a real niche for *your* new work.

Even if there are many already published books on your subject, Schowalter still thinks there is a chance for you. She believes a very well-written *writing sample* in that case might convince her that it would be all right to publish still another. And what would the sample do? It might show her, she says, that you can deal with the subject better than your competitors.

Charlotte Mayerson, of Random House, likes to see two sample chapters, plus as much more of the author's published work as possible—*included in the submission,* not just mentioned. What she looks for in the samples are indications that the "writer knows how to write" and "has a thesis that comes out in the material." She also wants to find out if the subject can bear expansion into a book-length work, rather than a magazine article. She tries to determine if "the writer knows how to organize his material."

Tom Miller, whom I interviewed when he was at McGraw-Hill, is more concerned about the whole proposal than the sample material, but he wants both. He likes to get a proposal which is 25 to 100 pages long, including sample material, and believes that samples of other published writing by the author can be sufficient for him to judge the quality of the writer's work.

Miller wants the proposal to have unusual ideas and reflect "a premise—something not done before." As for the additional exhibits to go along with the proposal, he wants the author to have done "a market survey, and detail the competition." He also wants the writer to emphasize his credentials, "not in two lines."

These requests should not bother you because you have just read in Chapter 4, "Targeting Your Audience—the Vital First Step," how to survey the market—your targeted readership—and how to find competing books at the library. And you have just finished reading about your author's biography, earlier in this chapter.

As for what else Miller wants, these items, too, are not unreasonable. He wants to see a detailed table of contents—"it must be in chapters." He needs a "statement of intent, why the author wants to write it." In any sample material he looks for "good writing, clarity of thought, organized structure" so he can be assured the author can put his book together. He wants books that have a "narrative argument—a thesis," so that the "book says something, points to something."

As you can see, all these editors emphasized strongly that the presentation itself has to be convincing first—the sample material is included mainly to prove that you can write with authority.

HOW IMPORTANT ARE EXHIBITS AND BULK?

Once upon a time I handed a first-rate four-page proposal to an editor in his office and asked him to read it on the spot. He did read it, said it was excellent, and then added, "It's not a very weighty proposal."

Outraged, I replied, "What do you mean it's not weighty! This will be a thorough definitive treatment of the subject."

Holding the thin proposal in his hand and lifting it up and down, he answered, "I mean it doesn't weigh much. I don't know if I can get a lot of money for so few pages. Isn't there anything you can add to it?"

I called the author and asked him if he had any newspaper and magazine articles about his subject in his research collection. "Tons of them," he said. "Any photos?" "Plenty." "Didn't you write two articles on this?" "Actually, it was three."

The writer sent me photocopies of six newspaper and magazine stories covering his subject, five photographs, and copies of his own three articles. To his very brief author's bio, we added a complete list of his writings, and his extensively presented job résumé. The proposal, his expanded bio, and the additional material—*exhibits* to show the importance of his subject and his mastery of it—made the whole thing weigh over half a pound, rather than one ounce.

I put it in a heavy cardboard folder and added a two-page letter of my own on top of that. We made the sale, and for money that motivated the writer to get right to work.

Afterward, I reflected on my own days as an acquiring editor who had to impress management with the importance of a subject and the qualifications of the author. I remembered how I got a proposal for a chess book past the jaundiced eye of a non-games-playing president of my company by laying out—completely covering his large desk—newspaper and magazine feature stories about its chess-champion author, Lisa Lane.

I recalled proving, as an agent, that a New York City

detective had had an exciting career by attaching to her well-written proposal full-sized photocopies of almost a dozen different front pages of the New York *Daily News*, all saying, "LADY COP CATCHES . . ." and receiving two offers to contract for her book—*Detective Marie Cirile*—from Doubleday and from Crown.

Exhibits that show the author has a good track record in almost anything can help impress the publisher or editor you are dealing with.

ADDITIONAL EXHIBITS

So now it's time to think about what else you can add to provide your editor and publisher with flash and bulk and prove that yours is indeed a weighty, important book.

Do you have sample illustrations? Photos? Charts and graphs? Diagrams? Cartoons and other art? If yours is an action or how-to book, do you have photographs of yourself in action, illustrating your subject?

Do you have news articles about your subject? Magazine features about it?

Do you have published samples of your writing?

Have you already assembled a bibliography?

Do you have videos of yourself on television, or yourself delivering a lecture or speech?

Do you have tapes of radio interviews, or of your speeches?

ARE YOU IN *WHO'S WHO* OR OTHER REFERENCE BOOKS?

If you are, photocopy the insert on you and send it along. If you are an engineer and are acknowledged as an outstanding one by being included in an important reference book, that will surely sell the publisher on your competence to write a book on engineering or a related subject.

SAMPLE ILLUSTRATIONS—PHOTO, ART

It is best not to send valuable original photos, original art, or any only copy of your material to a publisher or agent, as it might get lost or damaged. Better to send photocopies. But remember that some photocopy machines make *much* better copies of photos and art than others. Take the trouble to locate the right kind of machine—don't be lazy about this. It is a good idea to put captions on the photocopies if they are needed for an understanding of the material.

Should you include a photo of yourself? Yes, if it truly contributes to the presentation. If you are a potter and your book is about pottery making, photos of yourself at the pottery wheel at work, surrounded by beautiful examples of your craft, will add a lot to your presentation. But if you are, say, a geologist, unless you are famous for your public lectures and TV commentaries, there is really no need for a photo of you (except for a photo that is an illustration in one of your published articles). Including one might make you appear vain.

Another exception is if you are writing a book on a new theory of exercise or a beauty book. A good photograph of you, in that case, is mandatory. The publisher wants to know if you look good enough to be a spokesman for your theory.

Also, if you maintain in your proposal that your book can be best promoted by a TV publicity tour by you, then include a good *informal* photo of recent vintage. A video cassette would be better still.

Diagrams, plans, and maps may be the right illustrations to include for a scientific or technical work.

Any cartoons or other art submitted should be of the highest professional quality—better to have none than some casual art done quickly by a friend as a favor to you. Editors can be very literal-minded and will think that what they see is what they will get, and they may turn down the book because they didn't like the art.

ARTICLES ON YOUR SUBJECT

The best exhibits are your own articles. Don't be shy about including them if they came from a small publication. The main thing is that they show you *in print*. Next, select articles and news stories about your subject by others, as these will show that the subject is interesting to the press and your book might get publicity. A summary of TV and radio coverage of your subject might be useful also.

OTHER WRITING BY YOU

If you have published printed pieces on other subjects in a style similar to the one you'll use in your book, be sure to include them—and label them with the publication's name and date. If you received cover credit, make sure you attach a copy of the magazine cover as well.

But *don't* include typewritten *manuscript* copies of your articles on other subjects that are not published yet—not even if they have been accepted. Manuscript material can confuse the editor—he might think the material, because it is type-written, is part of the sample chapters, and find it irrelevant, and wonder what the point is.

VIDEO AND AUDIO CASSETTES

A video cassette showing you appearing on TV, or an audio tape of a radio interview, can be an impressive exhibit. Be sure such enclosures are labeled with date, station (or network), and program name. And don't send your only copy! You can have copies made at a studio.

The best exhibit of this type is a professional video cassette made by a producer and offered for sale. When Carol Cartaino as the agent was selling a series of new books by "America's Number One Cleaning Expert," Don Aslett, she was able to prove he was a great lecturer and TV guest by showing him in action on a commercial cassette that had sold thousands of copies.

This exhibit, together with a massive collection of articles about him, helped her get a six-figure guarantee for him from New American Library.

Next best to a cassette would be tapes of interviews on programs, and finally, you might consider having a cassette made showing you in action, or one that is a collection of your TV interviews, with commentary by you or by a professional announcer.

LETTERS OF RECOMMENDATION

Unless the writers of such letters are *truly* famous or influential in your field, better skip these. Letters from obscure people make you look small-time.

No matter how favorable a rejection letter is from an editor or publisher, I would leave it out of any presentation. The editor now considering your project will have to think, "Why did they *really* reject it?"

ARE YOU FINALLY READY?

You have four impressive things:

- You have a powerful proposal to write your nonfiction book.

- You have either some sample chapters or a few excerpts—good strong anecdotes that will be in the book, or details of new discoveries, or whatever is appropriate.

- You have a good author biography to attach.

- You have put supporting exhibits with it.

Don't try to be fancy in the way you package these items. As mentioned previously, put them all in a plain or colored file folder and type a label on the front, with manuscript title, your name, your address and phone numbers. Don't bind it.

Don't have it set in type. Leave it loose, each section paper-clipped, so your editor can take out any part he wants to copy and circulate within his publishing house.

You're ready for market. So next we are going to decide *who* is to do that marketing of your book project.

Part III

The Road to Publication

7

Money Talk—Agent Talk

MONEY TALK

I hope that I have convinced you that money is not your first consideration in choosing the subject of your first nonfiction book. Still you need to know what the going rates are for books and what you can expect.

If you are a Tip O'Neill or a Nancy Reagan or a T. Boone Pickens or an Elizabeth Taylor or a president of the United States, writing your life story—a one-shot tell-all book about yourself—a publisher will pay you one million or two million or three million dollars to publish your book.

But now let's get down out of the clouds. Let's talk money when the subject does not have a name known around the world. The average nonfiction book advance, at this writing, for a first-time writer is in the range of $5,000 to $10,000. If the first-time writer gets a $12,000 advance, that's very nice.

My own experience, handling contracts as an agent, is that most advances are in the five-figure range with a small percentage in six figures.

It's always good to keep in mind that the advance is only the first payment of earnings on the book. When a paperback is sold, that adds to the earnings. And any sales to big and small book clubs add to the earnings. The publisher must earn back all of that advance, however, before you, the writer, get any of the subsidiary earnings under the terms of most contracts.

But you can't earn until you've sold the book. So let's get to a very important question:

SEARCH FOR AN AGENT OR MARKET IT YOURSELF?

Robert Skimin, a successful writer of both fiction—including fictionalized history—and nonfiction, used an agent for years but now acts as his own agent. "I like the board room, I like the negotiation," he told Fran. "And who cares more about my manuscript than I do? Nobody. Therefore I will protect it myself."

On the other hand, Frances Spatz Leighton went the other way. For years she did not use an agent. Now she does, and she says, "Only a fool acts as his own lawyer, and only a fool acts as his own literary agent." She adds, "If you speak highly of yourself, that's bragging. If an agent says it, that's the considered opinion of an expert. Anyway, I'm so thrilled at any publisher's saying yes that I would grab at the first offer and not try for a penny more. I'd be ten times richer today if I'd had an agent."

And listen to this comment from still another first-rate writer, Steven Linakis. "Agents did help me, but most are cold bastards and not very smart."

So who's right? Who's wrong? Do *you* need an agent?

There is truth in what all three writers say. Agents are a mixed bag. Some are benevolent and are genuinely interested in the person behind the manuscript. Some can't see you for the dollar signs in their eyes. And some are cranky and hard to get along with, as are some writers, some editors, some publishers. You'll just have to rely on signposts and your own gut feeling to decide if a certain agent is for you.

98

But first, let's consider if *any* agent is for you? Should you try to find an agent?

Who Should Not Work with an Agent?

If you cannot trust someone else to handle your money or you think everyone is trying to cheat you, you don't want an agent. It is the function of the agent to serve as the business end of the book sale. You would have to trust him. If you could not stand to have a real estate broker sell your house but would insist on doing it yourself, even if you knew you'd get less money, then you probably would not like anyone speaking for you and you had better try marketing your book yourself. What it comes down to is can you delegate responsibility to someone else? If you can't, don't even try to get an agent.

WHAT DOES AN AGENT DO?

Though an agent is not a magician, in many cases he has made the difference between getting a manuscript sold or not. And he or she can sometimes increase your earnings substantially. And he plans for the long haul. First, he will study your plan for your book project, and if he likes your outline, he will take the time to read your sample chapter or chapters. He will tell you what he thinks is good and bad about it, what is strong, what is weak.

If he thinks the book outline and sample chapter are ready to go to a publisher, often he will already know which publisher might be interested. It is his business to know which publisher favors which subjects and the advance that is apt to be offered. If you have shown the agent only an outline or book proposal, he will give his opinion of whether this particular project needs a sample chapter or two.

When the agent is satisfied with the outline and samples, he will submit the idea to the publisher he chooses. And with it, he will send a letter telling about you and your qualifications and urging the publisher to make a bid. Since he knows many individual publishers, he might phone them first to talk about you and your project.

In some cases the agent of your first book will deal with only one publisher at a time—to see how the publisher reacts and determine if there is some flaw you and he didn't notice. In other cases, when he thinks your subject is hot and delay will date it, he will put the book up for auction. This means he sends it to several publishers—perhaps half a dozen, or even fifteen or twenty—and tells them that if they are interested, he must have a bid by a certain date. If several publishers end up bidding, the agent is able to drive up the advance offered by telling each publisher the size of the offer the others have tendered—but usually not the rival publishers' names until after the auction is over.

High bid does not always get the book. Sometimes other considerations enhance the second highest bid and makes it the better choice. The high bid may want 10 percent of any movie rights while the other will settle for none. Also, one may make the highest offer based on including both North American and foreign book rights, while the other lets the agent sell the foreign rights separately, making it possible to get an additional advance for each foreign country.

If the hardback company also controls paperback rights, the hardback company can sometimes presell the paperback rights for such a large amount of money that all its expenses in putting out the hardback are already taken care of—and then some. A lazy or *fast-buck* publisher might not even bother to promote the hardback book or make a large printing of it because he has already made his profit. An agent works in your behalf to pin down what the publisher's plans are, as he knows his habits.

Another important consideration for choosing to use an agent is that before the book is even published, the literary agent may be able to line up a magazine or newspaper sale of excerpts from the book. Magazine publication of the first serial excerpts must be timed to be before publication date of the book to avoid contractual problems with the book publisher, who may control second serial rights—the right to sell excerpts after publication.

And speaking of legal troubles—which you would have if

you broke the publisher's contract—here is another bit of advice. If you choose not to use an agent, be sure to have a lawyer look at your book contract and explain it to you. Agents understand the fine print. So do lawyers who do work in the publishing field. It could happen that you have signed away rights on future books that you don't even know about.

Whole books are written about the trouble you can get into if you don't understand the publisher's contract. Most publishers are ethical and so are their contracts, but you need a protector when you walk in that legal mine field.

After the book is out—and sometimes before—the agent works on selling the book, the manuscript, or galleys to Hollywood for the big screen or for TV use. And those contracts are another mine field. Generally, an East Coast literary agent has a tie-in with a Hollywood agent. The Hollywood agent usually shares the agent's fee with the book agent, so you, the writer, pay nothing extra for that service.

Foreign sales are another lucrative field. Your agent has contacts with agents abroad, and some books end up translated into many languages.

There is nothing to stop you from contacting agents or publishers abroad, but your agent already has credibility since he has dealt with them in the past, usually through a network of foreign agents on the spot. Foreign publishers may not want to take a chance on dealing with an unknown so far away, nor should you take a chance on not being able to check up on whether you are getting all your royalties. Your agent's foreign co-agents will be on the spot, protecting your interests.

An agent can think of ways to get additional money for your book that may not even occur to you. Did you know that extra money can be earned by selling the right to have the book republished in large-size print for those with eye problems?

WHERE TO FIND AN AGENT

If you are convinced you need an agent, there are several ways to go about getting one.

1. *The phone book* is one way. I am one of those agents who used to have my office in Manhattan, but now have moved in favor of enjoying the wide open spaces of the country. But even though I have my office in a barn near Cincinnati, Ohio, I list my agency in the Yellow Pages of the New York phone book. The Manhattan Yellow Pages lists more than one hundred literary agents.

So, whatever city you live in, look in the New York Yellow Pages.

On the subject of out-of-New York agents, I remember an instance, when I was still in New York, when my then partner, James Seligmann, received a pretty good manuscript from an author in Minneapolis. He liked it, but thought it wasn't quite right for our agency, and I agreed. He returned it to the author, mentioning in his letter that there was a local agent right there in Minneapolis the author might want to contact. The author wrote back and said, "I had already contacted him, and he refused me because he had too many clients already." That proved to me that it wasn't necessary for an agent to be in New York to succeed.

You may form opinions about an agent by talking on the phone, but it is reassuring to visit the agent's office. Often agents will have framed covers of their clients' books on the wall, or large bookcases full of books they have sold. If you see no books or covers, don't hesitate to ask for the names of some of the books they have handled.

2. *Ask the editor* of the book review section of your newspaper if he or she knows a good agent for such-and-such kind of book—a history, or whatever.

You may get several names, and if the editor is a friend, he may also steer you away from a dubious agent.

3. *Publishers* can give you the names of many agents if they want to. Try writing to the editor in chief or a senior editor, and say that you have a proposal on your particular subject, which you want to submit, but you want to go through an agent. Most publishers will then mail you a list of agents—though sometimes you may get a phone call saying send it in right away!

4. *Lists of agents* can be found in reference books, which your library has:

Literary Market Place lists more than 200 agents.

Literary Agents of North America lists about 800 literary agents, including 14 in Canada.

Writer's Market has a section for literary agents.

The Authors Guild will send you a list. Write to 234 West 44th Street, New York, N.Y. 10036.

The Society of Authors' Representatives, Inc. (SAR) can supply some—the address is: 10 Astor Place, New York, N.Y. 10003. It is an association of literary agents that has been around for sixty years.

Independent Literary Agents Association (ILAA) can also help. Mailing address: c/o Ellen Levine Literary Agency, 432 Park Avenue South, Suite 1205, New York, N.Y. 10016.

HOW DO YOU KNOW YOUR AGENT IS COMPETENT, HONEST?

Once you have signed with an agent, only time will tell if he is honest as well as good at handling or placing your book and making money for you. Every field has suffered incidents when respected members have been accused of dishonesty, and there is no way you can absolutely predict it won't happen with your agent. You have to take a chance—you trust your stockbroker, don't you?—after checking the agent out before signing with him or her.

The way you do this is to get acquainted with the agent and his books. When he tells you what books he has handled, go to the library and take a look at those books. Did any become best-sellers? Are they significant works in their fields?

You might go so far as to call one or two publishers he has dealt with and try to speak to the editor who worked with the author mentioned. Say you are considering signing with an agent they have dealt with, Mr. So-and-so, and you would like their recommendation of him. Do they think you would do well to sign with him? Publishers are not going to say anything derogatory that will make them legally vulnerable, but you may be able to tell by their attitude whether you have a lemon.

The editor may say, "Well, he is certainly one of many agents we deal with. It is against our policy to recommend particular agents." This is hardly a warm recommendation, so you might want to seek further information from others.

Be sure to ask the agent how long he has been in business, and don't be distressed if he is brand-new in the field. Ask what he did before. It could be that he was an editor or executive in a publishing house—jobs that would give him good training for agenting.

Ask the agent what professional organizations dealing with agenting he belongs to. You can check with them for verification as well as finding out if he is a member in good standing.

On the Handling of Money

An ethical agent sends you the moneys coming to you from the publisher just as soon as he has received the check and it has cleared his bank. He also sends an accounting that shows how much he received from the publisher in royalties, advances, or whatever, how much he deducted for his commission, and the amount he is sending you, plus a copy of the publisher's statement.

It is perfectly all right for you to tell your agent you want to see the accounting statement he has received from the publisher, if for some reason he has failed to send it to you. That way you can know your agent's account is correct. If you have any suspicions of the accounting you receive, it is perfectly proper for you or your lawyer to request a copy of the statement directly from the publisher.

If You Have a Coauthor

It is much better to have the agent handle the coauthor's money than for you to get the full amount due the authors and give your collaborator a check. This can make for hard feelings and ruin a friendship. Fran Leighton, for example, never has money dealings with her coauthors, other than signing a letter of agreement with them. (This is outlined in Chapter 3, "Should You Go It Alone or Get a Coauthor?) Even if it is a matter of deducting the cost of typing or photocopying or Federal Express charges that they have agreed to share, Fran sends me the list of her expenses and lets me present it to the coauthor for approval and deduct for it.

Agent's Commissions

More than half of all agents charge 10 percent of the earnings of a manuscript from any source, for sales in the United States—and more for sales abroad. But if *you* don't earn, *they* don't earn, so most agents will try to do their best for you. Currently, the rates have gone up to 15 percent in many literary agencies. I, myself, now charge 15 percent for clients who signed with me after January 1, 1987, and 10 percent for those who have been with me for years. I charge 20 percent for foreign sales.

There are agents who want you to pay fees, such as $200 or more, just to read your manuscript and critique it. You can make up your mind whether to go along. A publisher, of course, charges nothing to read your manuscript. However, if the material is obviously poor or presented in an unappetizing way, the publisher probably will just return it without analytical comment.

ABOUT GETTING ALONG WITH AGENTS

The best advice I can give you is don't be intimidated by your agent. Remember, he cannot earn a penny if you aren't good, and he wouldn't be trying to sell you if you weren't good. Agents are proud of their big-name clients, and you may become one someday—and perhaps sooner than you think. So keep that in mind.

As for his irritability, sometimes it's just because he is overworked. He is like a warrior taking the slings and arrows when a publisher doesn't like something. Rejection is his everyday fare, and it doesn't taste good. Publishers know and blame him if writers don't make their deadlines or fail to live up to the promise of the outline and sample chapter.

Authors who hate rejection are better off working through an agent. I know Fran reminds me, "Don't tell me if anyone doesn't like it or says *no*. I don't want to know where it is—at what publisher. Just call me when you get a sale."

So now you have a glimpse of the agent's world. Be diplomatic. Thank the agent if he makes a sale and, if he seems not to be getting anywhere yet, say a kind word—"I know you are doing your best for me," or "I appreciate the effort you are making." It can't hurt, and it might help. I know I can use a kind word now and then—it might even inspire me to make more submissions.

WHAT YOUR LITERARY AGENT CAN'T DO FOR YOU

There is just one thing. Can you guess? The one thing the agent can't do for you is place a poorly written or poorly conceived book with a publisher. But it is not hopeless. If the writing is poor but the idea good, he can help you find a coauthor with the necessary expertise. Or if it is borderline writing and only parts are bad, he might come up with the right "book doctor" to help you—but the "book doctor" will charge a fee.

If you are determined to have a career in nonfiction writing, your agent may point you toward the proper places to go and courses to take to rub the rough edges off your writing style and your manner with people in the field. Georgetown University Summer Conference, in Washington, D.C., where Fran has given seminars, is one of the best, as is Bread Loaf Writers' Conference, which is associated with Middlebury College in Vermont. A third is the Pacific Northwest Writers' Conference, located in Seattle, Washington.

At some writers' conferences you will live on campus and experience dormitory life. You will hob nob with other writers, literary agents, editors of various publishing houses. By the end of the conference you will be much more at ease in the writing world, and you will have gotten bits of advice you had never wondered about or even knew you needed.

IF YOUR AGENT STRIKES OUT, WHAT THEN? SELF-MARKETING

If your agent can't sell your book, that doesn't mean you should give up. When I offered the manuscript of Thomas DeTitta to publishers, they wrote me wonderful letters praising his account of going all over the United States as a hitch-hiker—but they didn't make offers.

They were right to praise it. It held their attention. DeTitta had a good command of the language, honed by his years as a newspaper reporter. Living in the South, he had absorbed enough of its atmosphere to write a successful regional outdoor play.

None of this helped me place his nonfiction book, and after I had rejections from all the major publishers I usually deal with, I regretfully returned his fine manuscript to him.

DeTitta did not just throw it in a drawer. Energetically, he himself submitted his manuscript to several regional Southern publishers, including a few that were only recently established. Not long ago he called and said that Cherokee Publishers of Marietta, Georgia, was contracting to publish his book and even offering an advance on his royalty. I said I was happy for him and hoped his book sells a million. Stranger things have happened to first-time writers. And many fine books are published without an agent.

As you can see, not every agent is right for every book. And not every agent will submit to regional publishers or small houses that do not pay as well. Remember, the only earnings of the book that you can count on is in the advance— it may not earn more.

If the advance is only $1,000 or $2,000, all the small publisher can afford, the agent earns only $100 or $200—or a little more if he charges a 15 percent commission—hardly enough to pay his rent and Federal Express bills.

Now you begin to understand what may be the inside

107

story if, when you write or call agents and tell them about your manuscript or project, they say, "I'm sorry, that's not the kind of work I handle." Even if this happens many times, it doesn't necessarily mean your book is not publishable—it just means it is not suitable for agents who are looking for works that can be sold easily or that might become giant successes with large publishers.

On a plane flying to the American Booksellers Convention, an annual event where publishers show their wares to booksellers, I met a woman dressed in a beautiful wool dress. I asked her about it, and she said she raised sheep, sheared their wool, wove her own cloth—and wrote books about how to do this. Her books were published by a small local publisher in the Pacific Northwest, and several had sold many thousands of copies. No agent. She didn't have one. She didn't need one.

So, you see, a lot depends on what you are selling. If it is regional, you can handle it yourself, dealing with regional publishers who operate on a lower budget than "the big boys" of New York and Boston—and now and then surprise the world with a blockbuster of a regional book.

But generally, to deal with the publishing titans of New York, an agent is better equipped to do battle for a client or simply to convince the publisher of the book's merit.

A SAMPLE AGENT'S CONTRACT

Here are the points covered in the Agent's Agreement I use:

1. I become your exclusive agent for not only your books, but the dramatic rights to your work.

2. The only works of yours I can collect commissions from are those put under contract while I represent you (whether I made the sale or you made it alone makes no difference—it's just *when* the deal was made that matters)—not things you sold before you engaged me or after we have parted company.

3. If I sell a book of yours to a publisher, I get to be the agent of it, forever, for the dramatic rights and foreign sales.

To make dramatic rights sales and foreign sales, I can use co-agents.

4. Money earned by your work is paid to me, not you. I then deduct my commission and pay you your share promptly (which means *after* the check has cleared in my authors' account).

5. If you ask me to make copies of your work, or I order up to twenty books of yours from your publisher, or send you something by Express Mail, or otherwise engage in some unusual expense at your request, you must pay the cost.

6. You can fire me, or I can resign, anytime. Otherwise, the agreement runs on indefinitely. But even if you fire me or I resign, I still get commissions from earnings of agreements made while I was your agent, and I am still authorized to handle dramatic and foreign rights to books published under those agreements.

7. I'm not responsible if your work is lost, stolen, or damaged.

The commission charged is, of course, spelled out—in line with the discussion earlier in this chapter. Incidentally, when your agent uses a dramatic rights co-agent, your agent and the dramatic rights co-agent usually split the 10 percent or 15 percent commission, so this costs you nothing extra. And keep in mind that TV needs an endless supply of new material, frequently based on books.

Proof that agents are not ogres and that great friendships can develop with much good-natured kidding is shown in the dedication that the writing team of Stephen Goldin and Kathleen Sky wrote for their book, *The Business of Being a Writer*: "Dedicated to our agent Joseph Elder in the fond hope he'll become a multimillionaire on his 10 percent commission."

8

How to Target Publishers
and Get Their Attention

Attitude is everything. It can make or break your chances of getting your book published if you are acting as your own literary agent. Let me put it another way.

There are two approaches to the problem of deciding which publishers to submit your manuscript to. One is, "How on earth am I going to find a publisher?" The other is, "Which of the many good publishers should I aim it at?"

With the first, you are practically defeated before you start—with great effort, you come up with a publisher's name and address. You write a letter addressed to "Editor in Chief" and send it off, hoping for the best.

When it comes back, all too soon, maybe with a rejection slip or a letter saying they only read manuscripts sent by agents, you are crushed, and it is months or maybe years before you try again.

PLAN A CAMPAIGN

The other approach—the one I use as an agent—is to make a good list of publishers I will submit a project to before

I make a single submission. I plan a *campaign* to get the book under contract and published.

I force myself to be realistic—I know that the most likely outcome of any single submission I, *or anyone*, makes is a rejection. So I don't depend on inspiration or luck—I plan to try to prevail by good planning and steady work.

If I were defeated by rejections, I would have gone out of business long ago. I know that every mail will bring rejections—*and* some checks for royalties—and that from time to time I will get a phone call with an offer to publish a book. Yes, I have sold books with a single submission—but it's the exception, not the rule.

UNDERSTANDING REJECTION

Why do publishers reject book proposals and manuscripts? One reason is that they might think the project is not much good. I remember a classic session sitting with a publisher who arrived in his office in a bad humor.

Seizing a book proposal—an unsolicited submission—he leafed through it, stopping to read here and there. Then he dictated this letter to his secretary:

"Looking over your book idea, I see that it is not presented in a good style. Inspecting it further, I see that the content is not very good either. Since neither the style nor the content is satisfactory, I must return it to you." Fortunately, his secretary substituted a polite form rejection for his gruff turndown.

But there are other reasons you may get a rejection of your perfectly sound proposal, such as:

- Your work is not the kind of book they usually publish.

- They have a competing book, not just the same as yours, but similar in some way, already under contract.

- They already have a two-year supply of books to publish.

- The editor has an unreasonable prejudice against your kind of book. The editor in chief of a major paperback house once wrote to me, "I have to confess I just don't like books about California."

- The editor or publisher you selected is "hot" and is being flooded with good projects—many more than they can accept.

- The publisher is undergoing a reorganization.

- The publisher is strapped for funds.

- The editor you submitted to lacks clout, and can't get many books through, or is about to be fired, or has already decided to leave in a couple of months.

When you get a rejection letter, usually the editor won't tell you any of these reasons except the first, that it's the wrong kind of book for that publisher. Most likely, he'll say, "It's not right for us at this time."

So if you have written a sound proposal and your research shows there is a need for or a market for your book, don't take rejection letters personally.

When I'm tempted to give up too soon, I'm reminded of the story a worldly lady who had a coffee house in Greenwich Village told me. A personable but shy young man confided in her, in deep melancholy, "I just can't get women to go out on dates with me."

"How many women have you asked?"

"Two."

"Try two more," she advised.

MAKE A LITTLE LIST

With a list of potential publishers, you won't be in the same mood as that discouraged young fellow if you get a few rejections.

How do you make such a list?

First, consider what you know already. What publishers

have published books of the same type as yours, that you have read, and maybe have on your bookshelves, or read when you were doing some research? Put them on your list.

Look in *Subject Guide to Books in Print*, under headings related to your subject, and make notes on the publishers who have published the books listed there. You might want to go to the library and actually look at the books themselves. Maybe the author has put in his acknowledgments a grateful word to his editor—so you'll have not only a publisher's name but an editor's name as well. Or if you can find only a reprint, on the copyright page the name of the original publisher might be mentioned, as in "Published by arrangement with Random House."

Some book publishing directories give lists of publishers who publish books in particular categories. For example, *Literary Market Place: The Directory of American Book Publishing*, an annual, is so completely organized that it even has seventeen pages devoted to "Book Publishers, Classified by Subject Matter" in its 1988 volume.

Less expensive annual directories are *Writer's Market* and *Writer's Handbook*. All are helpful to the new author. After you look up the names of the publishers, turn to the detailed entries about them in the front of the book, to learn much more about these publishers and their addresses and personnel.

Librarians and booksellers are good sources of information about the kinds of books publishers have been doing recently.

Book reviews in your local paper and in *The New York Times Book Review* can be helpful. Also, consider reading such industry publications as *Library Journal* and *Publishers Weekly*, which review many books in brief form, or read those publications related to your subject, which may review books and give you a hint as to which publishers publish books in your field.

Professors who specialize in your subject may be helpful.

Other authors may be willing to share information with you.

Other experts in your field may have ideas.

So, using the methods listed above, you have assembled a list of target publishers, together with their addresses, and possibly some of their editors' names.

LOCATING EDITORS

Incidentally, if you have an editor's name and affiliation, either from the acknowledgments of a book, or from a newspaper or magazine article, or from attending a writers' conference or other meeting at which the editor spoke or circulated, it is a good idea to check out his present job—editors move around frequently from publisher to publisher.

One way to do this is to look up the editor's name in "Names and Numbers," the yellow pages at the back of *Literary Market Place,* the annual directory of American book publishing, mentioned in the Suggested Reading and Reference section at the end of this book. There you may find his current publisher affiliation, if his name is in the directory. Be sure to consult the latest volume!

Now that you have your list of target publishers—and I hope you have as many as a dozen or so publishers on it—how do you get their attention?

The two main methods are 1) through introductions or referrals from someone who knows an editor at one of your target publishers, and 2) through query letters and/or query phone calls followed by a query letter.

When I was an editor a Prentice-Hall, my son-in-law, Professor Melvin Fitting, a logician, introduced me to Professor Raymond A. Smullyan, his associate and mentor. Ray Smullyan, who taught logic and philosophy, had a book of logical puzzles he wanted published, called *What Is the Name of This Book?* I was delighted with his book and even more delighted when a few discreet inquiries revealed that he had an excellent reputation in his field and was a sought-after speaker for meetings of logicians and philosophers. We published his book to great acclaim and strong sales, and he followed up with a second book, *This Book Has No Title,* also a success, selling not only in the United States but internationally in various translations including a Soviet edition in Russian.

Sources of introductions to publishers and referrals are not only professors, but authors, reviewers, magazine and newspaper editors and publishers, booksellers, librarians, lawyers, free-lance editors, and anyone who knows people in book publishing. They might include advertising, insurance, and real estate agents who deal with publishers; paper manufacturers and merchants, printers and typesetters; designers, publicists, building contractors—and maybe even your barber or hairdresser. Bantam editors were reported to have met Lee Iacocca through their mutual barber.

Of course, you can attract a publisher simply by getting a lot of publicity—and then the publishers will seek *you* out, as has happened with many famous trial lawyers.

QUERIES

But if you can't find anyone to introduce you to an editor or publisher, not to worry—you can introduce yourself. The most common way, and a good one if you do it right, is to approach a publisher through query letters, or if you are bold, query phone calls followed by a query letter.

You can approach publishers in two steps or in one step. A two-step approach would be to send all the publishers on your prospect list a one-page query letter, briefly describing your book in a straightforward, businesslike way and possibly enclosing a short biography of yourself, or a newspaper or magazine clipping with a story about you, or a copy of one of your articles.

The *query letter* is a one-page digest of all the best points in your proposal—the name of your proposed book (don't hold back the title for fear it will be stolen, but if you are afraid give a lesser one), the need and market for the book, a description of its contents, and the most powerful of your qualifications.

Make *very* sure this letter is beautifully typed (never use

115

Xeroxes with the name of the editor or publisher typed in—I usually just throw such letters away), is grammatically correct, and has no misspellings. No matter how good a letter I receive, if it has several misspellings, I'm inclined to skip it.

You'll still need such a letter if you decide on the more expensive one-step method in which you send everything at one time. Here you end your query letter by stating that your proposal and sample chapters are enclosed. The proposal should be a clear photocopy.

Be sure to send with the query, or query and proposal, a self-addressed, stamped envelope with sufficient postage for reply or return of your material—otherwise you may never hear about it and won't even be sure it reached the publishers.

First-class mail for a letter, or letter and proposal, or UPS for a letter and proposal, is fine. I find it overly dramatic to receive an Express Mail or Federal Express package from someone I don't even know. But if you made a telephone query first and were encouraged to send your material in, these fast-delivery methods are appropriate, though not necessary.

TELEPHONE QUERIES

There is really no need for telephone queries in most cases, and they can irritate an editor or agent who is busy. Remember that you are a *writer* and not a telephone salesman. And editors are *readers*, so communicating with them in writing is appropriate.

But if your project is urgent and timely and you can be brief, convincing, and to the point on the telephone, you might want to call your list of publishers and try to talk to a suitable editor. Here are a few tricks that might help you.

- If you know of a good book recently published by the publisher, call the publicity department and ask for the name of the editor of the book, and then call him, saying you got his name from whoever gave it to you.

116

- Call the secretary or assistant to the editor in chief, and ask her or him who would be the best editor for your project.

- From a directory, select the name of a senior editor and try to reach him or her. If that editor turns out not to be the right one, ask for the name of the appropriate person.

For such calls, prepare notes. Tell your most important, attention-getting point first and the name of your project. Say immediately your chief qualification, and summarize the appeal of your book quickly. You're not trying to make a sale on the spot—you're just trying to get the editor to ask you to send in your presentation. When you have achieved that object, stop, thank the editor, and send it in—don't ramble on and waste the editor's valuable time.

Here is a query letter I received after such a succinct and effective call about a timely book:

Charles Shuttleworth
(address, with day and evening telephone numbers)

Oscar Collier
Collier Associates
(agency address)

Dear Oscar:

Enclosed are the first two chapters of the book I am writing in conjunction with Mark Lesly, one of the jurors in the trial of Bernhard Goetz, the subway gunman.

The outline for the remainder will become evident upon reading this text. I am following a chronological line. The next chapter will detail the opening statements of the prosecution and defense as the trial begins. Then the prosecution's case will be presented, followed by the defense's case, the final arguments, and the jury's deliberations, ending with an "Aftermath" concerning the public's reaction and Lesly's experiences with the media. It will be an extremely detailed, factual account of the trial proceedings, flavored by Lesly's particular observations and insights. As his opinions about the facts of the Goetz case take shape, so may the reader's, and his interpretation will not so shade the facts that the reader will not be able to make up his or her own mind.

It is interesting to note that Lesly in his diary believed Goetz guilty according to the evidence up until the judge's charge to the jury was given and the jurors began deliberating, when it became clear that, according to the law and how it was interpreted to them by the judge, Goetz was indeed an innocent man.

I'll look forward to hearing from you.

Yours truly,

Charles Shuttleworth

With the submission were the first two chapters (31 pages), and a one-page, impressive biography of Charles Shuttleworth. From the bio, I learned that he was twenty-eight, had a B.A. in Journalism and English, and an M.A. taken on a fellowship, during which he taught Freshman Composition. He had worked his way through college, but still was able to graduate magna cum laude, had won a writing prize, and was elected to honor societies. He had worked briefly for a magazine and was a legal proofreader. He had written a screenplay under contract to a producer.

After meeting him and Mark Lesly, a juror in the Bernhard Goetz trial who had made a number of TV appearances after the trial was over and had written a feature in the New York *Post* about his experiences, I arranged to represent them. After many submissions, including near-misses at Macmillan and McGraw-Hill, during which Charles and Mark

agreed orally—governs the outcome of that dispute. Even so, when your publisher makes a verbal offer to publish your book and goes on to discuss contract terms, listen closely, make notes, labeled with the date and nature of the discussion: "Telephone conversation with Wendy Jones, senior editor of Monster House Books, 8/8/89. Made offer of advance royalties, $12,500, payable ⅓ on signing, ⅓ on delivery of first half of manuscript, ⅓ on publisher's acceptance of final manuscript. . . . Promised to pay half of bill for photos needed. . . . Said I have until next Monday to reply."

Then, when the contract arrives, be sure that all the points you agreed to orally are down in black and white. It won't help you in a dispute if you say, "Well, you promised and I thought you put it in the contract." As the saying goes, "What you sees is what you gets." And it's all you gets!

Money isn't the only consideration in a contract. There are deadlines and promises of when the book will be published. And possibly the budget or plan for promotion of the book. And on and on.

While I won't go into great detail about negotiating tactics, I will just mention one point that you should bear in mind. You are negotiating with an editor. The editor isn't boss. He has to get approval of others—perhaps a board of editors, or perhaps his top superior, the president of the company, and/or the legal department. In dealing with you, he is acting as the front man for his publishing house. So he may use "nice guy, tough guy" tactics—that is, he may appear to be on your side (and might actually be on your side) but say "I wish I could," or, "I can't give you an answer until I check it out." He has to satisfy "them"—"the legal department" or "the publisher"—and don't be surprised if he calls you back to say, "I'm sorry, they just won't do that. It's against company policy." Sometimes it's true, or you may be making what they consider to be an unreasonable demand, such as asking the publisher to publish in two months when they want a year. Fast publishing costs the publisher much more money.

If you ask, "But haven't you published in a few months before?" you may get the reply, "Well, we did do a fast job a

123

couple of times, a few years ago, but I don't think it's warranted in this case." That is the time to say, "Please take it up with management. I think this is a special case—it's justified by the urgency of my exclusive material. Someone else could come out first." And you might get what you want, or at least a partial speedup.

The advantage of having an agent or attorney is that in arguing various points you can be a nice guy also. You can say, "It seems okay to me, but my adviser said I should absolutely hold the line on this one," and let your adviser be the tough guy. Or better yet, let your agent fight it out in a nice way.

While you and your editor will naturally want to reach agreement quickly, remember it is not unusual for negotiation of major contracts to go on for one or two weeks or longer. I know of a few instances when long delays were caused by two *publishers* negotiating with each other. In a paperback reprint contract between a hardcover publisher and a reprinter the discussion over fine print went on for several months, even though the general outline of the major terms had been quickly reached.

HOW MUCH CAN YOU RELY ON YOUR EDITOR'S ASSURANCES?

Your editor might say, on some point, such as when you ask for a publicity tour, "I can't get that in the contract, but I assure you I will get it done." Usually the editor truly means it and is being genuinely helpful. But remember, his superiors may veto him, or he may be fired or quit or be promoted to an administrative job, where he can't help you very much anymore. Still, make notes of what he promises so you can remind him of it later. Exact quotes are best, with dates! But again, remember that such assurances aren't part of the contract.

I am happy to say that from time to time an editor has written to me, as the agent, or to an author I represent, backing up the verbal promise in a carefully worded letter. "Our present intentions, which naturally might change, are . . ." or "company policy at this time is to advertise and promote this work extensively, subject to bookseller acceptance and distribution success. . . ."

So your editor's assurances do have some value, in a reputable firm, even if they lack the force of being part of the contract. In my own experience as agent, I try to get even verbal editor assurances, as they show he or she really does believe in the book and will try his or her best to make it succeed.

WHAT ARE THE MAIN ELEMENTS OF A BOOK CONTRACT?

Publisher's contracts cover the following points:

1. *Names of Contracting Parties*—author and publisher—and their addresses, provisional title of book, date of agreement.

2. *The Grant.* This covers what the publisher contracts to get from the author, and in what territory. This tells in general terms what rights the publisher is acquiring under exclusive and nonexclusive license from the author (or rarely, through outright purchase), such as "English language book rights" and certain "subsidiary rights" in either "the U.S.A. and its territories and possessions and Canada" or "throughout the world," or whatever, and for how long—often "duration of copyright" if the "work" is previously unpublished, or sometimes for a period of five, seven, or nine years if it is being reprinted.

3. *Copyright.* The copyright should be in the author's name, or if there are joint authors, the authors' names.

4. *Advance.* This details how the publisher will advance moneys to the author in advance of publication. The advance should be nonreturnable if the author delivers the manuscript and the publisher accepts it.

The amount of the advance and how it will be paid is subject to negotiation. If the work is unfinished, usually a part of the advance is paid on signing and the rest on completion. Sometimes the installments are broken down to three, four, or five parts, particularly when the advance is very large.

If possible, get your entire advance by the time of delivery of the final manuscript and its acceptance by the publisher, rather than letting part of it be deferred to "publication" or "six months after publication." The advance is important because it is the only money you are sure to get for your manuscript. It could happen that the book never gets published—at least by that publishing house.

5. *Royalties.* This details what royalties you will receive on the sale of each copy. These royalties are charged against the advance until the advance is paid off, after which you get additional payments from the publisher, based on the sales.

Typical trade book hardcover book royalties are 10 percent of list price for the first 5,000 copies sold; 12½ percent on the next 5,000 sold, and 15 percent on all sold over 10,000, but your publisher might say that for your kind of book, he will offer you a lesser deal because of special expenses for composition of complicated copy or perhaps use of many color illustrations.

Trade paperback royalties range from 5 percent (not too good) to 10 percent or more. Typically they would be 6 percent for the first 15,000, and 7½ percent thereafter, or a straight 6 percent or a straight 7½ percent of the catalog price.

Mass market paperback royalties range from 4 percent to 10 percent and up; a typical deal would be 6 percent for the first 150,000, 8 percent for the next 150,000, and 10 percent for all over 300,000. But many publishers would balk at the 10 percent part. If they do, try for a straight 8 percent.

The publisher's justification for paying lesser royalties on the first batch of books sold is that he wants to recover his "plant cost" that is, the cost of setting the book into type, hiring an artist to do the cover design, plates for illustrations, etc.

He has to sell a certain number of copies just to break even. But after "plant cost" has been recovered, the cost of reprinting additional copies is less, and he can afford to pay more royalties in most cases.

Usually the publisher pays lesser royalties for books sold at very high discounts, for books sold in Canada and abroad, for mail-order sales, and premium sales or other "special sales to nontraditional outlets."

Some publishers will offer a contract based on "actual cash received" rather than the catalog price of the book. This means that if the publisher sells a $10 book to a bookseller for a 40 percent discount ($6), you get a percentage of $6, not a percentage of $10.

Say royalties were 10 percent, then instead of getting $1 per book royalties, you would get 60¢. While this is an unattractive idea, if the publisher is highly qualified to sell your particular kind of book, and other publishers who offer higher royalties are not as successful with your type of book, you might still go along with the less advantageous deal, because authors are paid in dollars, not percentage points.

For example, if the "actual-cash-received" publisher, who pays less royalties per copy sold 100,000 copies, and you got $60,000, it still would be better to be with him than with a "catalog-price royalties" publisher who sold only 40,000, giving you $40,000 royalties. This example is rather simplified; in actual contracts there may be escalating royalties for some sales.

Textbook publishers, some how-to and technical publishers, and some just-plain-greedy publishers pay these lesser royalties, and almost all publishers pay them on high-discount sales.

6. *Subsidiary Rights.* The publisher will want to control additional rights, such as first and second serialization (the right to publish in a magazine or newspaper), book club rights, reprint rights, foreign English language rights, translation rights, selection and quotation rights, dramatic rights, movie and TV rights,

merchandising and commercial rights. If you have an agent, or have special qualifications in these fields, you might be able to retain some or all of these rights, but usually the publisher controls at least some of them and will try for a 50 percent–50 percent split of earnings from most of them. I consider the following fair if the book is unagented, and your first one; 90 percent to the author if publisher handles first serial rights, dramatic, movie, and TV rights; 75 percent to author for British and translation rights, and 50–50 on the rest.

If you want to *act as your own agent*, then study the books on publisher's contracts and decide what rights you yourself might be able to sell. If you are a magazine writer, you might want to retain the first serial rights and sell them yourself to your regular magazine customers.

If you are an actor, director, screenwriter, or movie producer, you will certainly want to hold on to dramatic, movie, TV, and allied rights, and try to place them yourself, or through an agent. If you are in the mail-order business, you might want to work out a special deal for mail-order rights, and so on.

If you don't know how to sell and handle these rights and don't want the bother, let the publisher handle them for you. However, you might want to have the publisher agree to consult with you on larger deals (say for over $1,000), and have him agree to inform you of each such sale and give you a copy of the contract for it if you ask.

Or you might want to restrict the publisher to handling dramatic and allied rights and foreign rights for a certain period of time—and be able to get the rights back if the publisher hasn't been able to sell them.

The publisher, of course, will resist these suggestions, but they are legitimate sources of negotiation, on all except the smallest contracts.

The philosophy you should adopt about subsidiary rights is "plan for success." While you are writing a seemingly narrow-interest book on, say, the subject of hydraulic pumps in irrigation, a video cassette, or movie sale, or TV documentary, or sale of rights in Pakistan, or the right to use the title on a T-shirt might seem remote. However, with some quaint or far-out title, say *Pumping for You*, it could happen. And if such opportunities arise, you want to have a contract that gives you ownership or control. Only then can you be sure you will get your rightful share as creator of the material on which a rights deal is based, or be able to kill the deal if it would damage your reputation.

7. *Publication Date.* The contract should state that your book will be published within a definite period of time after acceptance—two years is the acknowledged maximum. But try for an earlier publication date, say one year or eighteen months from the date the manuscript is accepted.

8. *Free Copies.* The publisher will offer you a small number of free copies and let you buy more at a discount. If you have a legitimate reason for asking for additional free copies—such as that you know many reviewers or other influential persons who might praise the book if you sent them autographed copies—then ask for additional free copies, and you might get them.

9. *Statements and Payments.* The publisher usually will agree to send you a royalty statement and settle all outstanding royalties due you (if any) after your book's publication, every six months. But actually, you often will get them three or four months after the end of the six-month period involved. For example, after the period from January 1 to June 30, the publisher should send you a statement around September, showing sales and other earnings in that period, and pay you any moneys owed at that time.

10. *Delivery of the Manuscript.* The contract will provide when you must deliver the manuscript, and in

what condition, how many words long, number of illustrations, and detail what happens if you fail to deliver (such as return of advance money).

Usually, if you are making good progress on your manuscript and can prove it (by showing a substantial part of the completed work), most publishers will make reasonable extensions of delivery dates if you apply for such extensions—but you cannot absolutely rely on this.

When I was first an agent, I helped author/attorney Mark Lane sell a brief presentation of his first book, *Rush to Judgment*, to Grove Press. It was 1963 and President Kennedy had just been assassinated. Mark Lane wanted to show how he, as defense attorney, would have defended the accused assassin, Lee Harvey Oswald, to cast doubt on his guilt.

The contract called for delivery of the finished manuscript within one year of the contract date. Mark started the book, but before he had finished, the Warren Commission stole the show.

It issued a twenty-six-volume report on its findings about the assassination, and reported it thought Oswald was the lone assassin. Mark Lane, reasonably, I thought, said to his publisher that he needed additional time to study this lengthy report, which he felt was the "prosecution case."

On the very day when one year was up, Grove ended the contract and asked for its advance back.

One of its editors told me that Grove's view was that interest in the assassination would be gone if it gave the author another year, or more, to finish his book.

Mark Lane continued to work on the book, sold it himself to a British publisher during a period when I had ceased being an agent, and it was published in the United States by Holt. It became a No. 1 best-seller. So there are two morals to the story: deliver on time, or your publisher may end your contract; but stick to your project anyway, as it may still become a big seller!

11. *Proofs.* The author usually gets to read proof. That means the typeset pages of the book, and the author

must agree to return them promptly. If you make a lot of changes in proof (say in excess of 10 percent of the cost of composition), the publisher will usually charge you for these changes. So try to make your changes in the manuscript, for which there is no publisher charge.

12. *Competing Works.* You hereby agree not to write a truly similar work for some other publisher. This clause is a problem for experts, who plan to write only on a single subject. Usually this clause is interpreted narrowly, so if you are an expert on contract bridge, you can legally write a book called *Competitive Bidding in Modern Bridge,* and later write a second book, *Contract Bridge Complete* (with only a section on bidding, in different words from those used in the first book) without violating the noncompetition clause. Bridge champion Edgar Kaplan did just that.

13. *The Warranty.* You must guarantee that your work is original; that it is your property (or that you have secured permission to quote any copyright material included); that it has not been previously published (or if it has been, that you have the right to make this contract); that it contains no harmful "recipe, formula, or instruction"; and that it does not libel anyone or invade anyone's privacy. The warranty clause is usually terrifying to an author, but it is pretty hard to get a publisher to change it.

If you are truly concerned, then discuss your worries with the publisher, and if you are still worried, with an attorney familiar with publishing matters. To help avoid libel and invasion of privacy difficulties, you might want to consult one of the legal guides listed in the Suggested Reading and Reference section at the end of this book.

14. *Termination.* The contract should provide that if the publisher does not keep the work in print, you can end the contract. You may be able to make new sales— perhaps revise or update the book.

15. *Option*. Most publishers will seek an option on your next book. You should try to delete this provision of the contract, or if you cannot, get it restricted to very simple language, such as "on terms to be arranged between Author and Publisher." Particularly, watch out for provisions that you have to deliver a complete manuscript, rather than a presentation, before the publisher will even look at it, and that you have to wait a long period of time before being able to submit a new work.

16. *Miscellaneous Provisions*. There are a number of other desirable elements you might want to have included, such as a "bankruptcy clause" that spells out your rights if the publisher becomes bankrupt; an auditing clause that lets you examine the publisher's books of account; approval of the final title of the book; approval of editing and copyediting (hard to get); approval of cover design (very hard to get); approval of your author biography and advertising (might be important to a doctor, minister, or someone else whose reputation is very valuable—or who must adhere to a code of ethics); approval of quotation permissions (a feminist might be outraged seeing her work being quoted in men's pictorial skin magazines).

If you believe in arbitration to settle disputes, some publishers will agree to an arbitration clause, provided the arbitration is in their home city, and others will not. I believe arbitration is of advantage to an author, as it is a cheaper and quicker way to settle a dispute than a court battle, where the publisher's superior experience and wealth give that side an advantage.

THE BOTTOM LINE

The most important thing is to get published. Keep this end result in mind when you try to get a publisher to change the contract. *You want to win publication more than you want to make minor points in the negotiation.* Therefore, focus on the main points—*how much* the advance is, *how soon* it is paid, and the *royalty terms.*

And most important of all, don't promise what you are not sure you can deliver, such as permissions to quote letters from a collection controlled by someone else, or photographs owned by other people. Say you will try to get these things. Allow yourself enough time to write the book, *including time for setbacks.*

This brief overview of book publishers' contracts is merely an introduction to this complex subject. You should not rely on it for complete information, but rather also consult an attorney, agent, or, if you wish to do it yourself, read one or more book-length treatments of the subject.

In most cases, your editor will be willing to spend a reasonable amount of time to explain the contract to you. Be sure to *read it yourself,* several times before signing. Then be prepared to live by it during your book's life. Save it as a collector's item in case your book—and you—make literary history. All of Fran's contracts are scheduled to go eventually to a university library, along with all her manuscripts and research notes.

Part IV

—◆—

Gathering Your Material and Actually Writing It

10

The Art of the Interview

I have seen a lot of book projects falter because the writer did not know how to handle his interviews—he was too abrasive or too casual or simply did not know how to behave on someone else's turf. Or, as in one case I know, the interview never took place because the writer phoning for the interview antagonized the subject's press secretary.

It is never too early to learn the art of the interview and never too late. This chapter may be the making of your future success in nonfiction.

Let's say that you have decided to do a biography of a famous person. Or the person is an expert in the field in which you have chosen to do a book. You need to have a serious interview with him or her. How do you go about that *first interview?* What if you *already know* the famous person or at least have met at several gatherings? What if you've *never met?*

GETTING THAT FIRST INTERVIEW

Don't think that you can pop into someone's office—a senator or business tycoon—and he will drop everything and see you. And don't think that if you wait and catch him walking down the hall or in a parking lot, he will stop and talk with you. He will most likely rush off with a "Sorry," or "Call my office."

So be realistic. Do things in acceptable style.

INTERVIEW WITH A STRANGER

If you've decided you need to interview a certain person for your book, here are the points to keep in mind:

1. You might not be able to reach him on the phone and will have to make an appointment through his secretary or public relations assistant. Either person will demand to know what you want him for, and you cannot be secretive or you may never get through.

Have written out, in front of you, a brief statement of what the book is about so you don't hem and haw. You might say, "I'm writing a book for St. Martin's Press, a major New York publisher, and I would like to interview him because he is an expert in the field of _____." Or, "I'm planning to do a book on the late _____, and since they were colleagues, he may have some anecdotes and good background material that only he can supply." Or, "I'm doing a book on his life and career, and I would like his cooperation on it, if possible."

If the assistant says, "Mr. So-and-so is never quoted," you can say, "That's fine. I will use the anecdotes without attribution then." Or, "It will be an off-the-record interview."

2. If you can't reach anyone by phone, you will have to write a letter and ask for an interview. In this case, address it directly to your interview subject. You may even have trouble getting the man's address. You may have to write him in care of a university where he is part of a research team. Or you may have to check scholarly journals to find his affiliation.

Say your expert has written an article in *Scientific Amer-*

ican. You have the article, and that is why you must interview him. On the Contributors Page of the magazine it will say, "So-and-so is a professor of metallurgy at California Institute of Technology." But when you try to reach him by phone, they tell you he's on leave doing independent research. So again you must ask for his address, and the university will undoubtedly give it to you or agree to forward your letter if they do not give out addresses.

3. Let's assume you get your appointment. Now you must prepare to meet this personage. You do some research on him. You look him up in directories of his field, in *Who's Who*, and you use your library's on-line computer research facility to assemble a bibliography of his work. At least scan abstracts of his articles and books.

If he's famous and has been in the news, you can look him up in *The New York Times Index* or the indexes of the newspapers of his city. You can also check and see if there are entries on him in the *Reader's Guide to Periodicals*.

There are various scholarly journals, directories, almanacs, biographical volumes, encyclopedias, and of course, books treating the subject you are dealing with. What you find you can check against the material you receive from the on-line computer resources of your library. If your library does not have such computer service, your librarian can refer you to another library that does.

In Chapter 11, "The Art of Research—Search and Seize," you're going to get more information on the use of computers. The important thing to know now is that certain materials and information can be gathered entirely through the on-line computer. This means that the computer will not only help you find the material but will spill it out—printing it out line by line as it is stored in the computer's memory from the various source books.

But since the computer has only what has been fed into it, it may be incomplete and not up-to-date. So don't expect it to contain everything. You had still better look around at the shelves and the card catalog of the library.

Also, remember that the library computer service is not

free. I am told that some libraries charge $15 an hour for assembling a bibliography of sources for a subject.

Now for one little warning—titles don't tell everything. Just because a title doesn't sound promising, don't ignore it. You may be surprised at the nuggets you will find. So at least glance through every book and article.

Now you are ready for your interview—except for one more tip:

If in the course of your scanning this material you spot names of people you already know, you can call them up and ask questions about this man and his work. By the time you go for the interview, you will feel you already know him.

IF THE PERSON IS AN ACQUAINTANCE

If you actually know an expert in a certain field or a famous person about whom the public is eager to know more than they get in newspapers and tabloids, you are lucky. Phone that person. Or write a friendly note reminding him or her of where you met and asking for an interview.

You have to use your own judgment about whether the person will be negative if you immediately say you want to make him or her a part of or the subject of a book. You might say instead that you are contemplating writing an article but that you are also exploring whether there is enough material for a book.

That should stir the competitive spirit. He may want to prove there *is* enough. He or she may think the field has been neglected long enough, or that there are many misconceptions about the field or his or her life.

TREATMENT OF YOUR SUBJECT

Here is a little warning. When it comes to the interview and the writing of a book, treat everyone—whether you are acquainted or not—alike. *Do not take advantage of friendships.*

1. Never be late.

2. Never be discourteous or too familiar.

3. Never fail to keep your promises of showing them certain material or whatever.

THE ACTUAL INTERVIEW

Your place or mine? Let the subject decide. Fran starts by saying she would like to come see the person, but if he hems and haws or indicates there are a lot of people around, she switches and asks if he can come to her home or office.

The point is you have to be very flexible and ready to go to great lengths to make your subject feel good. When Fran was working with Mary Gallagher on the book, *My Life with Jacqueline Kennedy*, Jackie's former secretary wanted to work in secret. So every day found Fran at a card table in Mary's lovely bedroom, working away at the typewriter while Mary talked.

Secrecy is terribly important to many subjects of books. Fishbait Miller, whom you met in Chapter 5, "Writing a Nonfiction Book Proposal," was in hiding from the press and his Capitol Hill peers. He also did not want the interview to take place in his home or neighborhood.

Fran would have met him anywhere, but Fish chose to meet her at the National Press Building every day, trying to look inconspicuous as he took the elevator up to her office. If reporters cornered him, he did not let on that he was writing a book, but just that he was visiting around. Never would he and Fran leave together. Sometimes they would drive around in Fish's antique car so that he could show Fran his world, but she would meet him on some corner on Capitol Hill for those occasions.

All right, you have your first appointment and you are getting ready for it when you suddenly panic. You have a problem. Here are the answers to the questions I am asked most frequently concerning that crucial interview:

IMPORTANT QUESTIONS

1. *What to wear?*

Dress to blend in. If you are going to an average home, wear something fairly conservative. If you are going to a senator's office, be even more conservative. Suits for men. Dresses or skirts for women. In some senatorial offices women do wear slacks—but that's not the usual attire. On the other hand, if you are going to interview a rock star, don't dress like a business exec. If you are a man, wear a casual shirt and jeans or turtleneck and slacks. Come to think of it, the same type of outfit would be fine for a female writer as well—a skirt is optional.

Whatever you do, don't try to outshine your subject. Low-key colors are best.

2. *Should You Take a Tape Recorder Along?*

It's not necessary unless you know the person you are going to interview is prone to file lawsuits. Protect yourself from litigious people every way you can. You might consider showing the person you are interviewing exactly what you are saying about him in the book and having him initial every page. But that is not necessary if you have the tape that proves what he said. In general, it makes for poor writing to write as if you are nervously watching to see if you are angering someone. Write the truth without malice and there are usually no grounds for suit. The one suing must prove malice.

If you take a tape recorder, let it be a small, inconspicuous one and ask your subject if he minds having it on. If he is upset, don't use it, and if necessary, show that it is not on and put it in another room or in the hall beside the door.

3. *Should You Smoke?*

Don't smoke unless your subject is smoking. Don't chew gum. Don't snap your fingers or distract your subject with nervous mannerisms.

4. *How Do You Go About Getting Acquainted?*

Don't spend too long in opening gambits to get acquainted. Your subject may think you are more interested in his possessions than you are in him or her. Or that you are a slow worker or a time waster. Being friendly but businesslike is the ticket.

5. Should You Act "at Home"?

Not really—not even if you are urged to. Don't touch things in the subject's house or office. If you admire something, look at it but don't pick it up. Your subject may not want you around if you do—he's thinking of how you could destroy his prize possession—his Ming vase—and not about the interview.

6. Should You Bring a List of Questions?

Here's an important tip for when you are making your appointment for that first interview. Always make clear that you are bringing or have a list of questions you'd like to ask, but also make clear that the subject is not bound by them. He doesn't want to waste his time with you fishing around because you don't know what to ask. But on the other hand, he doesn't want to be badgered by a writer who is doggedly following some list *ad infinitum*. The key is to be flexible. Follow his lead.

Okay. You are sitting with the person and you have in your pocket or purse a bunch of written questions. Don't bring them out yet. Get acquainted if the person seems at all friendly. Even if he doesn't, it's your job to break the ice. If you see a Chinese vase and you have a few bits of Oriental bric-a-brac around the house, say so. Ask about the vase.

Show yourself mildly interested in whatever your subject is interested in. If he says he hates the vase but it's something his wife insists on keeping there, say, "Oh, I see. You care more for American style art," or, "Oh, do you collect something else?"

If he does, he will probably be happy to show you his gun collection, his stamp collection, or his collection of lead soldiers. Friendships have started with just such a beginning.

143

And if you happen to know where he can add to his collection, speak up. But don't be pushy.

This is your first book. By your second or third you'll be more experienced at breaking the ice. If there's no art around, talk about the cheerful colors of the room. "This seems a happy atmosphere in which to work," or if it is dark paneling, "What a thoughtful atmosphere this room creates." Or just say, "I'm glad you could give me this time."

If your subject says he has very little time, skip any more small talk and haul out those questions right away. But even so, don't follow your line of questioning slavishly. Let him lead. Ask if there is a particular point he'd like you to cover or clear up in the book.

7. Should You Stop Him If He's Not Giving You What You Want or He's Leaving Things Out?

No way, José! Don't interrupt, and if there is something you don't understand, make a note to ask him later.

Author Max Gunther, who has done a lot of interviewing, advises against a writer's "jumping in with questions, as though he were a lawyer cross-examining a witness." Gunther also quotes the warning on the subject given by A. J. Liebling, whose pieces appeared in *The New Yorker*. Liebling compares the situation with a horseback rider who keeps alternately spurring and curbing his horse, saying, "If you make a man stop to explain everything, he will soon quit on you."

I have watched Fran Leighton conducting an interview and noticed that she seemed very much in charge, yet did not interrupt. She just looked interested and expectant as the person talked and as he paused to think. But each time he seemed to run out of steam, she voiced great interest in what he had said and had a new question for him.

She had a little folded piece of paper in front of her, and you could hardly tell she was making any notes because her eyes hardly ever left the man's face. He seemed to respond to her complete absorption in his story by telling it with enthusiasm.

144

8. *What Should You Make Your Notes on—a Steno Pad?*

The steno pad is for reporters going in to interview the president or any other important figure having a press conference. For a first interview with a person who may turn out to be very gun-shy, have the least conspicuous thing—and the least noisy. I noticed Fran used regular writing paper folded into fourths. It was almost smaller than her hand. You can also use those small notebooks with spiral bindings so there is no noise when you turn the page.

The important thing is that you do not want to distract your subject or make him too aware that you are capturing his words. In fact, if you notice that your subject seems all upset or gets tongue-tied when you write something down, casually put the notebook away and just smile reassuringly and say, "I guess I don't need that," or just keep listening. Make notes when you get home.

On the other hand, if your subject has music blasting in the background and seems happy with it, while it is irritating you, bite your tongue. You want your quotes, don't you? Whatever makes him happy will make him more cooperative.

9. *Shouldn't You Start Out with the Most Important Question First, Even If It Might Embarrass Him?*

No. Hold your fire. I'm thinking of a great bit of advice given by Winzola McLendon, columnist and author of several books, including the definitive book on Martha Mitchell, *Martha*.

Winnie, as she is called, told Fran, "Don't ask what you really want to know. Ask everything *but*. Just let it evolve."

What *I* tell writers is, "Don't come on like gangbusters. You're there as a friend, not an adversary."

Save the tough questions for last. Don't antagonize your subject by asking embarrassing questions right off. You may ruin the whole project that way. Toward the end ask the mean question, but ask it in a gentle way—"What do you say to people who ask about the child abuse accusation? I'd like to set the record straight." He may say he's getting psychiatric help. He may deny the charge angrily. He may say it was all a misunderstanding and have you talk to his child. You never know what reaction you will get, and that's what makes non-fiction writing so interesting. Each book gives you a fresh slice of life.

Now let's zero in on a specialized kind of interview that you may get involved in if you write any kind of biography.

INTERVIEWING FOR A MEMOIR OR BIOGRAPHY

If you are interviewing someone because you hope to help him write his or her own story and share the profit, it's an entirely different ball game. In a way it's easier, and in another way it's harder. It's easier because a gold mine of material you need is sitting right in front of you. But it's harder because you must write to please the other person—it's his life, *his* byline that comes ahead of *yours*.

Now you have two masters—the coauthor *and* the publisher.

This circumstance hasn't intimidated Fran, however, and she has made a great success of helping various famous and even unknown people write their memoirs. She considers writing other people's memoirs the most exciting work of all because it enables her to delve deeply into another person's life and thoughts and way of looking at the world.

To write a memoir of someone else's life you must have total immersion. Fran says she always feels as if the things she is writing about had happened to her. This is real trans-ference.

When she wrote the memoir of June Allyson, she went to Hollywood and lived in the household of the movie star.

To show that movie stars can be like ordinary people, June then came to Washington to work on the editing part of the book with Fran—sharing the travel burden and furthering a friendship.

146

When Fran wrote the memoir of Beverly Slater, an amnesia victim—*Stranger in My Bed*—Fran went to the home of Beverly, in the Philadelphia area, for several weeks at a time, following her around and encouraging her to think aloud. Also interviewing the people in her past.

The intriguing thing was that Beverly was two people—the old Beverly and the new Beverly who lived in her body but knew nothing about her past. The book was made into a TV movie.

If you cannot be part of the household of your subject, stay in a lodge nearby and visit your subject every day for a short period in order to get the flow of his or her life.

An important bit of advice that I can give you concerns the letter of agreement you are going to use if you are helping someone write his memoir or if you are going to be a ghost or credited coauthor in the writing of a biography or autobiography. It is this: Even before your first interview have some idea of how you would like the book earnings to be shared.

If things go well in this first interview, tell your subject you like the idea of working with him on the book and are seriously interested. Say that you work with a simple letter of agreement so that each person feels protected. Say you would like to draw this up and bring it on the next visit. Or, if he seemed anxious to do the book when you phoned for the appointment, you may have the agreement with you. Give him a copy to keep and go over with his lawyer. Or he may just sign it. If he seems dubious, tell him he can show it to anyone he cares to and get back to you. A sample of this agreement is in Chapter 3, "Should You Go It Alone or Get a Coauthor?"

INTERVIEWING INSIDER SOURCES

So far we have been talking about interviewing the person we plan to write about, whether in his voice—first-person memoir—or yours—third-person biography.

Now let's consider another kind of interviewing. Background. You want to interview people who know the living subject of your book. You need to confirm claims he has made.

You need to know his impact on people around him and his dealings with people.

Or it might be that a movie superstar like Rock Hudson or a rock star like Elvis Presley has just died and you want to do a book on him, fast. Or you want to write about an interesting figure of history, now dead for ten years. Where do you get your material?

Relatives. Go see the widow, the children, the man's brothers and sisters. Any friends and relatives you can find. And don't go with a chip on your shoulder. Go with an open mind. Tell them you are simply searching for material and would appreciate facts as well as their insights.

If they ask if this is going to be a friendly book, say merely that you have an open mind. That you are going to let the facts take you wherever they lead. That you plan a fair book. Only if they are to receive credit as a coauthor do they have the right to okay the material you write.

Tell them you will respect their privacy if they want to speak off the record and that you can use their material without revealing their names. But if you need their quotes a good incentive is to point out they will be part of literary or show biz history if they let you use their names.

HOW TRUTHFUL SHOULD YOU BE?

A matter of ethics must be faced. Is it proper or within the bounds of ethics—or even within the law—to pretend that you are on the side of the subject to receive his or her cooperation and then do a hostile book that paints the subject in the poorest light?

Such trickery can have very serious consequences. I am thinking now of the case of the book *Fatal Vision*, written by Joe McGinniss about a man accused and convicted of murder. The point here is that McGinniss, by his own admission, let Jeffrey MacDonald, the accused murderer, think that the book would be on his side and show that he was innocent, whereas the book that was published painted him as a despicable killer.

MacDonald, who even had effusive letters from McGinniss clearly indicating he felt MacDonald was innocent, sued the author.

I feel that it is a mistake to betray sources—to be less than candid with the source. The better thing is to say something like, "I must tell the story the way I see it, but at this time I lean toward the feeling of your innocence."

McGinniss, in discussing his book, said that it is an author's duty to tell "the unpleasant truth." I agree that the book should tell the truth as the author sees it, but this does not mean that he needs to mislead his source.

WHAT ABOUT SECRETS?

In the course of a third-person interview, you might find that someone is on the verge of spilling a secret about the subject of your book. If someone says, "I'll tell you a shocking thing if you promise not to put it in this book you are writing about my old boss" (or relative or friend or neighbor), you'd better hold off listening. Say that you will listen only if it is understood that if you find the same thing from other sources or in your research he must understand you will use it—and that you will, if the source permits it, tell him where you got it.

That seems fair enough. Always be fair. Always thank people for being willing to tell you something even if you are at the same time refusing to listen. Something like, "I appreciate your willingness to tell me what you know, but I'm afraid I'd better decline—that is, unless you agree that if I unearth this skeleton in the closet from some other source, you will not think I have violated your confidence by publishing it."

This is not the only book you are going to write. Your reputation for reliability is very valuable. Word gets around if you break confidences.

Now you have your interviews behind you. But there are a lot of gaps. What are you going to do about the missing bits of information?

The name of the game is "Research."

11

The Art of Research—
Search and Seize

A CAUTIONARY TALE

I think that nothing is more embarrassing or distressing in a writing career than for an author to have his book published just at the time a major news story breaks with new information on his subject. Invariably, the reviewers will point out that the book is not complete because it doesn't contain the latest developments.

It happens all too often. But the good news is that through the most diligent research, *you* might be the one who first reveals the exciting new information. Your diligence in research can help your book get widespread attention. So you see, those long hours of "search and seize" can have a big cash value to you as well as offer you assurance that the publisher will be pleased—as will you—at how well you have covered your subject.

United States, was equally colorful in his legendary tightness—tipping only a thin dime.

Say you are helping someone write his memoirs. Even if that person cooperates with you completely in telling all he thinks he knows, you may find you don't have enough good material for a book. The answer to the problem is research. Frances Spatz Leighton always researches the persons whose memoirs she is writing—both by reading about them and talking with people who know them.

There are good reasons for this. She can remind the subject of things that happened that he has forgotten and he can give his version of the story. "That rascal? Let me tell you the real story and why we had that scuffle in his office."

If someone tells her a derogatory story about her subject, Fran may ask, "May I tell him you said this?" She abides by that person's decision. Often the subject does not know where the damaging material came from that Fran reports to him.

Neighborhoods

Get the feel of the neighborhood. The sound and smell. The ambience, the feeling of wealth or poverty. The kind of people—WASP? Ethnic? Insular? Sophisticated? Sinister? Open? Happy? Cheerful and friendly? Suspicious and sullen? Do you want to smile? Do you get goose bumps of fear as a young man lurches past you?

You'd be surprised what you can learn from the neighbors. Columnist-author Ken Hoyt happened to grow up near William Jennings Bryan. As a little boy, he would pass Bryan's house and be impressed with the fact that the orator always kept a bottle of grape juice on his windowsill.

The anti-evolutionist was also anti-alcohol. As Ken explains it, "He was trying to make the point that Jesus was turning water into wine but it was unfermented grape."

From Ken also comes an anecdote about Bryan's changing attitude toward money as he became wealthy. Bryan, filled with righteousness, once told a man, "You know and I know that no man can make a million dollars honestly." Then some years later when he had become rich and famous, he told the same man, "You know and I know that no man can make *ten* million dollars honestly."

These stories would be nuggets if you happened to be doing a bio of the great orator. Let's see how else you could research such a figure of the past.

Audio Research

Listen to old radio recordings of your subject. Some libraries have sections devoted to old recordings. Stations may be able to help you, especially if they know you will give full credit to them among your list of sources.

Presidential libraries have recordings of the speeches of modern presidents—and some not so modern.

Visual Research

If the subject is long dead, you will have to read old newspapers to get the feel of the time and to know what life was like and what people were interested in. And there may be collections of letters or diaries by or about your subject in a library where the subject lived.

If the letters and rights to them are owned by a private person or collector, you may still be able to make a deal—you can give credit in your book to the owner of the collection or you can offer to pay for the use of the letters. Many collectors are happy with just an acknowledgment in the book.

Oral Histories

If your subject, or coauthor, has been interviewed for an oral history collection, the material may be very useful. When I was editor of Eleanor Lansing Dulles's autobiography, I liked her manuscript that told of her work as a pioneer economist investigating money systems, and her account of her famous family members, such as her grandfather, Secretary of State Lansing, her brothers, John Foster Dulles and Allen Dulles, and her account of her role in rebuilding Germany and Austria after World War II.

But the manuscript was not as colorful as her anecdote-filled conversation. When I discovered that there was an 800-page transcript of an oral history interview of her done for Columbia University, I got a copy of it from her and found just the material lacking in her manuscript. At my request she wove the additional material into her book, giving it more life and color.

LIBEL AND INVASION OF PRIVACY—AND PLAGIARISM

Good news to today's writers is the Freedom of Information Act, referred to as FOIA. Many new books have been written and continue to be written by those who get to a treasure chest of secrets first. You have to be clever. You have to know what to ask for.

Under the FOIA, you have the right to request the record of anyone from any federal government agency—FBI, CIA, or whatever. You may find that certain sections have been censored and blacked out, but you may still have enough for a hot book prospect. You must follow whatever rules are given for using the material. But you still cannot print just anything. You can be sued for libel if you cannot substantiate facts you learn. Just saying someone told the FBI this or that does not make you immune from suit. A good libel lawyer is important in keeping writers of controversial articles and books out of trouble.

Just because you don't hear or read about every suit doesn't mean that no legal action was taken. Most cases are settled out of court.

So walk boldly but go to print very carefully. If someone tells you something negative about your subject, ask if the person is willing to sign a statement about this material. Some *are* willing, so anxious are they to show your subject is a rascal.

Explain to your source that his signed statement will not be used unless there is a court case. Or unless the publisher asks for verification—in this case you will give your source to your publisher but the publisher may not necessarily want to include the name of the source in the book. You can have an agreement with your source that if the publisher insists on using his name as the source, he has the right to refuse to be mentioned by name in the book.

QUOTATIONS

If you find a passage you like in someone else's book, how much of it can you quote? There is no hard-and-fast rule. "Fair use" is the key phrase used by publishers and lawyers.

My coauthor, in her books, feels safe in quoting only 25 words, or maybe two or three words more, if the quote is from a long work, like a book. This is her interpretation of fair use, based on what she has been told by many editors and publishers over the years. And of course she gives the source credit. More usage, she believes, requires a written permission to quote. With songs and poems, even a single line requires permission to quote, since even one line is a substantial part of the whole work. Titles, however, can be mentioned without getting permission.

The literary rights to letters belong to the writer and not the recipient of the letter. If you want to quote letters you have received, you must get the permission of the writer, if he is still living, or his heirs. You can, however, paraphrase and say "I received a letter from J. J. Johnson telling me that he lived with the Duchess for two years but could not stand her condescension because he was a commoner. He said that by night and by day she was two different persons. He said the night person found him good enough to spend the nights in her bed, but the day person did not want him in her drawing room."

However, if you are going to paraphrase extensively from the letters which were sent to you, you had still better consult a good copyright attorney. You can also get books at the library on copyright aimed at helping writers.

A perfect example of how dangerous it is to quote letters is what happened to writer Ian Hamilton, who wrote a biography of the reclusive J. D. Salinger, author of the perennial favorite *The Catcher in the Rye*, using many unpublished letters written by Salinger as a source.

Random House already had the book in galleys, but a suit by Salinger brought the publication to a grinding halt. The court sided with Salinger, and the book, which eventually came out in June 1988, was a shadow of its former saucy self— *In Search of J. D. Salinger.* The court had ruled that quotation and extensive paraphrasing constituted a violation of Salinger's rights.

LIBRARIES

Libraries are worth their weight in gold. And there are fortunes to be made just in tying together little strands of information gleaned from them.

My coauthor is addicted to the Library of Congress and likens it to a sort of literary shopping mall. Almost anything you want to learn about can be found in its vast collection. The past comes alive in its Rare Book Section, and the art and music lover finds much to be thrilled about. Congress was probably thinking of its own desires—the Library is right across the street from the Capitol—but the fact remains it acted wisely when it decreed long ago that two copies of every copyrighted published book must be deposited in this federal library.

Every library is important—from the small town to the big city—and all the specialized libraries as well. Wherever you are, your library is your lifeline. And it will often contain that great new resource we have been talking about—computerized information—to speed up your work.

Before you start your book, go into your nearest library and look around. A good place to start is the *Reader's Guide to Periodicals*, which list most general-interest magazine articles. The *Reader's Guide* is published several times a year, and each year's list of articles is bound. It may be a painstaking job to go through the volumes year by year but well worth it for the helpful articles you may find.

Look under name or subject. If it's a disease you are writing about, look under Medical. There is a great array of subjects, from Agriculture to Political Campaigns to Music to the Occult. Back issues are in the memory bank of a computer.

There are also volumes of specialized source material— Engineering, Architecture, Science, Religion.

Libraries hire information experts skilled in helping you find what you are looking for. You don't have to tell the name of your own projected book to get help. Just tell the general subject. Some libraries will let you roam among the stacks. The Library of Congress does not let unauthorized people do this.

Most libraries let you take out all but their rare books. The Library of Congress does not let you take out anything unless you are a member of Congress or have other high government rank.

Even so, some writers go to Washington just to research at the Library of Congress. They stay for weeks or months. Some are lucky enough to get permits for office cubbyholes where they are furnished a desk and may bring a typewriter. Fran has worked there and has commented on the symphony of typewriter sounds around her.

ESTABLISHING AUTHORITY

When you are writing a book, your editors—and maybe reviewers later on—will want to know your authority for something. If you say you read it in a book somewhere, that isn't a good enough answer. As you work with each book, enter it in your log of sources. The title, the author, the date, the publisher, the city it was published in. And even—so it's easy to get out again—the library and the number of the book as shown in the card index. A good trick is to give a number to each book you use, starting with 1. If this is the tenth book you have worked on, call it 10.

Now in the margin, as you write your first draft, every place you have an important fact that comes from that book, simply write 10 in ink—perhaps in red to make it easy to find among your other notations. Hang on to your list even when you are finished writing because you will want to list the books you have read on the subject in your "Bibliography" or "List of Suggested Reading" at the end of the book.

And if you quote anything from the book, you must give the source, either in footnote or right along with your quote. The latter is what Fran prefers. She is one of the writers who abhors footnotes because she believes they frighten readers away.

I don't always agree with her on this point. But I do think footnotes can be overdone. David E. Koskoff, in his monumental biography, *Joseph P. Kennedy, A Life and Times*, started by stating there had been a potato famine in Ireland in 1846. He footnoted this, citing a source. As his agent I suggested that people would believe him without the footnote, as the fact was well-known.

But his editor, Bram Cavin, disagreed, and solved the problem (page 1 had seven notes) by putting all the notes at the end of the book—the 638-page book has 160 pages of small-print notes at the end—and I have to admit they make fascinating reading.

Did you know there are specialized libraries that may have what you need? There are architectural libraries, art libraries. There is a separate library for each of the more recent presidents and National Archives has material on earlier ones.

Did you know that the National Archives in Washington will let you do research but not take papers out? In researching the Roosevelt family, the Archives was of great help to Frances Leighton, who wrote *The Roosevelts, a Family in Turmoil*, as coauthor of Lillian Rogers Parks.

There are also private collections of papers that some civic-minded people will let you look at. To locate such collections, you must simply make call after call to people with an interest in the subject. Large companies sometimes have fine libraries in specialized subjects.

Then there are specialized magazine indexes for subjects such as psychology and psychiatry and science. Or engineering. Or education.

There are newsletters printed on a variety of subjects, including flying saucers and health research. Call someone in the field in which you are writing and ask for the names of several newsletters if your library can't help you. Then check the newsletter—even subscribing for a while if it will help.

There are newspaper indexes. *The New York Times Index* will fill you in on what happened on any given date, and you can get the article on microfilm to read the full version. *The Washington Post* also has its index, month by month and year by year.

Don't forget to check the *Encyclopedia Britannica* and other encyclopedias for basic facts and progress in various fields. Also you will find short biographies of people who changed the world.

To help you find facts in a hurry, nothing beats the various almanacs—*The Reader's Digest, The World Almanac, The New York Times Almanac.*

While we are on the subject, I advise you to buy a good big dictionary as well as having normal-sized dictionaries and even a tiny pocket edition to carry around. The big one amounts to a one-volume encyclopedia. And it wouldn't hurt to have a full set of those around your house, too.

Also, get and keep handy a thesaurus and several books of quotations, including *Bartlett's Familiar Quotations*, and even collections of historic anecdotes.

Finally, remember the help Uncle Sam can give at the Government Printing Office. A visit there is an eye-opener. But you can write and ask for a list of publications on the subjects you are researching. The prices are low, and you will be surprised at what is there. The address is simply Government Printing Office, Washington, D.C. 20402.

Is your book about marriage and divorce? All the latest available statistics are gathered there. Do you need the facts about rivers and harbors? Or the racial mix of the United States? Uncle Sam is at your side to help you research.

Don't forget, too, that when you are trying to find someone who knows the subject of your biography, the phone book can be of surprising help. Libraries have phone books of other cities. So does the telephone company. Look up the name of your subject and see if there is a Jr. after some name. If the name is unusual, you might even try calling those with the same last name to see if they are related or have knowledge of the person you're writing about.

There are many reference books that can help you. For people living, *Who's Who in America* is important for giving all the facts and leads on where to look next. Frances Leighton and I are both in that, if you want to look us up. If you wanted to write about us, you could use organizations and people mentioned as leads for your research.

For people dead, there is *Who Was Who*—also put out by the *Who's Who in America* people, the Marquis division of Macmillan.

There are regional *Who's Whos*. There is a *Who's Who of American Women*.

Going back to people dead, there is also *The Dictionary of American Biography* and *Notable American Women*.

And for the living, you will want to check *Biography Index*, *Current Biography*, and the *National Cyclopedia of American Biography*.

Some writers make good use of the *American Genealogical Index* to find people related to their subject and facts about their subject.

WHEN ARE YOU THROUGH WITH THE RESEARCH?

The answer is NEVER. As someone put it, you're never finished; you just surrender.

The big point I'm making here is this: Do not get so immersed in research that you forget you are writing a book. It is not important to know everything there is to know before you start writing. Start writing as soon as you have something to say. Get the feel of it.

My advice is to do research and writing at the same time. Fran writes every morning rain or shine, hell or high water, and she would not think of going to the library until she has written her quota. She considers the library sessions the fun part. She writes first and earns the right to go there. So it is write in the morning, library in the afternoon in the early stages of her books.

Or, if she is simply interviewing someone, she writes in the early morning—sometimes even from four to eight—before rushing to her day's interview. It means that she is writing one part of the life story while interviewing on another segment of the life. If you think that would throw you, consider this: just because you are reading a book on another century that day doesn't mean you can't pause to read today's newspaper and concentrate on it, too, for a while.

The idea here is to start writing as soon as you have made a connection between events in the life of your subject. Something led to something or you have some insight. You are knitting together a life. You learn isolated facts. Knit your story as you go. Worry about tacking the pieces together later, just as the knitter knits the sleeve and attaches it later.

Or, if it's a how-to book, start telling how to do some phase of the operation as soon as you understand it yourself.

Use the mails

You may not realize how effectively you can use the mails. If you want to get comments from experts about a certain subject or anecdotes about a certain person, type out a list of questions. Leave space under each question for the answer, and make many photocopies of your questionnaire. Mail those to people from whom you want the stories or opinions—with self-addressed stamped envelope (SASE), of course. Postage is still cheaper than phones or long-distance trips.

Be sure to ask somewhere on the page if the person being queried has any objection to being quoted. Have him sign his name if he does not object. This will serve as your release.

Books on sex have, on occasion, relied heavily on replies to queries sent out randomly, inquiring about personal sex practices and attitudes toward the opposite sex. Sometimes telephone books of certain specific cities have been used to get the names and addresses from the general public. You could send your questionnaire to every tenth name from the phone directory, or to three from every page—however you want to do it. But in your book tell what your rules were in getting your statistics.

Be sure to start the questionnaire by explaining who you are. You might also tell why you are sending this query and give the subject of your book. Say you hope the recipients will help you in the writing of the book by filling in the blanks. Tell them you are on a deadline and need the material as soon as possible, and thank them for their help. When you mention the subject of your book, don't give the title. Titles are very precious to most writers and cannot be protected if someone comes out with a book by the same title ahead of you. The copyright law does not protect titles.

The lecture is over. Now go forth and search and seize and write as you go.

12

The Many Faces of
the Biography

Biography is one of the oldest forms of writing—its history extends back to tales of ancient heroes and saints, through successive stages of increasing revelation, to the tell-all form popular today, which includes gossip as well as public achievements.

There's always room for another look into someone's life. We flock to the bookstores to learn the details of how Elvis Presley's body ballooned as he became strung out on drugs. Or to learn what it is like to become a high-living modern Croesus—wheeling, dealing, outmaneuvering the competition—à la Donald Trump, whether in his own book or in the biography by Jerome Tuccille, *Trump*.

It brings out or satisfies the voyeur in us. We don't want to hide in the bushes and see what Elizabeth Taylor or Nancy Reagan is doing, but we read the book avidly when someone like Kitty Kelley or Frances Spatz Leighton writes a biography that, in effect, does it for us.

It is said that on his deathbed a British publisher whispered advice to his sons about how to succeed in publishing. "Always publish a book about the Queen every year, and never one about South America." That shows you how publishers feel about biography. (But just to show that times can change, currently books on South America are enjoying favor.)

There are several kinds of written biography. And then there is fictionalized biography which does not belong in this book. Before you start writing and before you start researching, you will want to consider the variations to see which is best for your book.

AUTOBIOGRAPHIES AND MEMOIRS

THE AUTOBIOGRAPHY

An autobiography is a full and detailed story of your own life telling almost anything and everything you care or dare to reveal. It is more complete and grand than a *memoir*.

I can show you with one simple illustration the basic difference between an autobiography and a memoir. My coauthor has twice been asked to write her memoir. The publishers who inquired both wanted Fran to tell the secrets and inside stories of all the famous, important, and fascinating people she has rubbed elbows with in the course of her unusual writing career. They wanted intimate details on such people as Elizabeth Ray, the Capitol Hill secretary who could not type and whose revelations toppled a congressman—Wayne Hays. They wanted Fran to talk about a man who claimed to be the illegitimate son of Henry Ford, the early developer of the automobile. And about a young man with a similar claim—his centering on President John F. Kennedy.

But neither publisher wanted intimate details about *Fran's* life, except in her relationship with these people who were involved in her career. Now you are ready to consider the memoir.

THE MEMOIR

A memoir is fun to read or write, or can be very moving, because it gives the author's intimate glimpses of important people he has known or some special world or event he was privy to. I knew the Pope. Or, I had power on Capitol Hill. Or, I was there at the great event. Or, more somberly, how I coped with a great loss—the death of a loved child. Memoir— memories of.

Many people confuse *memoir* with *autobiography*, and it's a natural mistake. A memoir is, of course, an autobiography but only of selected material. If you trek to the South Pole in the steps of the earlier explorers, you are in line to write a memoir. The reading public would not want every little detail of your life previous to that trek the way it wants every minute detail of the life of Lincoln or Pope John Paul II.

In general, the autobiography is the appropriate form only if you can record achievements in your life that changed the course of history or had great impact on the public. Some show business figures have had such impact that they have made the whole world eternally curious about them—megastars like Jane Fonda and Michael Jackson—as have some inventors, some writers, some notorious crime figures.

However, many whose lives have been less curiosity-provoking or historic have written autobiographies that have been important and have given pleasure to a small segment of readers. I am thinking of a man who recently called a writer I know and told her, "You've never heard of me. I'm just a successful small businessman, but I have a huge family and they would like to know my real life story. Can I hire you—and I know it wouldn't be cheap—to help me write it up? I'm not looking for a publisher. I'm just going to have it published myself and give it to all my clan."

Occasionally a book by an obscure person written for a limited circulation will be so well done, so amusing or full of insights that it will gain a wider audience.

Those are unusual cases. Facing the reality of the publishing world today, and in view of the vast number of books vying for the public's attention, there are few people for whom the general public will sit still long enough to probe their lives in great detail—from birth to time of writing. The likeliest candidates to write autobiographical books are presidents—after they have retired—and other prominent political figures, major scientists and inventors, major explorers, movers and shakers of the world of advertising, TV, and radio, or business and finance. Innovators of art and architecture. Record-breaking sports figures whose feats have captured the continuing fascination of the world—not just any record breaker but those on the order of Joe Louis and Babe Ruth.

DIARIES AS AUTOBIOGRAPHIES
AND BIOGRAPHY SOURCES

Diaries are, in effect, autobiographies. Samuel Pepys is popular today not for outstanding accomplishments—other than ravishing a large assortment of females—but for the intimate view he gave of his day-to-day struggle to survive in those long-gone times. To read him is to be transported through a time machine into the 1660s.

Hundreds of years after Samuel Pepys lived out his life as the staid Commissioner of the Navy in the time of Charles II, the life of Pepys lives on in his printed diaries. And why? Because of their stark truth about the intimate details of his life—of battles with head lice and nits. Of seducing servant girls and other men's wives. Of coping with his own righteous, angry, and barren wife.

He had no idea he was writing for the ages.

If you are lucky enough to know some famous person intimately, or, say, someone struggling with the greatest medical problem of the world, you might want to keep a diary and keep track of that person. If you don't end up writing a memoir about him, you will become well-known to other writers who might use you as a source. You will be mentioned in the resulting books.

Your own book can turn you into a celebrity. Consider A. E. Hotchner, whom Frances met and greatly admires. Hotchner struck up a close friendship with Ernest Hemingway in the course of a routine magazine assignment and started keeping a dairy of every day he was with or had contact

169

with the great novelist during the last thirteen years of Hemingway's life. *Papa Hemingway* has such intimate details as we were talking about, such as that Hemingway superstitiously put his faith in a horse chestnut, which he rubbed against his face.

You don't have to be a reporter to find your diary subject. Consider author Joseph Lash. He was a young liberal whose interests gave him the opportunity to meet and cultivate the friendship of First Lady Eleanor Roosevelt.

Lash spent a great deal of time at the White House. He was almost a member of the family. At the dinner table he listened to Eleanor and the President talk. Saw the tensions among the various members of the family.

He kept diaries. Years later those diaries were priceless in helping him write three books about the Roosevelts. First came *Eleanor Roosevelt; A Friend's Memoir, 1964.* Then *Eleanor and Franklin, 1971,* and finally, *Eleanor: The Years Alone, 1972.* In 1972 he received the Pulitzer prize for biography. Would it have been possible without his diaries? Probably not. How did he do it?

By being a sponge—an intelligent sponge. That's what *you* must be, too—a sponge. Don't be obvious. Most people don't appreciate having someone make notes in front of them. But when you are alone, write what you have just seen and heard.

THE BUILT-IN HAZARD IN FIRST-PERSON WRITING

Let's face it, if you are writing your own life story in whatever detail—complete autobiography or just a memoir—some people are going to think it's a bit conceited of you. So what's the answer to that problem?

The answer is that some show of modesty is in order—some explanatory word about why you are writing the story of your life. Even Benjamin Franklin, who was the spokesman for his generation and who had helped a government come into being, felt some excuse was due the reader.

In the opening of *The Autobiography of Benjamin*

Franklin he disarms the reader by admitting he is about to "gratify my own vanity" but that it is "natural to old men to be talking of themselves." What can you do with a man like that but forgive him and hope he *will* brag a little.

A memoir or autobiography must also give some solid reason early on for revealing the things you are about to read. Let's see what Fishbait Miller gave as his reason. "Well, I'm out now . . . kicked out or voted out, if you please, after forty-two years on Capitol Hill, twenty-eight of them as the door-keeper. And while it is all vividly clear in my mind, I'm ready to give you the true, unvarnished picture of life as it is lived on Capitol Hill. It's not the same as the sweet little newsletter that gets mailed to constituents back home. And it is the truth, so help me God, to the best of my ability."

Which is to say, he wants to *set the record straight,* and now that he's out of office, he is free to do it. Or you can say you want to *share with the world* your earlier view of someone who flashed to fame—"I knew him when . . ."

PICKING YOUR MEMOIR SUBJECT

I know that some of you are going to go into the field of collaboration in helping others write their memoirs. For you, the first job is picking the subject. Sometimes the subject picks you, and that is lucky! When Jackie Kennedy married Aristotle Onassis, Jackie's secretary, Mary Barelli Gallagher, who had worked for her in secret at the White House—no one knew Jackie had her own personal secretary paid by the Kennedys—came looking for Fran. Mary felt it was time to write the true story of what it was like at the White House when First Lady Jackie called the shots. Fran did not know of Mary Gallagher, but Mary was well aware of Fran Leighton.

But generally, it is you who are on the lookout for a good subject, taking advantage of friends or social gatherings to meet him or her. Then you might, in the course of a conversation, throw out a bold hint, "Have you ever thought of writing your memoir?" It is a flattering comment, and actually, some good prospects have *not* thought of it before.

So pick someone famous and go search him out and ask him. It doesn't matter if you don't already know him. Many writers pay special attention to newspaper articles that trumpet some star's arrival. But it doesn't have to be someone flashy. Your subject can be someone very mainstream. A teacher of the year. A doctor who conquered a disease. An economist. A golf pro. A poet.

BIOGRAPHIES

When a publisher uses the word "biography," he means a life story written in the third person. A biography is like an autobiography in that it is an in-depth study of a person who is considered to be of lasting interest. It used to be written after a person was dead—but more and more writers are tackling the lives of the living legends, as Kitty Kelley did Frank Sinatra's life.

It is interesting to see that Sigmund Freud, who is of lasting interest because of his own work, was also a biographer. And whom did he find important enough to write a book about—someone with lasting value? Leonardo da Vinci.

There are men and women long dead who are eternally interesting to the world—Gandhi, Buddha, Napoleon, Queen Elizabeth I, Cleopatra. The great inventors. During their lives they may not have seemed so important to the future. Did Edison, fiddling with materials that would hold electricity in a tiny container without burning up, seem important to those around him? Only some people are wise enough, clairvoyant enough to realize the importance of such people to the future.

The Profile

A special kind of third-person biography is a profile. It has been called a minibiography about a person or persons with the accent on showing why they are famous. It is not written with the detail and depth of a serious biography on, say, Thomas Jefferson. Profiles are important because they give a quick, precise view of their subject.

A perfect example is John Fitzgerald Kennedy's book, *Profiles in Courage*, which sketches various men in history who showed courage in their decisions and took heroic action.

A more modern illustration of a book of profiles is Marcia Cohen's *The Sisterhood—the True Story Behind the Women's Movement*. In tune with the times, the book gives not just laudatory details on the lives of women, including Gloria Steinem, Betty Friedan, Kate Millett, and Germaine Greer, but stories that might make them cringe. There is a story of one of them having been punched in the face and given a black eye by an angry husband, and another undergoing abortions, and another being bisexual.

If you want to write a book of profiles, find a theme and the men or women who exemplify it, and get going.

Collections of Letters

Yes, collections of letters can and frequently are biographies. Letters can be very revealing about private lives. Some people are absolutely fascinated by other people's letters and will buy almost any book that has a collection of letters by or about a famous person. What did Mozart write his friends? What did Martha Washington say to others about her husband—and what did she write to her husband when he was away at battle?

Usually in letter-collection biographies the life story is woven together between epistles by an author or "editor" so that the letters are thoroughly understood. Such a book is the touching story of Mary Wollstonecraft Shelley, wife of the great poet, Percy Shelley.

In the book, *The Letters of Mary Wollstonecraft Shelley, Vol. III: "What Years I Have Spent,"* edited by Betty T. Bennett, the reader learns many secrets of Mary Shelley through her letters. We learn that she is suspicious of her stepsister, Claire, and is afraid she is having an affair with her husband. Claire is not above an affair and has, in fact, had an illegitimate

173

daughter by their poet friend, Lord Byron. We learn that Mary Shelley is being blackmailed.

Health is also a matter under discussion in the letters. We find Mary Shelley recommending ginger as a medication and herself taking cod liver oil for what turns out to be a brain tumor.

You can become the editor of letter collections in libraries and universities if you haven't a famous ancestor. Search and seize!

All right, you've given the subject a lot of thought and you would like to write a straight biography about a famous living person. Or you want to do one on a personage of a past century. Well, before you expend too much energy, check it out at the library—there could be a hazard.

PICKING YOUR SUBJECT FOR A BIOGRAPHY

When picking your subject for a third-person biography, make sure there aren't lots of competing books out at the same time. Also beware of the one big book that is considered the definitive work on the life of your subject!

You face the danger that reviewers will dismiss your book with the comment that it is not as good as the other book, even though your book may have some important new material. Only if you think you can turn the opinion of the public toward your subject entirely around should you tackle such a formidable job. There have been instances where a writer has changed the public view of some figure, but it's always risky.

The best subjects for biographies are persons who have not been written about before but who are nevertheless well-known and important. In addition, if you have some special in with your subject or your subject's family, heirs, or intimates, you can expect to produce choice material.

One way of developing bookworthy biographical material is to write a Master's or Ph.D paper on your subject. That way you will get the benefit of academic review by experts without the danger of book reviewers panning your material. Then later, armed with tested and true information, you can use the material and expand it into a book aimed at the general public.

To bring it into a more popular style, you would, of course, have to get rid of much of the formal language and academic trappings.

Now that you have selected the right person, you still have one more important decision to make. Should it be an authorized or unauthorized book? Sometimes what starts out as one turns into the other. Let me tell you the story of how one such switch came about.

One day I had lunch with Robert Stewart, then a senior editor at Macmillan. We batted around a few ideas for new books and in a follow-up phone conversation decided that someone should do an in-depth biography of the First Lady, Nancy Reagan. Her popularity had plummeted because of stories of her expensive clothing, her expensive redecorating, her expensive lifestyle in general, her expensive friends—among whom she seemed almost poor—her worshipful look at her husband as he spoke. Could this picture be as perfect as it seemed?

Who could get the story from the White House and get it fast? Frances Leighton came to mind. She lived near Washington and was a former White House correspondent. She had written about other First Ladies.

Fran was to get what she could from the First Lady and follow the leads wherever they went. Her first surprise was that the White House was stonewalling her. She tried over and over to get to the First Lady, phoning and sending letters to Nancy Reagan's press secretary. It was clear that Mrs. Reagan did not want a book written about her.

I relayed this information to Robert Stewart, and he said, "Let it be an *unauthorized biography*. It's just as well, and it may be better."

Fran took the questions she had asked the White House and a list of more questions and set about getting her own answers.

She read whatever she could find of what others had said about Nancy—good things and bad—in defense and in condemnation of her. She checked reference books for information on the president when he was governor and hunted for bits about his wife. She checked old newspapers on microfilm. Old magazines. She checked books written on the president that also included stories about his life with Nancy.

While things were fresh in her mind, she wrote them up—working in the early morning so that she would feel free to go to the library in the afternoon.

Now she knew enough to talk intelligently with many who knew Nancy. To find people who knew her, Fran resorted to the social directories of the cities in which they had lived. Also the telephone books—most of the people she tried to contact, however, had unlisted phones. She tried, through the offices of their husbands, to leave messages for the wives in the hope they would return her call. A few did. She called relatives of the Reagans—on both sides—with some success.

She would hear of a woman who had lived in Nancy's neighborhood. She found women who had dealt with Nancy because of charity committees they had been on.

She found people—men and women—who had worked directly for Nancy or had worked for Governor or President Reagan but had been assigned to help Nancy. Some felt they had been pushed out of their jobs by Nancy, even after they had gone out of their way to help her and be her friend. Fran sought out wives of men who dealt with Governor or President Reagan and who heard various revealing stories from their husbands, as well as seeing Nancy socially themselves, on occasion.

The hardest part was getting information from Nancy's friends, and it was obvious that many had formed a protective wall around her. Some hung up on Fran when she finally reached them. Friends of friends sometimes gave telephone numbers on condition that Fran wouldn't tell how she had gotten the number. "I know who can tell you this great story about Nancy snubbing . . . but don't tell her you got the telephone number from me."

The unauthorized biography, *The Search for the Real*

Nancy Reagan, depicted a complicated, fearful, and feared woman who was a bundle of contradictions.

The Authorized Biography

If you are doing an authorized biography, prepare to spend as much time with and around your subject as possible. The experience of Lawrance Thompson, as told to me by R. H. Winnick, who completed Thompson's three-volume, authorized biography of Robert Frost, is instructive.

Robert Frost, at sixty-five, in 1939 appointed a young scholar, Lawrance Thompson, as his official biographer, with the provision that the biography was not to be published until after Frost's death. Thompson thought it no hardship to wait, as he was then in his thirties. But after a quarter century Thompson was no longer young, and one day Robert Frost said to him, "Larry, has it occurred to you that I might outlive you?"

Thompson replied that the thought had crossed his mind.

Frost then said, "That's all right—if I do, I'll write *your* biography."

Thompson did outlive his subject, and after bringing out a volume of Frost's letters in 1964, published the first volume of the biography in 1967, winning a Melville Cane award for the best biography of the year. This was followed by the more controversial volume two in 1970, which got a savage review attacking it in *The New York Times*, but also won the Pulitzer prize.

Roy Winnick met Thompson while taking his Ph.D. at Princeton, where Thompson taught. They became friends because of their mutual interest in Herman Melville. Winnick began to help Thompson with the research and planning of volume three of the Frost biography.

When Thompson had a stroke, Winnick lived in Thompson's house for the last ten months of Thompson's life—all the while continuing to work on the biography.

After Thompson died, with the assent of all concerned,

the publisher, Holt, Rinehart and Winston and its editor, Thomas Wallace; Thompson's wife; and representatives of the Frost estate, Winnick finished the biography, writing all of volume three except for the first few pages, though using Thompson's research and plan. It took him three and a half years—from age twenty-five to twenty-eight—to finish the book. He saw his task as not to whitewash Frost or to make him a monster, but rather to show him "as a complex person—obnoxious, lovable, generous all at once."

R. H. Winnick was gratified when *Robert Frost: The Later Years, 1938–1963* was published and *The New York Times* reviewer said, "It is impossible to tell when Thompson leaves off and Winnick begins," and that the three volumes were "seamless."

HOW TO APPROACH THE WRITING OF A BIOGRAPHY

There are three approaches you can take in writing a memoir or biography of any sort. One is the *strictly chronological*. Start at the beginning and tell the story according to the calendar. The weakness is that it's hard to show cause and effect. Something happens in 1968, but you will have to wait until 1982 to show what the effect of it was.

The second way is by *subject matter*. You take a phase of the subject's life and tell about that. If he collects paintings, you can have a chapter that is all about his collecting adventures no matter what the year. Or if he has had a lot of tragedies, you can have a chapter on all the blows he has sustained. The problem is that it may sound choppy, as if you were jumping around too much in time.

The third is the *mixed approach* technique. You can start chronologically and move along to a crucial event. Then, instead of dropping it and going on to events in an orderly fashion, you stick with the subject of that crucial event and don't worry about chronology.

You take what happens to him at that point in his life and follow it wherever it leads. You can look back and show times in the past that led up to it, and jump ahead to show how it will affect his future. Then, when you are through explaining that subject, you pick up the chronology at the approximate time you veered off.

You can say, "But back in 1862 he was not thinking of what the consequence could be. He roamed the mountain trails searching for . . ."

In the mixed approach technique, the life story is only loosely tied together by time. I prefer it—of the three techniques—because it seems the most natural. It avoids the straitjacket of the strict chronology and the jumpiness of the topical approach.

THE PARTS OF A BIOGRAPHY

We are talking now of any kind of biography—first or third person. It's the same as with any kind of book. Every biography is divided into three parts. It has a *beginning*, a *middle*, and an *end*.

Each is very important. Each has a function.

IN THE BEGINNING . . .

The job of the beginning is to catch the attention so that the reader is curious or compelled to go on. It can make a big statement: "I told myself when I was fourteen that I would not stop until I had five million dollars, and I knew just how I would get it . . . ."

Or you can set a mood: "It was a murky day, the kind that always filled me with foreboding—a day made for mystery and dark happenings. And before that day was over a woman lay dead and I had begun the life of a fugitive."

Or you can do it with an anecdote, as Fishbait does in his memoir of life on Capitol Hill. It must be an anecdote that somehow reveals the character of the subject of the biography and sets the tone of the book. Here it is:

One Saturday morning, I was standing in front of my doorkeeper's office in plaid shirt and stocking feet—I only permitted myself this luxury on the weekend—being friendly and maybe showing off a bit. A ramrodlike figure came by, and I thought I'd warm him up, maybe make a friend.

I pointed to the sign on the door and said proudly, "That's me." The man stopped, gave me a haughty look, reached into his pocket, and pulled out a Heath candy bar. "That's me," he said, and kept on walking.

Already, from the anecdote, you know you are going to read about a man with a sense of humor, a man who is brassy but sensitive, too.

NOW COMES THE MIDDLE . . .

This is the big juicy part. The whole story. It pours out or it flows slowly—but it MOVES. We know where you are going because we have already talked about the three approaches you can take and you have chosen one. There are a few questions you have as you go along and a few problems that are almost universal with first-time biographers. So let's take a look at them:

How Do You Switch from One Subject to Another?

1. There are many ways to let the reader know you are through with one subject for the moment and are going on to something else. If it is a clear break, you can simply skip three or four lines and start a new paragraph. That can indicate a change of time, place, subject. It can show that a flashback is about to begin. At the end of it you again skip three or four lines to show you are going back to the flow.

2. You can ask a question. "And what was So-and-so doing? Or, "What difference could it make that So-and-so had become his enemy—what harm could he do?" Then the scene shifts to So-and-so and why he was a dangerous enemy.

Transition is simply the way you travel from one segment of a book to another.

180

3. A new chapter can indicate that some section is closed and a new phase is opening.

4. You can just say, "Meanwhile, at the camp, the plot was progressing."

5. Hinting at or forecasting events ahead is called *foreshadowing*. Just as in life, there are little indications that something is going to happen. The writer—you—must throw in a line here and there to indicate what is going to happen. You can say, "Her temper tantrum didn't seem so important then, especially when she laughed and immediately apologized. But he would remember it months later when there were more serious consequences that changed all their lives."

This way you hold you reader who is dying to know about that next temper tantrum.

How Do You Get Variety in a Biography?

By switching frequently from close-up to long-distance view to middle-distance views of your subject.

It is deadly dull to read every minute thing that happened to a person. It is equally dull if you never tell intimate details but always seem to be viewing your subject from afar.

To illustrate what I mean, let's look at *The Search for the Real Nancy Reagan* and view the romance of Nancy Davis and Ronald Reagan.

There is an intimate view of Nancy getting her first date with Ronnie. You hear the exact conversation. That's close up. He arrives. He stands at the door on crutches. You hear their banter. That's still close up. Then you have the actual date. You almost feel you are at the table with them at the night club, listening in. Still close up.

The flow of her days during the early days of the romance—middle distance.

You see them riding horses. You see her dressed to help him pitch manure during the courtship as she did to prove herself a good helpmate to a would-be cowboy. Middle distance.

General background about the ranch where the courtship progresses or views of what Ronnie was doing to earn a living during that time is long distance.

What About Quotes?

Too many quotes are tiresome. So is too much prose without a quote to brighten it. Keep mixing it—switching back and forth.

If your subject is long dead and you cannot get quotes from him, you will have to rely on the newspaper of the day to find what he said. Or you can use a small quote from another biographer, being sure to say, "Biographer So-and-so quotes Jefferson as saying, '. . . .'"

Another trick is to show you are making up a quote and use what you think he might have said. "It was as if he were saying, '. . .'"

Still another technique is to give your interpretation of the subject's action. You are the expert and you are permitted to have opinions. Or find an expert and quote him: My own view is that he was glad to have been found out so that he could stop the masquerade. Why else did he . . . ?"

How Do You Treat Scandal and Sensitive Material?

The old saying, "Never speak ill of the dead," does not hold when a biography is being written. If there is evil to speak of, speak of it.

To illustrate, consider the world-famed painter Pablo Picasso. Many books have been written about the many-faceted artist and his prolific works, which turned him into a billionaire—some of the books taking an almost reverential tone. But then, in 1988, came a new biographer of the artist who shocked the world by describing him as "a sexual sadist," and "a little monster ridden by rage."

The author, Arianna Stassinopoulos, claimed that Picasso was cruel to his wives and mistresses—had crushed out cigarettes on one lover's face—and that he had not spoken to his children for years. Further, that two wives had ended up committing suicide and that mistresses became mentally disturbed.

Some defenders of Picasso claimed the author of *Picasso: Creator and Destroyer* was actually motivated by a desire to denigrate Picasso's art, but Stassinopoulos maintained that, to the contrary, knowing the man helped *understand* the art. It might explain, for example, the ugliness of the women in some of his paintings. Stassinopoulos argued that she was not denying that Picasso was a great *artist*, but only that he was not a great *man*.

Every writer of biographies or memoirs has to decide how to handle hurtful material that makes the subject look bad. When Albert Goldman's book on John Lennon was published, fans were furious at the picture of Lennon as a selfish druggie. Author Goldman did not cave in under this outcry. He said, "The price of truth is high."

Some writers absolutely refuse to write anything derogatory about their subjects. Take the biography of President Eisenhower's secretary, written by Robert J. Donovan, a Washington reporter who is also the author of a two-volume biography of Harry Truman.

The name of the book is *Confidential Secretary—Ann Whitman's Twenty Years with Eisenhower and Rockefeller*, and it has no touch of scandal in it about the lives and loves of these men as other biographies of Whitman's bosses had.

No, in this book, about the meanest thing told about Ike is that on one trip he kept Ann working, typing thank-you notes, until she had to forego the thrill of seeing the Taj Mahal. But the book does prove again that it is not necessary to have scandal to make a biography interesting.

But a biography can be selective and just not talk about the dark underside of a famous person. That is different from lying and saying it could not be that the man has a dark side. What I'm saying is that a good biographer is honest. Of course, if you ignore sensitive material, your biography may appear old-fashioned. Times have changed. You don't have to be brutal, but you don't have to mince words either—or lie for the subject.

If you are writing a biography of the star of *Animal House* and you are showing the rise and fall of a fine actor, you simply can't say, "No, John Belushi could not have been on drugs." You have to accept the evidence. And the public has the right to know what the police or his friends learned. You just have to present the material that has been dug up and add any explanation you wish or mitigating circumstances.

Some biographers become like mother hens protecting their little chicks. They become defensive and refuse to write anything that will reflect on their subject's reputation. That may be noble but it is not good biography.

When Frances Leighton was writing *Dog Days at the White House*, the newsmaking memoir of the electrician-dogkeeper of the White House, Traphes Bryant, Bryant described scenes such as President Kennedy and pretty female guests skinny-dipping in the White House pool.

In one instance that Traphes relates, the message came that Jackie had doubled back and the staff was hard pressed to get all evidence of a party and girls removed before she arrived.

This was the first published account of Kennedy's penchant for dalliance, and some book reviewers and fans among the public were up in arms defending JFK—saying it could not be true and that such things *could not go on at the White House*.

Traphes Bryant and Fran rode out the storm and were vindicated when some of Kennedy's pretty, surreptitious visitors themselves stepped forward to say yes, they had been there, at the White House, and had made love with the president.

THE SATISFYING ENDING

The ending of any type of biographical book, whether written in first or third person, must leave the reader thoughtful or applauding or amused or happy at how it all turned out, or even slightly tearful—just as a good novel does. In other words, it leaves you satisfied.

If it is a sad way your biography ends, that's life. And the reader will understand and accept it—though sometimes

your publisher won't and will urge you to end on a happie
note. If something terrible happens to your subject at the en
of the book, there should have been some little arrow hidder
somewhere in the manuscript that points to it, so that the
reader can say, "I might have known." He isn't caught completely by surprise.

There are many ways to end a biography. Just answer
these questions and see which one seems aimed at your book:

Should you try to tie it in with the beginning? Has the
subject, perhaps, come full circle in the course of the life story
and is now back where he or she started?

Should you end with a telling anecdote?

Should you end with a quote saved for a thought-provok-
ing punchline finish? It can be what your subject tells someone. Or it can be a quote from someone else that amuses or
pithily sums up your subject's life.

Or should you end with the subject's funeral and the atmosphere there?

But if your subject is still living, should you have him
look back and try to make sense of what happened? Or glory
in the way he made everyone laugh or tricked the world or
became a billionaire?

Or should he look forward and still dream of some big,
seemingly impossible goal of the future that he is going to try
for no matter what anyone says?

All of the above can lead to very satisfying endings. You
will feel it when you come upon the one that is right for your
book.

13

Getting Down to the Actual Writing

Congratulations! You are ready to write. Then why are you suddenly afraid?

FEAR OF WRITING—THE NEMESIS OF AUTHORS

Lots of people are afraid of writing. You are not alone. Even Fran, with some thirty books behind her, had periods of self-doubt and fear.

But I am here to fight the fear with you and guide you through the book step by step. So let's see what the fears are—what's holding you back:

Fear of inadequacy—lack of education.

Fear that someone will laugh at you or pressure you.

Fear of not making the deadline.

Fear of not knowing what makes up a book.

Fear of not writing well enough.

All right, it's out in the open. Let me assure you there are solutions for each of these common fears.

1. *Lack of Education.* You haven't had enough education? You're in good company. Pulitzer prize-winner Fred Sparks,

mentioned in Chapter 1, "Write a Nonfiction Book and Gain Satisfaction, Authority, and Cash," told me that he quit school at fifteen to take a job as copy boy for a New York newspaper and never looked back. Art and film critic Parker Tyler, after finishing prep school, began writing reviews for a Chicago newspaper at seventeen and later was managing editor of *View* and *Art News*. When he turned in his 800-page biography of surrealist artist Pavel Tchelichew, I deleted one hyphen— much to his annoyance—and the editing was complete.

You will be comforted to know that even people with college educations can suddenly feel totally inadequate when faced with a book deadline. They say they are unprepared, lack a proper education.

And they have a point. Just schooling won't make anyone a writer. If you have a yen for writing, chances are you have a knack for it. What you need is confidence. Tell yourself you *can* and keep working on your nonfiction book. Consider this: if you hadn't exhibited some feeling for writing, a certain talent for expressing yourself, you wouldn't be sitting where you are now, ready to start a book, would you?

2. *The Laughter, Pity, or Envy of Others.* Don't tell friends and relatives you are writing a book. In keeping it secret, you have taken away half of the fear that anyone will undermine your confidence. People can do it to you. They might be amused that you dare to think you can write a book.

I can tell you this from personal experience. While I was working on my own first nonfiction book, I met a classmate I hadn't seen for many years at a party. When she asked what I was doing, I proudly said, "I'm working on a book—*How to Write and Sell Your First Novel.*"

"That's ludicrous," she replied. "You've never written a novel."

Crushed, I weakly replied, "It's a journalistic book— based on interviews with novelists and my experience as editor and agent."

Fortunately for my ego, a young writer listening in said, "Oh, an agent writing a book on how to sell a novel! I'll buy one!" But the criticism still rankles.

Even after writing many books, Fran Leighton does not talk about her current work. When people ask, "What are you working on now?" she says, "I'm superstitious. I can't tell you till I'm done."

So get your excuse for not revealing what you are doing ready—and don't hesitate to use it.

3. *The Specter of the Deadline.* Meeting a publisher's deadline is simply a matter of keeping a schedule so that you finish in plenty of time to study your work and improve it, and to retype it or have it retyped in final draft.

Your contract probably gives you about nine months to write your book. I am going to show you how you can have your first draft done in a little more than three months. Then you will have enough time left for editing, thinking, and making a clean copy. This will also give you time to show the finished manuscript to someone else if you want opinions and help in perfecting it.

We'll get to your work habits later in this chapter, but for now let's get on with the reasons for your apprehensions.

4. *You Don't Really Know How to Write That Kind of Book.* Well, that's easy to remedy. Get a book that is similar to the one you have in mind.

Take a close look at it. With a yellow legal pad beside you, go through it chapter by chapter to see how the author handled the material. It's called "on-the-job training." You are learning by doing. Make a line down the middle of your pad. In the left column put down how the author did it. In the right column put down how you are going to do it.

Say it's a how-to book. How does the writer handle the gathering of the materials the reader will need? When does he talk about the cost? How many sketches and pictures does he use?

If it's a biography of a historical character, where does he begin the story?

Write it down. Maybe he starts with the death scene and then flashes back to the beginning of the man's life. At what point in your subject's life do *you* want to open your story?

What does the writer accomplish in the first chapter? The second, and so forth? Write it down.

When does he get around to his main theme—that his subject was right in advocating war with England? Do you want to start your main thrust at the same place in the book? Maybe by seeing how he did it you suddenly have an idea for a different way to present your premise.

Remember, there is no right and no wrong way to weave your story. If it's interesting, if it holds the attention, it's the *right* way.

5. *What If the Publisher Rejects Your Manuscript?* That is perhaps the biggest fear of all. Rejection. Okay, we've said it. Fear of rejection. But how do you know it will be rejected if you don't write it?

Fear of failure keeps many a potentially fine writer from writing. Or from actually finishing a manuscript. As long as he doesn't finish it, he doesn't have to find out if it would or would not be accepted. Most manuscripts under contract are accepted. Let's look at the worst that can happen. Your first book did not sell. So what?

If it doesn't sell, you write another. And if that one doesn't sell, you write another. Years after Hemingway died, some of his early writings came to light and were published and well paid for. He hadn't thought they were good enough, but later others did. Our advice is don't throw old manuscripts away. They're like stocks and bonds. Store them where you can get them out and rework them after you are a published and successful writer. You will have developed better judgment and you will see what they need and fix them up— discarding the dull parts, perhaps reorganizing and adding a little.

Fran knew of one case in which a man wrote three books about the Vietnam war before he sold his first. Publishers were suddenly going back to take another look at the earlier books. Such things happen.

And there is another solution we'll get to in this chapter—you can call in a "book doctor." If *you* don't know everything you need to make that manuscript salable, *he* may be able to supply the missing ingredients or tell you what to do.

So now you are relieved because you know there is a way to overcome every problem you face. Let's get going on that manuscript.

WHERE TO BEGIN—WHAT TO DO FIRST

Would you believe the first thing you do is write the beginning and the end?

You need to know the limits of your book—the boundaries. You are going from here to there. So write the lead. Or a bunch of them. You can decide on the best one later. It can be some outrageous statement. Or a great truth of life. Or some promise to the reader—what you are going to do for him before the book is over. Whatever it is, it must grab the reader's attention.

Now write the ending. Your final statement. It can be some conclusion that can be drawn from all that has been said. It can be a philosophical statement. It can be how the subject's life or career ends. It can be inspirational. It can be practical and tell the reader what he can go out and do now that he has read your book.

Okay. Don't you feel good? You have the alpha and the omega. The beginning and the end.

Now, my friend, get out your tentative Table of Contents from your book presentation—and review the whole presentation. List the major points you want to make in the book. Is the original plan still right, or have you thought of a better way to make the major points hold together. Certain points will be grouped into distinct parts or segments that make your subject easier to follow, easier to understand.

Maybe you have uncovered five main phases of your subject's life. Or four phases in learning how to paint. Or three parts in explaining the development of America's sea power. Whatever parts your manuscript falls into, write down the parts, give them names, and then make a list of chapters that belong to each part.

Let's take an example to show how a biography can be divided into parts. Fran's book, *The Search for the Real Nancy Reagan*, is divided into six parts:

I. The Lonely Childhood of Anne Frances
II. The Hollywood Ending . . .
III. First Lady of California
IV. The Rocky Road to the White House
V. The Agony and the Ecstasy: The White House
VI. Once Is Not Enough

Each part contains several chapters—and incidentally, the numbering of the chapters for some publishers begins again with "1" in each Part. Each part has its own theme, and each chapter of that part advances that theme in some way.

Let's pick at random the third chapter of Part II, "The Hollywood Ending . . ." It starts with Hollywood gossip columnists not being impressed with the fact that Ronald Reagan was dating Nancy Davis and predicting that Ronnie and Jane Wyman would get back together.

The chapter ends with a small disaster on the way home from Ronnie and Nancy's honeymoon and shows Nancy jumping in and saving the situation. The last line points a little arrow at the future by posing the question, "Could it be a portent of things to come?"

So you have your beginning and your end and you know in a general way the flow of the middle section. Now let's talk about your work habits.

WHEN IS THE BEST TIME TO WRITE?

The important thing is to follow your own inclinations. If you are a night person, burn the midnight oil. Many do. One of my clients who so values his privacy, I won't tell you his name, often works all night. He will call me at six or seven in the evening, shortly after he gets up. Another writer, William Hoffman, author of *David: Report on a Rockefeller*, told me, "I get up at seven in the morning, have a cup of coffee, and write until I can't stand the hunger any longer." Frances

Leighton writes from 5:30 A.M. to 12. By noon she has put in six and a half hours. Though she drives herself to write only four pages, often she writes from eight to ten pages and still has the day ahead of her.

Some of my clients, who have switched from a nine-to-five job to writing, feel best keeping that nine-to-five schedule. What counts is production, and we'll get to that in a moment.

WHERE IS THE BEST PLACE TO WRITE?

One woman writes in her car, her portable on her lap. In New York there are writers' enclaves where you rent a cubbyhole and talk to no one. Just the presence of other sufferers, however, makes the ordeal bearable. Fran writes looking at water out of her home office window—a lake that comes within thirty feet of the window.

Every room you can mention has been used for writing, including the bathroom. In that case, the writer felt intimidated by large rooms but very safe and cozy sitting on the edge of the bathtub, pounding away on a typewriter that sat on a roll-away typing table. The room was tiny, bright, cheerful with much red paint. Also, there was a window he could look out of without having to stand up.

Any number of books have been done at kitchen tables and bars, dirty dishes strewn about. But that was what felt comfortable to the writer.

Don't tell yourself you can't start your book until you get a word processor, as one man keeps telling me. That's a dodge—and a poor one. I find I can write perfectly well on an upright Olympia manual typewriter. Several books have been written on an old portable that I lent to the authors. So don't get too fascinated by the mechanics. Allow yourself no excuses. If your typewriter konks out, use a pen until it gets fixed. Or rent a typewriter.

SHOULD YOU HAVE A WRITING QUOTA?

Absolutely. The only way to get the job done and have the feeling of security you need while writing it is to know that the manuscript is inching along every day. Sticking rigidly to your writing schedule will give you a great feeling of being on top of the project.

Writers have come to me in a panic, saying a book is just too big an undertaking and they can't handle it—it may never get done. I tell them not to think about the whole book but about only one little part at a time—the chapter or the segment they are working on for the day. And remember my advice to Fred Sparks in Chapter 1.

A nonfiction book is like a series of articles. Each article has its theme and is complete within itself. Just deal with that chapter and don't worry about the book. When you have about twenty or so articles—chapters—you have a book. By writing your chapters or segments, you have let the book take care of itself. Only after you have your first draft need you study each chapter and fine-tune the book.

Keep a small daily goal—one that you can easily handle.

Do you think you could write just three double-spaced pages a day? Just three pages. Of course you can. Many I tell this to laugh and say that they can easily write double that amount. I say, "Do that in the days you are in the mood to keep going, but you don't have to. You don't have to feel pushed." If you write just three pages a day, you will have 300 pages in 100 days—just a little over three months. That's your first draft. If your book is a little longer—360 pages—you will have your first draft in exactly four months.

Doesn't that make you sigh with relief?

Of course if you take Sundays off from writing, it will take you a little longer to finish your first draft. Some writers write every day of the week but never on weekends. One writer writes even on weekends, actually carrying his portable to the beach during the summer. He says, "I have this terrible feeling that if I ever broke the rhythm of my one or two hours of banging out three pages every day, I'd never be able to recapture it." Maybe he's right.

How do you know when you've filled your quota each day? That's part of the game. Each day before you start writing, you ceremoniously take out three sheets of paper and put them within easy reach. If you write an anecdote or bit of advice that fills only half a page, you will take a fourth sheet and be responsible for filling only half of that. The total is still three full pages.

If it's a good day and you are really rolling, keep going until you start to run down. Then stop immediately so that you will feel fresh for the next day. Never write to exhaustion. At least, not on your first draft. After the publisher has accepted it and wants certain things rewritten, there will be time enough to drive yourself. By then the excitement and triumph of having made the grade and knowing your book is slated for publication will spur you on.

How Do You Get in the Mood for Writing?

Just the routine of writing at the same time every day will help put you in the mood. It's like getting hungry for lunch automatically at the same time every day. Or excited at post time at the races. You will find yourself thinking of that typewriter as your starting time approaches.

But you can't allow yourself the luxury of moods. You are going to sit down at the typewriter as soon as the clock says, "Go."

"The good news," says Fran, "is that after you've sat there a few minutes and stumbled around writing a few things, some magic takes place and suddenly you are fascinated by the material and the sheer joy of finding a way to say something you're thinking. The sheer joy of self-expression. Loneliness is gone. People are alive in your mind. And, best of all, you're in charge. The power is yours."

Coffee is a great help to many writers in getting them started. Fran has talked about how she automatically wakes up and reaches for coffee at 5:00 A.M. and spends the first half hour drinking it and eating a single piece of toast with cheese and slices of green pepper on it.

It doesn't sound too appetizing to me, but that's her way. Then, her third cup of coffee in hand, she descends the stairs to her typewriter, in her special quarters.

By the time she has sipped the coffee while fiddling around and trying to figure out what to say first, she is hooked and needs no more props to keep her going.

There are a few tricks you can use to get the creative juices flowing. Decide what you want to tackle that day—which section of a cookbook or a housework-made-fun book, or which incident in a person's life, if it's a biography, you want to concentrate on. Don't feel you must pick up where you left off the day before—though, for some writers, it helps.

One particular writer reads the last few paragraphs of the previous day's work and this is enough to get her motivated to continue the flow.

Another writer actually retypes the last few paragraphs to get the feeling again, if he is not in the mood. This sets up a momentum. Also, he is apt to think "that sounds pretty good" and want to continue.

SHOULD YOU CORRECT OR IMPROVE YOUR FINISHED PAGES AS YOU GO?

Heavens, no! The best way is just to keep going. Don't get caught up in editing or being critical. Just put it away. It can shatter your confidence, and it can certainly throw you off your schedule. Fran writes a first draft without looking back. If she doesn't know which way to say something, she says it both ways or even three or four ways if they occur to her. But she keeps plowing ahead.

She does not stick with a particular sequence. She writes what she is in the mood for that day and sticks the pages into the proper folder. There is a folder for each chapter and also a folder called "Only God Knows Where." If it is just a clever phrase or an isolated anecdote that could go any number of places, she puts it into God's folder.

There is also a folder labeled "Need." If there is a question she needs answered, she makes a note of it and tosses it into that folder. Also in it is a general rough outline of the book and list of chapters so she can think about all the things she needs and should look into.

After Fran has written material for every folder and thinks she has enough, she stops. That's the first draft. She puts it away—still without reading a page of it. Then, flush with the thrill of accomplishment, she relaxes and clears her mind. She rewards herself with about two weeks of movies and reading other writers' books and rock gardening and visiting friends. Then with fresh mind and fresh approach, she starts reading the pages and putting them in order. She studies each chapter, makes notes about her feelings. She decides where the chapter is dull. Where it needs more facts, more quotes or anecdotes. Where a description is needed or a date or a transition.

She may decide that something belongs in a different chapter. She may decide something should be told in flashback.

She cuts and pastes, getting each chapter in shape, and then retypes, making final changes as she goes. Or she may turn it over to a typist, editing chapter by chapter as the typist makes a clean copy. You will be surprised at the typographical errors that creep in. Of course, if you use a word processor, making corrections and moving material around is much easier.

WARNING: GIVE CREDIT

As mentioned in Chapter 11, "The Art of Research—Search and Seize," it is of utmost importance to give specific credit to source when quoting someone else's material. Not doing so can ruin your career. It ruined one politician's chance at the presidency in the 1988 race, when Senator

196

Joseph Biden failed to give attribution for some very impressive statements. His credibility simply crumbled.

Similar neglect to give credit can ruin your reputation with publishers. It can result in bad reviews of your book. You can, of course, simply paraphrase a quote and say, "As it has been said," or "As someone once said." At least that shows you realize you are not making up the pithy comment yourself. But it is nicer to spread the credit if you know who said it first. You will not be diminished. You will actually be more respected for it.

There are two ways to give credits in your book. One is informal and the other formal. The informal way, which I prefer and which most modern writers prefer, is to mention the source in the same breath with the quote. "J. J. Johnson, in his book *Marilyn Monroe*, said it well, 'Thus and so'—giving the quote. Or if it is a newspaper or magazine quote, you can say, "J. J. Johnson, writing in *Ladies' Home Journal*, said, 'Marilyn Monroe hated men but simply manipulated them to help her career.'"

You can also simply give credit to the publication—"*The New York Times* said that thus and so." Or, "An article in *Good Housekeeping* holds that Marilyn Monroe actually hated men but manipulated them to further her career."

If, however, you find many sources that say the same things, you can say something like, "It has widely been said that Marilyn Monroe hated men and only . . . etc."

HOW MUCH CAN YOU QUOTE?

That's a money-loaded question—how much you can safely quote. The answer is very little if you have not secured *written* permission from the copyright holder or the author's publisher. There is such a thing as fair use—the amount that can be quoted without injuring the author's rights. As you have seen in Chapter 11, "The Art of Research—Search and Seize," Fran holds herself to a very strict guideline in quoting material—about 25 words.

To get permission to make a sizable quote, you must contact the publisher of the material. Put your request in writing. You may be surprised to learn that publishers are not so flattered that you want to quote from one of their books that they quickly give permission. They may charge as little as twenty-five dollars or as much as hundreds of dollars for the quotation, usually depending on its length and your intended use of it. Be sure to send them the excerpts that you want to use so they can make their judgment on whether to charge and how much to charge. And tell a little about the book in which it will appear. It may be that if they charge too much for you to pay, they will settle for less if you cut down the size of the excerpts.

Such matters are handled by the rights department of a publishing house, which is a good thing to know if you need permission in a hurry. It may be that they *are* willing to give their permission *gratis*, but inform you that you must strike your bargain with the author and they will give you the name of the author's agent.

SOME TIPS ON EDITING

1. *Don't Try to Think of What Your Publisher Will Like or Dislike When You Are Editing Your Own Work*. Edit to please yourself. You can seldom predict what a publisher will like or what he or she will object to.

2. *Don't Overdescribe*. Use adjectives and adverbs sparingly. She is smart or she is not smart. You don't have to say, "She was very smart." Unless you can cite her IQ of 175 or membership in Mensa, you won't impress the reader by adding "very." Getting rid of the excess words makes writing crisp and a faster read. Let's take an example. First the bad way: "She was very beautiful and very smart so it was strange that she was also extremely shy." That's long-winded, dull.

Look how much better it is if you simply say, "She was beautiful, smart, and strangely shy." That's crisp.

However, adverbs or adjectives sparingly used can make

a sentence more vivid. "'It's true,' he said apologetically." Or "His skeletal form . . ."

3. *Avoid Too Many Participles.* If you find yourself using "ing" endings, change them to more exciting verb forms. Let's say you have written, "She was crying and sputtering, but he was not paying attention to her." That's too roundabout.

Now read it this way: "She cried and sputtered, but he ignored her." That's the straightforward way to say the same thing.

4. *Don't Try to Find Substitutes for "Said."* "He said," "she said" can be used over and over without jarring the reader. But all those substitutes do irritate the reader: "avowed," "stated," "commented," "affirmed," "asserted," "declared," "renounced," and on and on. Only if the speaker is saying something in an unusual way need you make note of it. For example, if the woman is shouting, say so: "Get that ugly creature out of my sight!" she screamed.

5. *Do Not Use Black Marker Pens When Crossing Out Words in Your Manuscript.* Use a pencil to cross out a word with a single line and write the new word above it. The trouble with markers is that you can't read what is underneath— it's gone forever. You may change your mind and want to go back to the original way. A single thin line drawn through a word or sentence enables you to compare the two ways of saying something.

If you are using a word processor, it is important to "save" your original words as well as insert the new version.

6. *When You Move Something to a Different Chapter Folder, Make a Note of It.* On that page jot down where to find the material: "Moved instructions for mitering to Chapter 6." But don't try to figure out then and there exactly where it goes or how to fit it in. Which brings us to the next point:

7. *Give Your Attention to Only One Chapter at a Time.* Study Chapter 1 and make all the changes you want in it. Rearrange the order by cutting pages apart and putting the chapter together the way you want it, or rearrange it on your word processor.

If you're working with typed pages, spread the pages of the chapter on a table or kitchen bar or desk. That gives you an overview and makes it easier to see how the parts fit together. Cut and paste. Cut and staple. Make new pages. To show this is the edited chapter, you might want to staple the pieces to colored typing or duplicator paper, which you can buy by the ream. This way you know it is the first editing of the chapter. Then if it needs a second editing, you can staple your changed sheets to a different color paper.

Or if you use a word processor, put a note in your text, "First Edit."

8. *Colored Folders Are Worth Their Weight in Chocolate Chip Cookies, If Not Gold.* As you finish editing each chapter, number the pages in each chapter separately. (Yes, Chapter 2 also starts with Page 1) and put them in a colored folder—say green.

That's the trick. For your first editing, use the same color editing folders. If you reedit, switch to a different color, say red, so you will know what stage of editing the chapter is in. In each case—the first editing, the second editing—leave all the leftover pieces and pages in the old folder.

9. *Messy Pages?* Don't worry about how the pages look as long as you can read them. This is not a beauty contest. It's a brain contest. Editing is of paramount importance.

James Clavell put it tersely, "The art of writing is rewriting."

10. *Find Those Clinkers.* Read each chapter an extra time to get rid of repetitions of words—unless it's done for effect—and see if a better word can be found for those that strike you as pedestrian. This is the time to use your *Roget's Thesaurus,* your dictionary, and any other word book you can find.

11. *Pretend You Are a Reader.* Make notes in the margin of what you like and don't like, such as "great writing" or "paints a picture" "or "sounds fake" or "leaves me cold" or "boring." Or, "Isn't there a better word?" However, don't do this on the days you feel low, or you will have only nasty comments on the margin.

On happy days or good days, pep up and shape up the

bad parts and be proud of yourself for the nice touches you have managed to put in the manuscript.

On the days you are depressed, spend the time looking for better words in the thesaurus or just making a clean copy of something a typist will not be able to read if you are going to have it professionally typed. Or look up some fact you need for a particular page.

12. *Use the Same Work Schedule When Editing as You Did in Getting the First Draft Done.* Work at the same time, for the same amount of time, in the same place.

13. *When You Start Typing Clean Copy, Don't Start Clean-Copying the Chapters Until You Have Worked on Each and Every One.* That's because you may suddenly find something toward the end of the book that you want to put in an early chapter. You might not make the change because it would mess up the looks of the chapter. Don't worry about it, and never hesitate to improve something because it won't look as neat. When you photocopy the page, the cuts will not be visible. With a word processor all this is much easier.

14. *What About Half-Filled Pages? What About Extra Pages? Missing Pages?* If you make a change and you are left with an empty half page, after you cut and paste your clean copy, simply draw an arrow downward on the empty space to show it is not the end of the chapter.

If you have made an insert and had to use an extra sheet of paper between pages 16 and 17, for instance, just label the extra page 16A. On the other hand, if the manuscript now jumps from 15 to 17, indicate the missing page by adding the 16 to page 17, to make it read 16-17. Editors are used to this.

15. *Save Everything.* Save the folders with the material you did not use and all your notes from your research and interviews. You do not know when an editor may phone you to ask about something you left out or something that just doesn't ring true. You can go back to your original material and check it or add a few more paragraphs from the things you left out.

If it's a matter of accuracy, you will know what book or magazine article to consult. It is wise to keep a log of your sources in your original chapter folder that tells what pages of what book were used as your authority.

Even after the book comes out, readers or authorities in the field or book reviewers may challenge you. So keep everything for several years.

———— •• ——➤ •• ————

So your manuscript is done. If you are happy with it, see the instructions for preparing and mailing the manuscript and get it off. If you are not happy with it, or if it has had a number of rejections, you may need to use a "book doctor" before you run out of publishers.

BOOK DOCTORS

You may know that Hollywood turns to "film doctors" when a movie in the making seems not to work. Elaine May has on occasion doctored a film to box office success.

But did you know that there are also "book doctors"? If you are not satisfied with your manuscript but don't know why, or if you *know* it won't sell because half a dozen publishers have turned it down, you may need just such a person.

Maybe you want to make all the changes yourself—do all the rewriting. You just want guidance in knowing what to do. A free-lance editor can read your manuscript and tell you. For this, the charge will be anywhere from $750 to a thousand— and often more. But if you can afford it and if you feel you have the makings of a great book, it's a small price to pay.

Maybe you prefer to give up on the writing. You want an expert to take over, do the rewrite. Okay, that's possible, too. Some charge a flat fee—$1,000 to $1,500 or much more if it is a major rewrite job. Others charge by the hour—about $20 to $30 an hour is the sum I've heard of lately.

And who are these experts that you should have faith in them? And where do you find them? They are almost always former editors of major publishing houses who are now free-lancers working for publishers and authors. Yes, publishers call in outside editors, too, to edit books they have bought, when their own editors are busy.

Or maybe one of these outside editors is an expert in a certain field—medicine, architecture, psychiatry, cooking, and so forth.

It's hard to find these editors. Every literary agent knows one or two and what type of books they prefer or are best at editing. If you know anyone in a publishing house, he may give you the names of former editors there who are now freelancers.

You don't want to give your manuscript to some rip-off artist, so be sure you ask what other books the editor has worked on and check with the previous author-client or publisher-client on whether he recommends that person. It's a touchy subject, and a previous author-client may have forgotten or not want to acknowledge that he had help.

You can seek helpers in your local telephone directory. In the Manhattan Yellow Pages, the editorial helpers are listed under the category of "Editorial Services." Others are listed in *Literary Market Place*. Since these listings contain the names of editors with a wide variety of skills, you must be careful to match their ability with what your manuscript needs—perhaps they must have some knowledge of science or fine art. Ask about their expertise.

Then be sure to ask if they have edited books and ask for some titles and publishers. You might also inquire if they have had experience working at a publishing house—and in what capacity. Then do not hesitate to call the publisher and check it out. It's not being snoopy. Just basic self-protection to make sure you are dealing with proper professional persons. Ask if So-and-so ever worked for that company and what his position was.

INSTRUCTIONS CONCERNING THE MANUSCRIPT—
ITS PHYSICAL APPEARANCE

FIRST FOR SOME DO'S:

1. Use good, medium-weight white paper—8½ × 11 inches.

2. Put the page number in the upper-right corner about one-half inch from the top. If you have the number on the left, a paper clip will hide it if the publisher is clipping certain pages together. Now is the time to be sure you have numbered the pages throughout consecutively, from 1 to 300, or whatever. And be sure to white-out the previous chapter page numbers.

3. Use a title page. Not doing so labels you an amateur. Put the title, nicely centered, one-third of the page down. Under that, centered, the byline, several spaces below.

Put your name, address, and phone number at the bottom right or left side of the title page if you don't have an agent. If you have an agent, leave that blank because your agent will stamp his name and address there. You can also put the approximate number of words down near the bottom of the page. To find this, count the number of words on an average page. Then do it again on another page to be sure, and multiply the average number of words on a page by the number of pages.

4. The ideal margin is an inch at the top and bottom. A margin of 1¼ to 1½ inches at the left looks a little better. The margin at the right can be jagged, but should not come closer than a half-inch to the edge. Each page should look like a picture in a frame. You can put a dot at the bottom so that you know when to stop.

5. Double space. Indent paragraphs five spaces.

NOW FOR SOME DON'TS:

(Some of these are applicable only to typed rather than print-out manuscript.)

1. Don't use erasable bond unless you are adept at using it. It smudges too easily and has a slight stickiness.

2. Don't make a lot of corrections with pen, or even by typewriter. If you make corrections, cut and paste. That is, retype that set of paragraphs. Cut the page and insert the correct ones. Keep the page looking normal, and if there is now too much material to go on a page, start another one, calling it, for example, 131A. Editors are used to insert pages marked A, B, and C.

3. Editors don't want your name or another slug on the top of every page. That is because in getting ready for the printer, everything extraneous has to be crossed off.

4. Don't send your original. A good photocopy looks much better. Keep the original for yourself. It is legally safer since it's easy to see where the corrections were made.

Never send your only copy of anything written, even your covering letter. Make a photocopy.

Don't send photos until the editor wants them, and send them by registered mail—it is, the post office says, the safest way, and it can be insured. Certified mail can't be insured. Use a soft pencil to put identification on the back of the pictures to be sure no line shows through.

5. Don't staple the pages of each chapter. Don't even use paper clips to keep each chapter together. If the editor wants to take some section home to read, he will clip those pages and put them in his briefcase.

6. Use business-type stationery for your covering letter. Don't use stationery that shows you work in or own a clothing store or any other nonwriting profession unless your book is about that profession.

If you don't have plain business stationery, run, don't walk, to your closest printer. It is not expensive. You don't want fancy stationery. Just something easy to read, giving your name, address, and telephone number. It need not say you are a writer. It should be on white 8½ × 11 inches, good-quality paper—no fancy weaves—of medium weight.

7. If you are submitting the manuscript on speculation and have not made the sale, be sure to send the proper

amount of postage and a sturdy self-addressed mailing bag for the publisher to return it if the answer is no. Have it weighed at the post office and include the stamps in an envelope with your name and address on it and the name of your manuscript. Paper-clip that to your copy.

8. If you send the manuscript first class mail, always write "First Class Mail" on it in big letters to be sure it does not end up in the slow lane, going fourth class.

If you are short of money, don't hesitate to send the manuscript Special Fourth Class Book Rate—there's no stigma attached, but it's slow getting there. Postal rates change, but at this writing, Special Fourth Class is 90 cents for the first pound and 35 cents for each additional pound. A book manuscript weighs about three pounds. If you are including a letter, no additional postage is necessary.

Frances Leighton always sends her manuscripts certified mail with return receipt requested. That way she receives notice on a card that her manuscript was received.

9. Post offices no longer like string or twine and may charge extra if you use it. Strong postal tape is the best.

You should use a stationery box to hold your manuscript. Put your name, address, and title on the label and glue it to the cover of the box. Then put the box in a padded mailing bag or wrap it with strong wrapping paper, using mailing tape to seal it.

Mail it. Now may The Force be with you—and the Fates!

14

How to Deal with Editors
and Copy Editors

There are certain things you should know about the editors you will be working with. They are individuals and they have feelings. They want you to make them look good.

This brings us to the first basic truth. If you have a successful book—not necessarily a best-seller—they will look good. If your book is a lemon and loses money for the publishing house, they take up residence in the lemon grove. They may even end up being urged to resign—especially if they have had a finger in picking several lemons in a row.

Therefore, rest assured that when your editor suggests something, he is not trying to ruin your book because he is jealous of your talent, or any other such rubbish. He really thinks his suggestion will help the book.

The second basic truth is that practically no two editors will see a problem in exactly the same way. In fact, one may not even think there is a problem, while another will demand a change in organization or language—or may even want to throw one part out. But knowing that isn't going to help you, except to make you feel a little better. The fact is that you have to deal with the particular editor assigned to you, so try to see it his way. His way is the product of his background and training, just as yours is. So let's take a look at editors.

Book editors come in all sizes, sexes, shapes, and colors. They usually arrive at book publishing from other fields—music, art, newspapers and magazines, TV and movie companies, bookselling, sales and publicity, literary and ad agencies, academia, even from sports. I once met an editor of college textbooks of philosophy who had originally been a high school athletic coach. David Segal, a famous editor of the past who died young, told me that he came to book publishing from the clothing manufacturing business.

About the only things editors have in common are a fascination with books and reading, plus a belief that they know what the public wants—and minds stuffed with an extraordinary miscellany of information gained from the books they have edited. Editors (and agents), like authors, believe "If I like it, it's worth publishing." They feel they have the common touch. Some, indeed, seem even to have the Midas touch and make profits on almost every book they bring to their company.

But editors are rarely "company men"—or women—unable to see beyond the canons of their company and striving merely for their employers' maximum profits. Instead, they are would-be tastemakers and pacesetters, trying to get the books published that *they* like—books they will be proud to point to on their "lifetime list" of works they acquired, edited, or shepherded in some way.

Just as writers have their "list of published books" to feed their egos and show accomplishment, editors have their "lifetime lists" as their proud achievement. Their list not only feeds their egos, however; it also can put them in a higher earning bracket. Just as you are trying to further your *writing* career, so is the editor working on his *editing* career.

Your editor is usually a careerist who will not hesitate to move from publisher to publisher to advance his or her power and influence.

Howard Cady, one of the better-known editors in the

208

publishing world, for example, made ten moves in a distinguished career that saw him become editor in chief at Putnam's, Holt, and Little, Brown. He is now semiretired.

Phyllis Grann, who became president and publisher at Putnam's trade book division and chairman of the board, started as a secretary at Doubleday before becoming a rising editor at Morrow, David McKay, and then senior editor and vice president at Simon & Schuster.

Once, when I was applying for an editorial job at Charles Scribner's Sons and had passed the inspection of the editorial director, Burroughs Mitchell, Charles Scribner, Jr., himself declined to hire me because of the variety of jobs I had had in the past. He said, disapprovingly, "I don't want someone who, like a bee, will go from flower to flower and pollenize it and then move on."

Actually, that struck me as exactly what an editor *should* do. Scribner's has regained its vigor under the new ownership of Macmillan, where it is managed by such experienced and energetic people as editor in chief Robert Stewart, formerly with McGraw-Hill, Simon & Schuster, New American Library, and Prentice-Hall; and senior editorial consultant Edward T. Chase, who previously worked with New American Library, Putnam's, and Macmillan. Each brings distinctive and sometimes distinguished works to the company.

So expect your editor to be an individual, rather than just a type.

Now let's look at the categories of editors with whom you will be working.

NOT ALL EDITORS EDIT

The first editor you will deal with at a publishing house may, in some cases, be a person who has nothing to do with the actual editing of your book. Let me explain. A large publishing house hires a variety of editors with specialized jobs.

Writers talk about "the publisher," but the person they are really talking about is the editor assigned to their book— or editors. There are three editors who may be involved with you. First is the *acquisitions editor*. He is the one who studies your presentation and recommends that the publishing house makes you an offer. His or her reputation is built on which books he was able to bring in.

Once you have signed the contract at such a publishing house, another editor may be assigned to work with you on the book. This will be the person who phones you and says, "Welcome aboard. I'm so glad to be in charge of your book, and I think it will be a great success. It sounds very exciting." That's the *manuscript editor*.

Now is the time for you to say how pleased you are to be meeting your editor and how much you are looking forward to working with him or her.

Ask if he or she can send you the company's style book. If he says they do not have their own, say that you plan to follow *The Chicago Manual of Style*.

The editor will probably be delighted to hear this, since that is the most widely used writing style manual. And having said you would, go out and buy it at a bookstore and study it. Your library also has a copy of it. That editor will ask you to change this or that, or add or subtract. And he may take issue with your viewpoint and general tone.

After your manuscript is all done and the manuscript editor is satisfied with it, you may get a series of phone calls, if it is a rush project, from another person—the *copy editor*. Or what is more likely, your manuscript is in the mail to you with many "flags" asking questions and seeking clarifications. It's the copy editor who vets your manuscript, chapter by chapter, for style, grammar, consistency, and factual accuracy—as well as spelling accuracy.

There also are *production editors* who shepherd your manuscript through the book production process, but you are not likely to deal with them. Questions they have will probably be put to you by the manuscript or copy editor.

In practice, one person could do all these things, and often does in a small publishing house. Even in large houses, the acquiring and manuscript editors may be the same person.

So in the smaller house, usually, after your projected book is under contract, you will come in contact with only two editors—the one who works with you and guides you through your manuscript, and the one who copyedits it.

Now that you know who's who, let's talk about the realities of how to work with these experts assigned to you.

GETTING ALONG WITH EDITORS

To get along with your editor, the first rule is to keep in touch with him or her. Tell him or her of your progress with the manuscript, but don't show the editor anything not finished and polished. Editors are notorious for their lack of imagination—they may think your first draft, which you plan to polish and expand, is what they are going to get, and become upset.

To prove this point, here's a little confession I can make about myself as an editor. I had put under contract a biography of a famous tanker tycoon, by a writer of several well-received previous biographies. When a few months had passed, I called him and asked how the manuscript was coming. He said things were going well, and did I want to see a first draft of the first six chapters? "Certainly," I replied.

When he sent the first draft, I was terribly disappointed. This was not the sparkling prose, rich in detail, I had seen in his other books. This was bare-bones stuff, casually typed—and even with many corrections. I finally got up my courage to call him and tell him just that.

"Oscar," he answered, "this is first-draft material. Naturally I'll enrich and polish it later. My first drafts always look like this."

When I was still disturbed, he took the trouble to rewrite and polish the first three chapters, to prove what he meant, and had it perfectly typed. But this interrupted the flow of his work—and caused him to lose a couple of months and deliver his final manuscript later than scheduled. I felt like a fool—but I'll bet another editor would have reacted the same way, so be warned. This is not the only story of this type I know!

You, too, may get better results if you turn in a finished neat, beautifully typed manuscript.

CHANGING FROM THE ORIGINAL OUTLINE

You don't have to be rigid about writing each and every chapter that was in the outline you sent the publisher in getting your contract. Publishers and editors understand that in the writing things happen, something becomes clear. You may find that you need to write several chapters you didn't even mention or that you really don't have enough material for a chapter on a certain phase of the book.

Let's use this book you are now reading as an example. When I sold the publisher, St. Martin's Press, and editor, George Witte, on the book idea, my proposal lumped all the variety of nonfiction books into one chapter. Fran and I ended up doing a separate additional chapter on biography, however, for several reasons. First, because it is one of the most popular forms of nonfiction writing, and, second, because Fran has so much to share on the writing of bios that it would have made a single chapter ridiculously long.

On the other hand, we were going to have a separate chapter on *sample* chapters but found the few pages we had on it could better fit into other chapters dealing with the presentation package sent to the publisher to sell your book idea.

So you see, you can combine chapters or leave something out. However, if you make such changes, you should write down your reasons and have them handy by your phone for the next time you phone your editor or he phones you.

Just say, "I've decided to eliminate Chapter Ten. Shall I tell you why or would you rather have me mail it?" You may find that the editor still thinks the chapter you are eliminating is too important to be combined with something else or dropped entirely. In this case, I recommend that you tell him you will do more research to beef it up and write the chapter and then he can decide if he likes it.

Sometimes an editor does something that you really cannot go along with. This happened to Fran when an editor wanted to turn one of her books into one long chapter—he said this was "the new way." Fran appealed to me, and I told her to hold her ground and say she insisted on dividing the book into parts and chapters, using the chapter titles she and I considered appropriate and also, in many cases, quite clever. Though the editor scoffed at Fran's "old fashionedness," she won.

Now let's follow a manuscript as it arrives at the publishing house.

STEPS IN THE EDITING PROCESS

When the manuscript is finished and sent to your editor, be sure to write him a dated cover letter, and keep a copy so you have a record of your delivery date. If you have a literary agent and there is time, you might instead deliver two copies to your agent—one for him to deliver to the publisher, and one for the agent himself. In that case, to ensure that your editor knows you have finished, you may want to tell the editor you've given it to the agent, especially if the deadline is close. It's good if your agent reads it first—he may find small errors of typing or other mistakes that you can correct, or otherwise help by providing editorial input, especially if the agent is a former editor. He can make you look better at the publishing house.

Eventually your editor will read your manuscript and make notes. He'll watch out for errors, for possible libel and invasion of privacy. And he might want to see documentation that supports some of your claims, reports, and assertions. He might ask you to expand certain sections or cut and condense others.

Once in a while an editor gets so involved in a manuscript that he or she will want to rewrite it. I remember the instance in which an expert on a craft wrote a rather sketchy how-to manuscript. The editor said she wanted a rewrite, and we got in a coauthor who rewrote it. The editor was still not satisfied and rewrote it again, herself.

When she finished, she proudly showed it to the original

author, the craftsman. The craftsman said, "This is fine for style, but it makes me look ridiculous—there are some bad mistakes here about how to do things. It just isn't right. Now *I've* got to rewrite it." The editor, like a proud author, became quite huffy and didn't want her prose touched! As the craftsman's agent, I had to intervene, and at a conference with all of us present, the work was finally edited to everyone's satisfaction.

But such extensive work by an editor is the exception—most editors in today's publishing world don't have time to do much work on your manuscript. Therefore, it's up to you to do your own best work and perfect the manuscript yourself—or you face the danger that it might be rejected because your editor doesn't have the time to help you.

The work load of most present-day editors is enormous. They often have to do their real work—editing and reading manuscripts—at home at night or on weekends, because their days are filled with writing reports, meetings, sales conferences, phone calls, and lunches with agents and new authors they are pursuing.

So don't be surprised if your editor doesn't respond to your manuscript immediately when it is turned in. He or she may have to put it in a long line with other manuscripts. And there may be several readings—by assistants, experts, the legal department, and more than one reading by your editor.

But if there is no word for about a month, don't hesitate to call and say, "How are you coming with my manuscript?" Some authors can't wait a month; they have urgent bills to pay out of the "on-acceptance" advance royalty payment—expenses of research, typing bills, phone bills, and living expenses. But try to wait at least two weeks.

Once your manuscript is accepted (and don't forget to turn in the illustrations, and any permissions required), and you and your editor are happy with the final version, then it will be put into production, and a copy editor will go over it.

For many writers, the copy editor is an enemy, because it is the copy editor's job to nitpick and quibble about fine

214

points of your style, usage, grammar, spelling, consistency, and exactness of statement.

The copy editor will search for and find instances where you spell a word or name one way one place, and another way another place, and will create a "style sheet," with the spellings and usages decided on, either following "house style" of your publishing house, or some style manual, such as *The Chicago Manual of Style*. And the copy editor will seize on your clichés and note the places where you overused a word or phrase.

While reading, the copy editor will also look for factual errors—addresses, names, places, and check your math. But book publishers don't have "fact-checkers" as some magazines do, so don't rely on your publisher to catch your errors. It's *your* responsibility, according to the contract, to turn in a true and correct manuscript, and your name is on it as the author.

Copy editors sometimes revel in the havoc they can cause. This somewhat perverse satisfaction from finding errors in the work of others is illustrated by what a former copy editor for a reference publisher told me. She was copyediting the second volume of a reference series and found an important error in the manuscript. To make matters worse, it referred to the first volume, already in production. She checked the first volume and, sure enough, found *the same error*. When she pointed this out to management, all hell broke loose. The publisher literally had to stop the presses on a large run, destroy the incorrect printing, and start over—a very expensive action.

The copy editor was *proud* of causing all this trouble, even though it cost her employer many thousands of dollars. And I believe she should be proud because an otherwise valuable work would have damaged the reputations of the publisher and the author if she hadn't.

A serious error caught by a reviewer of a major newspaper or magazine can be and often is picked up by other publications all over the country. Errors have led to expensive legal actions and have resulted in books losing money instead of making money.

The important message to you in this story is that you must be grateful there is that copy editor standing between you and trouble with a capital *T.* No, your copy editor is not trying to show you up as an illiterate, ill-educated dunce. He or she is trying to save you—and the publisher—the embarrassment of producing an error-filled or otherwise flawed book.

When your manuscript arrives from the copy editor, it will have "flags" on it—little pieces of paper that ask questions or point out inconsistencies.

Don't destroy these flags—just answer the questions or make corrections and send the manuscript back with a letter of explanation. And if there is no flag—just a correction right on the manuscript—and you think the correction is wrong, write "stet" by it. That means restore the original. Explain in a note why you did this. A polite argument may ensue, but it's for the good of your book—you do want your readers to understand what you mean, as does your publisher.

In spite of what I've said, copy editors are not perfect, and it is finally *your* responsibility to make sure your manuscript is correct. At Prentice-Hall a longtime employee secretly, and with glee, showed me one of their older books, a biography of a baseball player. In it was a recipe for a stew. After the list of ingredients, the recipe began, "Put on two gallons of water and boil for two hours, then . . ." Several people had to be sleeping at the switch for that one to get by!

IMPORTANT GUIDELINES FOR DEALING WITH YOUR EDITOR

Treat editors with respect and insist they do the same with you. No matter how excited you get, don't curse and carry on. Stay cool and logical in explaining why you are sure that your way of solving a problem is best.

Unless there is some overriding reason why you disagree, try to do it the editor's way to a reasonable extent. The editor

has probably dealt with dozens of books and has developed a sense of what will work and what won't, what will sell and what won't.

If you have an agent, get his or her thinking on the disagreement with the editor. The agent is also tuned into what sells and what works. Sometimes the agent can explain to you in a better way why the change would be good. And sometimes the agent can intervene and talk with the editor, helping you plead your case.

Before you get on your high horse, ponder this: The editor has the upper hand because he speaks for the publishing house. If he thinks what you are doing ruins the book, and you are adamant, he can recommend to his superiors—such as the president of the publishing house—that they drop your project. After all, he doesn't want a failure to reflect on him. You may even have to return the advance. I'm not trying to frighten you or turn you into a wimp. In one instance, Frances and a coauthor *did* offer to return the advance, as a strategy to save their manuscript from an editor's rewrite. I'm just trying to show you the business side of being a selling author.

Like it or not, you are very dependent on others in getting your book published and enhancing its chance to succeed after it is published. The editor is the person through whom you communicate to the others who control the success of your book—the salespeople, the rights director, the advertising department, the publicity and promotion directors.

If you plan to write just one book, you can "use up" the goodwill and admiration that a good manuscript engenders. That's what can happen if you try to get results by blowing your stack or constantly voicing complaints. People may stop returning your phone calls.

So it isn't good to get a reputation for being difficult—in the end it will make you poison at the publishing house—and since publishing people move around, possibly at other publishing houses as well.

FIVE DON'TS IN DEALING WITH EDITORS

- *Bad Temper.* Avoid an argumentative style of dealing with those who are working on your manuscript.

- *Failure to Keep Deadlines.* If half a book is due at a certain time, make sure it is there. And if the whole book is due by the end of a certain month, that's what it means. Your contract can be canceled and you may be required to return the advance and any other moneys received. Publishers are used to allowing for a certain amount of lateness—but we are talking weeks, not seasons.

- *Poor-Looking Manuscript.* Using a dull ribbon is an insult to the editor. Editors must do a lot of reading, so they have little patience with manuscripts that can cause eyestrain.

- *Too Many Misspelled Words* is another insult to the editor. You can look the word up just as well as the editor can. If you really can't spell, hire a proofreader or an English teacher or a newspaper reporter.

- *Ignoring the Editor's Suggestions.* Take every suggestion seriously. If you hate the idea of the change that is being suggested to you over the phone or by letter, don't jump to say no. Say you want a little time to think about it. And then do think about it. The editor has a reason for the change he wants. Make a list of reasons why his way might work. Then make a list of reasons why it's a bad idea. Then with the lists in front of you, phone the editor and ask, "Is this a good time for us to talk?" If he wants to call you back, don't insist you must talk now. He'll get back to you. Then calmly point out the good and bad results the suggestion may have on your manuscript. Perhaps

there is something he hadn't realized and he finds himself agreeing with you.

In that case, thank him for seeing it your way.

● *Being a Good Loser.* If he is adamant and you see you had better agree with him, be a gracious loser. Say you will do it his way even though you think perhaps the other is better. Say that you are appreciative of his caring enough about your manuscript to take the time to explain why he wants this change to be made.

So go thou and sin no more.

15

Writing the Whole Manuscript on Speculation—With Notes on Self-Publishing

There's an exception to every rule. And now I'm about to make an exception that should make some of you very happy. It is that maybe you should go ahead and write your book no matter what anyone says.

It's a do-it-yourself message.

Though most nonfiction books are written after they are put under contract, and the theme of this book is that it is easier and more economically sound to sell your first nonfiction book from a presentation, some works so cry out to be written that their authors simply sit down and write them.

If you are such an author, you simply may not *care* what the market is. You *don't* want input from an editor—you want to write it your way, or write it for the joy of it.

Or maybe you did write a presentation and you showed it to agents and editors. Somehow, it just didn't sell at that stage. But you have the gut feeling the whole manuscript will be more convincing—so go ahead anyway. *If necessary, you'll publish it yourself,* even if it means running off a few Xerox copies to show to your friends, family, or professional associ-

220

ates, bound with holes punched through it and a red ribbon holding the pages together.

Or you will invest some money to have it printed up as a standard paperback with or without artwork on the soft cover—perhaps just the title and byline in suitable, interesting lettering that the printer has in stock.

Or you are determined to go all the way—hang the cost!—have it printed as a hardcover book and even hire an artist to paint an exciting scene for the book jacket.

Well, don't laugh. Don't sneer. Don't feel sheepish. Did you know that some best-sellers have started that way—*The Whole Earth Catalogue*, which won a National Book Award, for example. And I'll tell you about some others later in the chapter. But before you spend the first penny, let's try to get a publisher to do it for you so that you don't have to lay out the hard cash to become your own publisher.

SELLING YOUR MANUSCRIPT

All right, you have done it. You have your whole manuscript. Now you need to know how to sell it.

First, let me say that if you are marketing your manuscript yourself, there are a whole lot of publishers out there that *you* can approach, that an agent probably would never go to.

As an agent, I ordinarily deal with about fifty publishers at most—and almost all of my sales are made to a core list of about forty of them. The most extensive submission I ever made—and that was only once—was to sixty publishers, in three rounds of multiple submission of twenty copies each time. For the third round I found I was resubmitting to some of the same publishers, where personnel changes made it possible to try again. (Happily, on the third round, I got two offers.) For me, it is not profitable to keep trying with a single work after a certain number of submissions—I get only a 15 percent commission if I make a sale. But you are going to get 100 percent—and for you more is involved than money: your

221

reputation, your feelings, and most important, getting your message across through your manuscript.

So your target list of potential publishers (see Chapter 8, "How to Target Publishers and Get Their Attention") can become as big as several hundred commercial publishers, including regional ones, and several *thousand* "small presses" that publish only a few titles a year. In fact, there is a list of small publishing houses contained in *The International Directory of Little Magazines and Small Presses*.

Persistence can pay off. One author I know took over when his agent returned his manuscript after twenty submissions. He made a sale on the sixty-fifth submission—and this is by no means a record. For help on your list of publishers' names and addresses, consult the directories listed in the back-of-the-book material—"Suggested Reading and Reference."

SELLING TO COMMERCIAL PUBLISHERS

From time to time I get an anguished call from an editor who says, "We have two holes in our fall list because of projects that fell through. Do you have anything already finished you can tell me about?"

Such "holes in the list" are opportunities for you, who have a finished manuscript—if you can learn about them. Practically the only way you can hope to be the writer who fills such a need is to be in there plugging, keeping your work in front of the editors.

If you receive mildly encouraging turndowns, redo your manuscript. You might consider dropping a note to such editors from time to time. Update them on what is happening with you and your manuscript, ideally with a news peg to hang your letter on. You might say, "Because of the new developments recently announced in fusion reactors, I've updated my manuscript, *The Future of Energy*, and am ready to resubmit to interested publishers. When you read it last year, you said there was much merit in it. And I thought you would like to know that I've received three speaking invitations recently from major associations."

Another approach is to query new editors just after they join a publishing house. They're bound to begin buying books right away—they usually don't have a backlog of books already bought to work on. You can find out about such editor moves in *Publishers Weekly* and sometimes *The New York Times*.

NEW PUBLISHERS

Brand-new publishers are an excellent market for already finished manuscripts. They don't have time to wait for a couple of years while an author finishes his opus—they need manuscripts they can publish right away.

How safe is it to contract with a new publisher? In some cases, not safe at all. But there are advantages to being on the initial list of a well-financed new publisher. Your book will probably receive very strong promotion, as its publication is one of the means by which the new publishing house will try to establish itself in the book trade—show bookstores and famous writers that it advertises, promotes, and offers sound products.

If an important writer is dissatisfied with the treatment he is receiving from his current publisher, he just might give the new publisher his next book.

The key question about new publishers is, "Are they well-financed?" Will they be able to stay the course? What will happen if they end their company?" You can run a Dun & Bradstreet credit rating on the company before signing. Also, bookstore buyers and suppliers might tell you what the scuttlebutt is in the trade. Are good things or bad being said about their finances? In the case of *Subway Gunman* by Mark Lesly and Charles Shuttleworth, which I mentioned earlier in Chapter 8, "How to Target Publishers and Get Their Attention," I had no hesitation in recommending that they contract with the new publisher, British American Publishing Ltd.

I had known the chairman of this company, Bernard F. Conners, for several years, and knew that he was a very successful businessman. As he is also a successful author, he knew a lot about publishing. And he had the help of his friend, George Plimpton, a best-selling author and founder of *Paris Review*. Conners secured distribution from Simon & Schuster, one of the largest publishers. He hired experienced, competent people to help him in the company.

Obviously, every publisher has to get started sometime—Simon & Schuster began with the publication of one best-selling crossword puzzle book. Prentice-Hall started with the publication of one textbook.

I'm proud to say that long ago I met one of the founders of Simon & Schuster—Henry Simon. I recall reading later that he was asked what the greatest benefit was of the success of his company. Without a moment's hesitation he had replied, "Now I can afford to buy all the books I want."

Any new publisher who makes the grade deserves a lot of credit. It's hard for a publisher to pull himself up by his bootstraps, just from the profits of those first successful books. The reason is that he must lay out a lot of money to pay salaries, typesetters, printers, binders, and paper merchants up front—and of course, advance royalties to authors. And then he must wait a long time to be paid by booksellers and book wholesalers who are often slow to pay him, because they have his unsold books in their inventories and need capital, too.

So an excellent editor, like Tom Congdon, who started Congdon & Weed, or Larry Freundlich, who started Freundlich Books—even though he selects best-selling books—may have to close down his company after a few years, and that is a crisis for his authors, as well as for him and his staff.

What happens to the authors, you ask. Well, they may find that their contract now belongs to another company which bought the book list and the "goodwill." Or on some occasions the author can get his rights back and start afresh.

Assuming you are willing to take a chance on having a new publisher publish your manuscript, how do you find out about the publisher's coming debut in time to make a sale?

If you have an agent, he may be able to find out for you, though he may prefer not to deal with new publishers. However, if your agent hasn't been able to place your manuscript with his regular, well-established publisher customers, ask him, "Aren't there any new publishers out there willing to take a chance on it?"

Starting with many cautionary remarks, warnings, and dire stories first, your agent might be willing to go along and try a new outfit for you, after making sure you understand the risk.

But if you don't have an agent, what then? Again, *Publishers Weekly* is one source of information. Newsletters like *BP Reports* sometimes give advance information on new ventures. Or you can simply ask a great many people who are involved in the book world—other authors, publishers' salesmen, book dealers—"the usual suspects," as Claude Rains said in *Casablanca*.

UNIVERSITY PRESSES

You don't have to be a professor to be published by a university press, though it may help. The main point to consider is, "Does my manuscript treat a subject that is closely related to an academic discipline, or make a bridge between two disciplines?" If the answer is yes, and yours is a thorough and sound work on your subject, you might consider querying university presses.

Marlie P. Wasserman, editor in chief of Rutgers University Press, says, "Remember that university presses, like commercial publishers, tend to specialize in particular subjects." She suggests that you learn which university presses specialize in *your* subject by reading scholarly journals in the field—archaeology, entomology, history, electronics, whatever—and particularly, by inspecting the publishers' book ads in such journals. The lead book in the ad usually is one of the type the press specializes in.

To illustrate, Wasserman says, "If yours is a nonfiction cowboys-and-Indians history, then by looking in a journal devoted to American history, you might see that the University of Nebraska Press is publishing a new study of the battle at Little Big Horn, and realize that is a press you should approach."

The editor in chief admits that more than half of the material she considers is in the form of complete manuscripts. She does not think that a work has been rejected by other publishers just because it is a finished manuscript. Also, as she seldom deals with agents, you are at no disadvantage if you don't have one.

As when you are dealing with a commercial publisher, Wasserman wants a query first—don't first send your manuscript. She also says that university press editors are more likely to take your telephone query than are editors at standard publishers—and they will actually talk to you—though sometimes she gets tired of the time taken by telephone queries.

Rutgers University Press, located in New Brunswick, New Jersey, published a book I handled, *The Lindbergh Case* by Jim Fisher, a former FBI agent, detective, and professor of criminal justice. The fact that the kidnapping of the Lindbergh baby occurred in New Jersey enhanced the manuscript's publication chances at Rutgers University Press, since it was part of New Jersey history as well as American criminal and legal history.

Kenneth Arnold, director of Rutgers University Press, told me he liked the Lindbergh manuscript because it was the most complete work on the subject he had seen, incorporating much new material. He was anxious for it to succeed—university presses need good sellers just as other publishers do to help finance their operations.

Their contract, incidentally, was similar to a regular trade publisher's contract, and they paid an advance royalty. They also helped the author publicize the book—using promotion money for ads and setting up various interviews.

There were an extraordinary number of major reviews of *The Lindbergh Case*, as well as TV, radio, and bookstore appearances by author Fisher. When the furor was over, Rutgers had sold many copies and the author did well financially.

SELF-PUBLISHING

It's not too hard to become your own publisher. So say Tom and Marilyn Ross, the authors of a book on self-publishing. How's this for a success story? The Ross team self-published their *Encyclopedia of Self-Publishing*. It then was turned into a commercially published book, *The Complete Guide to Self-Publishing*, after Carol Cartaino, then editor in chief of Writer's Digest Books, made them an offer they couldn't refuse. And there are other good books on the subject.

If you want to publish your own book, you will learn that it will cost you from $3,500 to $5,000 to manufacture—print up or produce—1,000 hardcover books. It will cost $1,500 to $2,000 to produce 1,000 paperbacks—softcover copies of your book. Those figures are for the current economy, subject to change, and also they assume you compose the type yourself with a computer. If you get someone to set type, that's extra.

WHAT IS THE DIFFERENCE BETWEEN VANITY PRESS AND SELF-PUBLISHING?

Self-publishing is not the same as publishing your book through a subsidy publisher or "vanity press," where you pay a certain (usually hefty) sum to a publisher to bring out your book—often to very few sales indeed.

A vanity press contracts with you to publish a certain number of your books—usually 5,000 of them—at a cost of about $35,000 or $40,000 or up. They usually agree to store half the books in their warehouse and send you the additional copies as you need them.

Sometimes they let *you* pay for an ad which they place in newspapers or magazines, and sometimes *they* pay for the ad.

However, if it is their ad, you may find your book is just one of a whole list of books shown in the ad.

They do send books to book reviewers, but reviewers rarely treat their books with enthusiasm. Even so, occasionally a book published by a vanity press does skyrocket.

John Rahn Braue, a good example, went on to commercial success with his *Uncle John's Original Bread Book*. John, an itinerant German-American baker, who simply loved his work, wrote a schmaltzy book about the many ways to make good breads. Many feel it is the best book on bread baking that was ever written.

Though it was published by a subsidy publisher, later Pyramid Books and other paperback publishers reprinted it in full or partial editions.

That's the story of vanity presses. The publisher does everything necessary and does produce the book, but you pay a lump sum, and sales and reviews may be scanty.

In contrast, with a self-publishing program you literally do everything yourself. You edit your manuscript, design your book, set it in type yourself or hire a typesetter, proofread it, have it printed and bound, warehouse it, publicize it. Then you sell it to the public through stores—and perhaps little ads—and ship it yourself to through-the-mail buyers, bookstores, wholesalers, libraries, and organizations. You do your own credit checking and billing, and collect the money for your sales.

Among originally self-published books are not only such classics as *Robert's Rules of Order* and *Bartlett's Familiar Quotations*, but such big best-sellers as *How to Avoid Probate, Looking Out for Number One, What Color Is Your Parachute?*, and *How to Keep Your VW Alive*. Some of these were later taken over by commercial publishers and went on to even larger sales.

But you don't have to have a potential best-seller to self-publish and make a profit. When I was a book editor, a woman sent me her collection of recipes, which she had published as a trade paperback entitled *The Joy of Chicken*. She had sold 20,000 copies, and it was handled by big bookstore chains.

Though it was a sound book, it didn't strike me as exceptional, so I recommended she keep doing it herself; she could make more money that way.

Making a book out of your family's history is an idea that many would-be authors come up with. As readers of Fawn Brodie and a few other historians know, there is early nineteenth-century newspaper evidence that Thomas Jefferson, who did not remarry after his wife died, had a romantic liaison with a beautiful slave girl who was the half sister of his wife. Of that union was said to have come several light-colored children, the first of whom was a redheaded son, as Jefferson was redheaded.

Minnie Woodson is married to the descendant of that redheaded son and collected all the family oral histories to write a fictionalized version of the story. She chose to publish the book herself. She is now considering writing a second, nonfiction straight historical account, based on the family oral history.

Has your business firm or association ever published a book? Martin Weiss approached Collier Associates with his financial book, *The Money Panic*, which his organization had self-published and sold successfully through the mail. Lisa Collier Cool liked it, and helped him place it with Arlington House, where it has sold many more copies.

So even if you self-publish successfully, in some cases you can still find a commercial publisher to take over your book when you need your storeroom back, or your garage cleared to return it to its original purpose—hard to remember what that was, oh, yes—to store your car.

Part V

Helping Your
Book Succeed

16

Publicity: Gravy Train
or Treadmill?

Let me tell you first off, a publicity campaign for a book is a little of both. It's a gravy train because you will get to see the country—usually with all expenses paid by your publisher. But it's a treadmill because you won't be able to stop long enough to *see* the country—and your mind will be fully occupied with doing well on this interview and getting yourself to the next.

When former First Lady Betty Ford was touring the country publicizing her memoir, *Betty, a Glad Awakening*, written with Chris Chase, she never failed to mention how hard she was working for her meal at book luncheons and made it clear she'd much rather be relaxing and paying for her lunch herself.

So will you, I'll bet, before your tour is over, but let me further explain that if it weren't for the publicity tour, your chance of big sales or getting on the best-seller lists would be considerably lessened. If fact, be grateful you were invited by the publisher to go.

Don't assume that just because you are getting your book published, the publisher is going to send you around the country, putting you up in top hotels. Or that you will be on Phil Donahue, Oprah, or Charlie Rose's talk show.

No, no, it's not that easy. The way it works is that the publisher's publicity department drums up interest by first sending around its catalog of new books. The publicity director keeps in touch with major TV shows, important magazines and newspapers, and radio interview shows, and tells them of upcoming books, noting which ones they may be interested in. Then the publisher sends out advance copies of your book—sometimes just in bound proofs, with or without a copy of its jacket or cover, and a press release.

If the interviewers jump on the bandwagon and phone to ask the publicity department to schedule interviews or appearances by you, you may get your exciting trip.

But if nobody picks up the phone, you don't get it. However, your book can still be a good money-maker; or a bestseller. It just may take a little or a lot longer. It's the book about some weird or wonderful theory or person, or the by-line of some public icon or public enemy that gets the attention.

They may tell your publisher, in passing, that the book by Roxanne Pulitzer or George Burns is well written, but that isn't the reason they picked up the phone. That is secondary.

Good writing will make your book live longer and become part of posterity. But a flashy angle, hot information, or flashy fame will make your book earn big bucks quickly in the world of today.

The pressure when you have a hot book is unbelievable.

Massive national-media publicity can be so important to the success of a certain kind of book that Mary Barelli Gallagher, Jackie Kennedy's former secretary, turned down—after conferring with her publisher—an offer to pay her for the documentary film rights to an exclusive thirty-minute interview. And why? Because accepting the offer would put her publicity in the hands of the filmmaker. Instead, she chose to devote several weeks out of her life, for no payment, to a lengthy and strenuous book publicity tour, managed by her publisher, that put her on many national and local TV and radio shows and saw her interviewed by many major newspapers and magazines.

It worked. The immediate publicity campaign shot her book, written with Fran Leighton—*My Life with Jacqueline Kennedy*—onto *The New York Times* best-seller list, where it settled in for a stay. The Jackie Kennedy book is a perfect example of a "hot news, publicity-propelled" best-seller.

But the gravy-train trail of interviews on news and entertainment shows, and newspaper and magazine gossip and news stories are not the only road to success. The author of *My Dog Tulip*, J. R. Ackerley, had been dead twenty years when Ann Patty of Poseidon Press contracted with the hardcover publisher to bring out a new, elegant trade paperback edition of his book, and Martin Asher, then at Quality Paperback Book Club, decided to use it as a selection.

The New York Times Book Review quickly published a long, glowing review, as did other publications—often, as was the case with the *Times*, for the second time. (The hardcover had received good reviews twenty years before.) The new edition succeeded because reviewers loved it and wrote of their admiration in long, memorable, and quotable reviews.

My Dog Tulip also benefited from another kind of publicity: strong praise in cover quotes from famous writers—E. M. Forster, Christopher Isherwood, Irving Kristol, Elizabeth Bowen, and more. They were part of the "cult" following of readers who treasured the unique memoir for the truthful, no-holds-barred way it told everything about the experience of living with Tulip, an Alsatian dog, for her whole life of eighteen years.

Now you've seen two ways a book can succeed—a great publicity drive on TV and personal appearances, or simply great book reviews in newspapers and periodicals that reflect how the book has captured the heart or the mind of the reviewers.

But there is a third way, available to all—success through word-of-mouth recommendations by enthusiastic readers to their friends and associates.

A word-of-mouth-propelled success involves a kind of

contagion—a belief in its virtues passes from person to person. "Hey, you have to get this book," one friend tells another. For this contagion to begin there had to be at least one original person infected with it—often the book's own editor, or sometimes its publicist, a book salesman, a bookseller, or anyone who is a "communicator," that is, a person who talks to a lot of other people and leads them to new things.

Say it is the editor. The editor convinces the publishing staff, including the publicity director and salesmen, that they have something great and must push it. Eventually, in cases of the biggest successes of this type, the contagion becomes an epidemic, spread wherever people meet—at parties, on the street, in buses and airplanes and their terminals, and best of all, in bookstores.

No mere book reviewer, scoffing that it is a "stupid book" or that he fails to see the "charm" of it, can stop the stampede.

Jonathan Livingston Seagull by Richard Bach is a famous example of a giant success based on word-of-mouth recommendations. Its editor, Eleanor Friede, practically bludgeoned her associates at Macmillan into accepting it, because she loved it so herself.

Finally they agreed to a small printing—but with no promotion budget. They didn't initially get the contagion. But Eleanor Friede was undeterred.

She thought of a way she could promote the book herself, on her own time if necessary. She thought it would appeal to aviators—after all, she was a pilot herself.

So she sat down and wrote scores of personal letters to other pilots and told them what a great book it was, how it expressed all her feelings about flying.

Some of those she wrote to bought the book—and loved it as much as she did. They recommended it to their friends, and their friends recommended it, too.

Soon the book's fans were not just aviators. There were eventually more than a million buyers of the book. And this success happened without any of the usual initial pushes given a book by its publisher. All because Eleanor Friede had identified a strong core audience and reached them! And because of them everybody suddenly wanted to feel the thrill of being in the air, wings spread and flying.

Actually, in the success of any big-selling book, word-of-mouth publicity plays a role. And it can play a *negative* role. When publishers promise too much in their promotions, for example. If readers who buy it are disappointed and think they have been taken in by hype, they tell their friends and colleagues *not* to buy it. The book then quickly falls off the best-seller list and later turns up on remainder tables.

Note the kind of words I'm using—national media, hype, news, reviews, blurbs and cover quotes, interviews, word-of-mouth, core audience, communicators. This is the language of publicity, and if you get involved in publicizing your book you'll hear such words again and again.

You'll learn of "press kits." That's a packet of information about your book and you, with photos of you, your book, and maybe a sample illustration. In it will be a press release (written like a book review) and anything else the publicist thinks will attract the attention of reporters or reviewers.

Press kits are used only for books the publisher thinks are major—for the less publicizable books, there may be only a review mailing with just a "review slip" inserted in the book, stating the book's title, author, price, and publication date, with a request for two tear sheets of any reviews published.

To learn more about this world of book publicity, let's fantasize awhile, and consider the life history of a book you write that is *ideal* for publicity, and see all the good (and some bad) things that can happen to it. And afterward we can look at a smaller, more practical, scaled-down version of such a campaign.

PREPUBLICATION PUBLICITY

Your book's publicity can start even before you write it. You yourself—or your hired publicist, or your organization's publicity department—may manage to get you in the public eye, through sending out or telephoning in news stories, or by inviting the press to meet you. Why? Because you are news;

you just discovered a treasure trove of fascinating information—a new set of notebooks by Leonardo da Vinci, with drawings and plans for inventions. Or you have just come back from two years as a hostage. Or you have been the surprise recipient of a major award—say the Nobel prize or a lesser-known scientific award—for your previously little-known but now considered spectacular achievements in space, medicine, whatever.

ON-SIGNING PUBLICITY

Then, when your book is put under contract, you or your publisher announce it—unless there is reason for secrecy—and perhaps a reporter who covers the book scene, like Edwin McDowell of *The New York Times*, or one of the reporters at *Time* or *Newsweek*, writes a story about it, as news. And it should be announced in a newsy way—maybe you got a record advance for a book of its type. Or the publisher won it in an unusual auction, conducted on the slopes of Mount Everest. Don't laugh. That's exactly what happened to Tenzing, the Sherpa guide who pulled Edmund Hillary to the top of that highest mountain.

THE PUBLISHER'S PUBLICITY QUESTIONNAIRE

Behind the scenes, when your publisher sends you your contract, or soon after, he'll also send a "publisher's publicity questionnaire." This will have blanks for you to fill in dozens of facts about yourself. But don't rely on his actually using it much—often it is filed and forgotten. What he'll really use is the author's biography we talked about earlier.

CATALOG COPY AND COVER COPY

After you turn in your book manuscript, and when the publisher schedules its publication, your editor, or a copywriter, will start to write copy for the publisher's catalog, and later for your book's jacket or cover. If there is any way on earth you can get to see this copy, you should—to correct errors in it.

Don't complain about its length—that is decided before you get to see it, and it is written to fit the space available. The publisher's catalog blurb about *your* book is traditionally a short one unless it is the publisher's lead book of the season. There is only a brief mention of many books.

The same is true about the written material on the book jacket. There is only so much room on the jacket, no more. So just make sure the copy is correct, your name is spelled right, the title you agreed on is used, and that other facts are exact and to the point. Fran has caught several misspellings of her name on the jacket in time, but once failed to catch a misspelling of a word in the title.

QUOTES ABOUT YOUR BOOK FOR THE JACKET AND ADS

At some point your publisher (or you, yourself) may send out copies of your manuscript, or bound proofs of it, to famous writers, celebrities, experts and authorities, and political figures, asking them to read it and make short comments suitable for quotation on the book jacket or cover, and in advertisements.

Usually you have to send many of these out, as the people you send them to may be busy with writing their own books, or have a policy of no comment (because they receive so many such requests), or just plain be slow to answer.

Or they might not like your book or its attitude toward their friend, and ignore the request or write you a polite refusal. It is usually a race to see if you can get some good quotes in time for them to be used on the jacket—a race you often will lose. But if you get them, they do help. If only to impress reviewers and make them more likely to review the book. Having many such quotes on a jacket is a sort of signal to reviewers that the book may be an important one.

FIRST SERIAL USE OF YOUR MANUSCRIPT

This amounts to getting publicity and being paid for it. Your agent or publisher may be able to sell one or more installments or excerpts from your prepublished manuscript to a magazine or newspaper syndicate. The amount of your story used is usually only a small part of the whole manuscript. If your agent made the sale, you will get most of the money. If the publisher controls first serial rights, you will usually share this, split according to the contract. In either case the publication gives you and your publisher credit and publicity by saying the article or articles will shortly be part of a new book.

THE PUBLICATION SPLASH

When your book's publication date arrives, you may be confused—the book has already been in the stores for a week or two or even a month. Why is "publication date" as long as six weeks after the book has been actually printed, bound, and shipped?

There are two dates involved here—"in stock" date, which is when the book is in the publisher's warehouse, and "pub date," which is the "official date" on which, theoretically, reviewers now have the go-ahead to write about it and the booksellers to sell it.

In practice, booksellers usually put the book on their shelves whenever they receive it and get around to unpacking it. Reviewers sometimes take the fact that the book is now available in bookstores as a de facto publication date, and review it when they please, particularly if the book is a hot news item—as was David Stockman's book after he left the Reagan administration and blasted "Reaganomics," of which he had been a major architect. Reviewers treated the Stockman book, *The Triumph of Politics*, as the top news of the day, ignoring the future release date.

The reason the two dates are different is to allow time for the bookstores that are far away from the publisher's warehouse to receive their shipments. It allows all reviewers a reasonable amount of time to receive and read the book, and to publish their reviews at the same time—or shortly after—the "pub date."

PUBLICATION PARTIES AND HOOPLA

On publication date there may be a publication party or other event, such as a news conference. It can be a news breakfast or luncheon, usually buffet style. Publication date parties are less fashionable than they used to be—often the only result of a press party is that a lot of lower-level newspeople attend, and drink a lot, and never get around to writing about the author. For a truly news-packed book, a news conference with only coffee and pastries served can be appropriate, and it often does result in many news stories, sometimes appearing all over the world.

By way of contrast, at another news conference I held for the author of a biography, only one reporter came. The author and I were miffed, but by good fortune, the reporter was delighted. He did a long, thoughtful interview, and a fine, newspacked story appeared in his publication. Parts of it were then picked up by other publications so it worked out all right anyway.

The publisher's publicity person will sometimes plant items about the book—amusing little anecdotes or bits of news from it, with favored columnists.

Another approach is simply to have the author appear for an interview on a major news program, such as *Today* or *Good Morning, America*, or the CBS morning show. Ideally, at the same time, an AP or other news service story will run and be picked up by papers all over the country, and some of the larger papers—*The New York Times*, *The Washington Post*, *Los Angeles Times*, *Chicago Tribune*, will have their own "exclusive" interviews, which they too will syndicate to other newspapers.

ATTACKS ON YOUR BOOK

At this stage you might begin to get a new kind of publicity you don't much like: attacks on your book, charging you stole material, that something in it is false or mistaken, that you have violated confidences you should have kept private—Larry Speakes, the White House press secretary, revealing that he made up quotes in the name of President Reagan, for example—or that you are commercially exploiting a sacred institution, or whatever. You should be well prepared for such attacks, and ready to strike back by having your argument ready—"The public has the right to know"—or pulling out documentation that proves your book is absolutely correct and that you may have even soft-pedaled the truth a bit.

For example, when the book mentioned earlier, *My Thirty Years Backstairs at the White House*, by retired White House maid, Lillian Rogers Parks, as told to Frances Spatz Leighton, was published, a front-page story appeared in *The New York Times*, reporting that Jacqueline Kennedy, wife of the then new President John F. Kennedy, was requiring White House employees to a sign a pledge not to write such memoirs—and Lillian's book was the reason.

"Little Lillian," as her friends called her, was able to counter Mrs. Kennedy's implied criticism of her book. She pointed out that it was the wife of another, and even more famous, president who had first suggested to her mother, also a White House maid—and then to her—that she write the book and record what she knew of White House history. That woman was Eleanor Roosevelt.

When the story came out about who had inspired the book, Mrs. Roosevelt kindly allowed herself to be photographed accepting an autographed copy of Lillian's book. The former First Lady said to Lillian in a loud, clear voice in her inimitable upper-class New York accent—for the benefit of the reporters present—"Lillian, I'm so glad you finally wrote your book." The picture and quote appeared widely even on newspaper front pages. Thus did Eleanor, one of the truly great First Ladies of American history, the protector and patron of minorities and the humble, gently offer the new First Lady a lesson in democracy. Later another distinguished former First Lady, Bess Truman, invited Lilian to visit her and her husband, Harry, in their home in Independence, Mis-

242

souri. The flak from the Kennedy White House suddenly quieted.

Sometimes the hassle comes from the news media. I recall author Stephen Shadegg in his book, *What Happened to Goldwater?*, referred to a news bureau's dispatch, which he labeled as "totally false" and said the bureau had later issued a retraction.

The news bureau's attorney called the publisher, Holt, and threatened to sue if the book was not withdrawn. Shadegg was able to produce an original copy of the teletype dispatch in question, which he had saved, and the news bureau withdrew its threat.

Such criticism and attacks go with the territory. If you get a lot of attention from the press, there will be people who envy you, or call it unsuitable. If you survive such an attack, you may find that the additional publicity helped rather than hurt you, simply by giving you additional attention.

NEGATIVE REVIEWS

Some of the reviews will attack your book—perhaps your chief rival expert has been assigned to do the review, and he points out how you are all wrong, and his theory is the correct one.

If his review has obvious mistakes and misstatements, you might want to reply, in a letter to the editor, as Fran once did. But if his sarcastic criticism is based on his taste, tough turkey. He doesn't challenge your facts—he just says you are a bad writer, a lousy writer, a naive writer, an amateurish writer, and cites a couple of awkward constructions of your sentences. So don't complain. Just ignore him.

It was your right to write the book. It's his right to state his opinion, and the publication's right to hire him to do it.

I must say, before we leave the subject, that book bashing is a popular sport among certain book reviewers. The purpose seems to be to keep the reader amused at the expense of the author. It matters not whose book it is. Sometimes the reviewer gets more of a kick the bigger the name of the author.

Fortunately readers buy books in spite of reviewers, and that is the message for you. Many a bashed book has landed on the best-seller list none the worse for it—and the author, as Liberace used to say, can "cry all the way to the bank."

PUBLICITY TOURS

Now that your book is launched, your publisher may decide to send you on a national publicity tour for one, two, three weeks, or even a month or more. Be prepared for many strenuous days—sometimes starting at five in the morning and continuing past midnight—the interviews, TV and radio appearances, visits to bookstores to autograph your book, looks-in at major book wholesalers, and speeches for book and author luncheons.

HITTING THE BEST-SELLER LISTS

But finally your effort pays off—your book hits the best-seller lists. It has taken weeks—after all, you're a new face, and it takes time and many repetitions of your name and your book's title to reach enough people. It sold well from the start, but the sales were spotty. A "best-seller" is not a book that, *over the long run*, sells an enormous number of copies. It is a book that is *selling fast*, in many bookstores across the nation, all during the same week. That is why you need repeated national publicity, concentrated in a short time period, so that many people will buy your book *at the same time*. If a book is selling like hotcakes in Chicago, it will get on the local Chicago list—but not the national lists unless it is doing the same thing all over the country. This is true even if its sales per week in Chicago are larger than those of another book that is on the national best-seller list. It's hard for some authors to realize this fact.

BOOK ADVERTISING

Now, suddenly, your publisher begins to advertise your book. You wondered why he had held back, doing no advertising except for a small "announcement" ad here and there. If you asked, he explained he was using his ad budget in "co-op" ads with bookstores, to make sure the book actually was bought and displayed in major bookstores.

You never happened to see such ads—which were scattered over the nation. Also, he said, "We don't have anything to say in the ads." Now he has something to say: "National Best-seller!" And the reviews are finally coming in—and some of them are quotable.

Most publishers believe that ads should be used to pour fuel on an already burning fire—not to start the fire originally. Most authors disagree. If readers don't know about the book, how can they buy it? Even tiny ads would help. But then, authors rarely run publishing houses.

PUBLICITY FOR REPRINTS

Eventually, exhausted and tired of talking about the book, you quit touring. But wait! The paperback reprint of your book is coming out next month, because finally, after an eleven-month run, your book has fallen off the hardcover best-seller list.

The usual publisher's contract says that the paperback can come out one year after the hardcover publication date, unless the hardcover is still on the best-seller list. Then the paperback publisher must wait. For the paperback, you have to do it all over again! Run the publicity marathon. And maybe in England, and other countries, too.

Possibly the paperback publisher will record a video of you speaking and send it to bookstores to display or to small stations to put on the air. He might even buy TV and radio ads—for his is truly a "mass-market" approach. Now he's pursuing really huge sales and has put many books in thousands, rather than hundreds, of locations.

ARTICLES ON YOUR SUBJECT

If you can find the time, you might, while all this is going on, write a few articles related to your subject, and sell them to magazines and newspapers, to keep your name and book before the public.

When the controversy was raging over Mary Gallagher's tell-all book about her old boss, Jackie Kennedy, Fran Leighton was asked by a Sunday supplement to write the inside story of how the book had come about and how she and Mary had worked in secret. The story went out to a readership of 20 million people.

A SMALLER CAMPAIGN

Now back to reality. Maybe you think that kind of treadmill or rat race is impossible for you—your book could never command so much attention. And you don't have time to leave your job for all that. Or you're too shy for it.

So do it on a smaller scale. Select the parts that fit your life, your work, your subject.

Some people with family obligations tell the publisher, "I can be away only three days of the week," and the publicity office will work around your schedule. Or you can say, "I will do whatever you want for two weeks, but then my vacation's over and I must get back to my office." And they will honor that, flying you here and there to make the most of the two weeks.

Afterward they may schedule radio interviews that you can do from your home telephone. Some interviewers tell the listeners it is a telephone interview and some do not.

Or, if you are a busy professional for example, you may do everything without leaving your home town. Let's see what can happen.

A chapter of your book may be published in a professional journal. You get a write-up in the house organ or the trade paper of your business.

You autograph books in your local bookstores. You persuade the stationery store in your neighborhood to stock your book. Your local newspaper runs a story on you. You speak before the Chamber of Commerce, or a local author's group, or to a women's club.

Your friends, who are also experts in your field, endorse your book. Six publications run reviews, small publications, but they go right to the audience you are reaching for. A telephone call-in radio program has you as a guest to answer questions about your specialty. You appear on local TV news accepting an award.

Your library features your book in the rack of "Local Authors." There are countless small opportunities for publicity, as well as a few giant ones.

Both ways sell books—the national and the local approach—and help you find your audience of readers who will warm to your message. And maybe that small core of satisfied readers will spread the word—and through their contagious enthusiasm, break your book out of its local fame, into a regional and then national arena.

DOING YOUR OWN PUBLICITY

If your publisher isn't doing much, because of expected modest sales, and has spent the tiny promotion budget on sending out review copies and listings in trade publication ads, you might either hire a publicist—there are lists of them in publishing directories—or start trying to do it yourself.

I know it is possible for a beginner to get a lot of publicity because when I first had the job of being a book publicist myself, I knew almost nothing about that kind of work.

What happened was that suddenly I was drafted to move from sales to publicity by the publisher. Through study and trial and error, I was able to get authors on major and minor TV and radio programs, and arrange interviews with newspapers and magazines.

If *I* could do it, you can, too. I'll give you a hint of my method—maybe it will work for you, too. I first made a list of every program and every even remotely likely publication I could find out about, from lists in directories and from publicity services.

Then I called the programs and publications, described the book and its author, and if they were interested, followed up by sending a copy of the book, with a press release and author bio and photo enclosed, marked "For the Personal Attention of . . ."

A few days later I called them again, asked if they had received the book, and if they wanted to interview the author or invite him to appear. A good many said yes. That's all there was to it! It really was a case of "ask and ye shall receive."

PROMOTION TIPS

Here are three small points about publicity that are very important:

About Stage Fright. Most people don't get stage fright if they are talking to just one person. So if you are comfortable in one-on-one meetings, but get stage fright in front of TV cameras or a large audience, probably you should confine your publicity to interviews by individual newspaper and magazine reporters, or taped radio interviews—unless you panic at sight of any microphone. In that case, especially if you foresee your future in writing, you really should consider taking a course in public speaking, joining a speakers' club, and even, perhaps, consulting a psychologist to get you over the hump.

2. *Mention Your Book.* Don't count on others to do it for you. Some talk show hosts may never mention it.

During interviews always talk about the subject of your book and mention your book's title several times—don't give in to the temptation to pontificate on some other matter or ride some hobbyhorse.

3. *Beware of the Photo You Use.* Get a good, professionally shot author photo that says something about you. If you like, you can have some symbol of your craft or the subject of the book in the picture as long as it does not steal the

limelight from your face—a typewriter, a word processor, a model plane, a mixing bowl.

The point is, don't use a formal shot or a snapshot of you—if you are a man—in some loud-patterned shirt standing in front of a busy background. Or, if you are a woman, in some childish-looking outfit or a fabric design so busy that the viewer can't find your face.

Your author-photo should help readers—when they spot your book in a bookstore—recognize that they saw you on TV or lecturing.

Curiously, not all photographs resemble their subjects—it takes a special art to show you as you ordinarily appear. That's why a professional may take dozens of shots of you, in the hope that at least one will *actually catch some vital and typical pose* true to your normal expression.

Unless you are the author of a book on beauty, an entertainer, or an exercise instructor, don't worry about being beautiful or handsome or cute. Even if you are a comedian, you want to project *authority* and *credibility*—to be someone the reader will trust and respect—not a clown, nor a formal figurehead, nor airbrushed beauty queen.

So now your book is published and you've done what you can to publicize it. It's a couple or more years later. The original hardcover or trade paperback has stopped selling, and your publisher has either failed to reprint it when all his copies sold, or remaindered it as a slow seller and not worth expensive warehouse space. The mass-market reprint is nowhere to be found. How do you keep your book alive? Read on.

17

Keeping Your Book Alive

Will your book live on and on?

In the libraries, yes. On bookstore shelves, only maybe yes, probably no. Let's be realistic and see what we can do to keep a book alive or give it mouth-to-mouth resuscitation if it lies there, for years, almost dead.

Yes, let's see what happens to books.

Initially you rely on your publisher to keep your nonfiction book alive—to publish it and put it in bookstores, sell it to libraries, offer it to book clubs, and fill mail orders. When he has sold all he can of the original edition, you hope he will bring it out in a cheaper edition, or license it for reprint in a trade quality paperback or mass-market, rack-size paperback version.

You want it continuously listed in *Books in Print*, so that anyone can find out how to get a copy. Sometimes the publisher does so for the life of the copyright of the book, or even longer.

How-to books like *The Joy of Cooking*, by Irma S. Rombauer, or *Etiquette*, by Emily Post, have survived in revised

and updated editions more than fifty years. And, for that matter, another how-to book, *The Prince*, by Niccolò Machiavelli, published in 1513, is still selling, almost five hundred years later.

Self-help books like the previously mentioned *How to Win Friends and Influence People*, as well as *The Power of Positive Thinking*, though published many years ago, are still in print offering their enduring messages. Biographical works like Benjamin Franklin's autobiography and Anne Frank's diary continue to be available and read.

I hope your book endures as well as these.

But with most of the 40,000 or more nonfiction books published each year, there comes a time when the original publisher loses interest. Sales have fallen to a dozen or so a month, or even lower.

Since it costs the publisher money to keep the book in a warehouse, list it in *Books in Print*, and fill orders in quantities of ones and twos, rather than tens and twenties, his business manager may think the company can't afford to keep it in print any longer.

If they have a large supply, he may want to "remainder" it—that is, sell all or most of the remaining copies to a remainder dealer for a dollar or so a copy, to be offered on "bargain books" tables at a low price in bookstores that sell cut-price books.

Or if it is a mass market paperback, he may sell it by the pound to be ground up as pulp for new, recycled paper. The publisher's contract lets him do this.

However, if you had thought ahead, in the case of a hardcover or trade paperback, your contract would provide that the publisher has to offer the books to you, and maybe the plates or films from which it was printed, at manufacturing cost, or even at the price a remainder dealer would pay. Usually the contract would provide, if it covers this eventuality, that you must act quickly or lose the right to buy.

Should you buy the remaining copies? Unless you can think of some way to sell them, probably you would only want to buy twenty or thirty. But if you give lectures or seminars and can offer your books for sale to your listeners, you might be able to sell them to your students.

Or you just might have an entrepreneurial talent and be able to think of ways to sell your books that the publisher hasn't tried. And if you have bought the plates or film, you can print more if your sales method succeeds.

Some authors have sold more than a thousand copies of their book—and others have been unable to sell a single one. I don't think there is any disgrace in seeing your book on the remainder table—it's part of the book business, and with it you will see hardcover copies of major best-sellers that are now available in cheap paperback editions.

Even if *you* are the author of the best-seller, you have to realize that though your book sold 200,000 in hardcover, there was no way your publisher could tell when it would stop selling.

Like a good soldier, he just kept on printing them and putting them out in bookstores—but sales finally stopped, a little before he thought they would. Now he has 4,500 copies more than he needs. He remaindered 3,500, and kept 1,000 for the continuing trickle of hardcover sales.

Or your publisher may have sold all the copies he printed—and decided, because sales were slow and he has few reorders, not to print any more. When you ask him about it, he says, "There is no demand."

If your contract is properly drawn, it has a clause that allows *you* to demand, in writing, that the publisher reprint. And if he doesn't within six months (or some other time period), the contract ends, except for foreign rights sales he has made, and you get your book rights back.

Should you make such a formal demand? Here are the arguments for and against it. Probably you should end your contract only if you think you or your agent can do something with the rights you have regained—make a movie sale, find another publisher, write a revised edition, or reprint it yourself.

It's safer to take back your rights if you have an agent—

because if anyone wants to find you and you have moved, he calls the publisher, the publisher will look up your contract, and tell the searcher your agent's name and address—or forward letters to your agent.

END OF CONTRACT

If you end the contract and *don't* have an agent, be sure to keep telling your publisher your changes of address. Send this information to the contract department as well as to your editor or the editor in chief, in case someone wants to get permission (for which you can charge a fee) to quote from your book, or make it into a TV movie, or whatever. And if you do have an agent, be sure to tell your agent your new address—even if you never write another book.

I have had, several times, to refuse to sell permissions to quote from old, out-of-print books I handled, because the author failed to give me his or her new address, and because my agreement with authors does not let me make sales without their explicit permission.

Also, even if I had such permission, I would not want to collect money for such an author and simply have to hold it, maybe forever.

When one author approached me to handle his second book, I asked him if he previously had an agent for his first, fairly successful coauthored book. He said he did, but did not want to use that agent again, because he regarded her as his coauthor's, rather than his own agent.

I recommended that before he engage me, he write his first agent a letter, politely telling her than he was ending the relationship and was planning to engage another agent, namely me. He did write such a letter, but didn't put his return address on it.

The agent called me and asked for his address. "We have been holding several hundred dollars in royalties for him for three years, because he didn't give us his new address," she reported, "and mail to him was returned."

If you don't have an agent and don't have any plans to try

253

to resell or reuse your book rights, probably it is just as well to leave the contract with your publisher alone. Sometimes a publisher makes a paperback sale, years later, and the publisher can handle permissions to quote, or perhaps be able even to republish the book because it has finally established a paperback publishing division.

If you get some marvelous new publicity or new fame, suddenly your words are again in demand. That happened with Ronald Reagan. A memoir he had written before he was even Governor of California suddenly came back to life and was reprinted when he became President.

You're better off with an agent because in some very large companies, with enormous back lists, the publisher can forget that he has your rights and queer a permission request and your joint fee by being slow to reply. Because there is a large backlog of requests being handled by a small rights and permissions staff, the deal that is small gets attention last. In fairness, I just add that most rights and permissions departments are usually competent.

But don't count on it! In one case where I requested a reversion of rights more than ten years after a book went out of print, the publisher's legal department called me and asked for a copy of the contract—they couldn't find one or any record they had published the book.

RECYCLING OR POSSIBLY REPUBLISHING YOUR BOOK

Okay, you have decided to get back the rights to your book and have done so. What should you do with it? Here are ten ideas.

1. *A Revised Edition.* Look at your book carefully. Is it out of print because it is out-of-date? If you revised and updated it, would it be useful again and worth republishing? You might make a plan for such revision and updating, send it around to appropriate other publishers, and make a sale. I'm currently offering such a plan for a new edition, revised and

updated, of an old book by authors I represent, and hope to get the book in the stores again.

2. *A New Kind of Edition.* Could your book be reprinted in a new kind of edition? Maybe the paperback rights were never sold—and you can find a new publisher.

Lewis Paper did just that with his biography, *Brandeis*, the life of an important Supreme Court Associate Justice. When Prentice-Hall let it go out of print, he reclaimed the rights and sold it to Citadel for a trade paperback edition.

If it is an illustrated book and you have the plates, you might be able to get a "bargain book" reprinter to republish it in a cheap hardcover edition. Occasionally, even a book club, like Paperback Book Club, will republish a book in a trade paperback edition so it can use it as a selection.

3. *An Edition for a Special Market.* Do you know of some special market that is perhaps too small for a regular publisher—but that you can fill with your own small printing? Rear Adm. F. Julian Becton, U.S.N. (ret.) wrote, with co-author Joseph Morschauser, a fine book about his experiences in World War II as captain of the *Laffey*, a brand-new destroyer. *The Ship that Would Not Die* tells the story of the *Laffey* and her heroic crew—how many of them survived and won a tremendous battle during the biggest and most sustained kamikaze attack of Japanese suicide planes ever mounted against any ship, while the *Laffey* was on picket duty in the sea off Japan.

After Prentice-Hall published his book, and Military Book Club used it as a selection, it finally went out of print, and he regained the rights and bought the plates of the book.

Admiral Becton felt that because the restored *Laffey* had finally found a peaceful and safe harbor as a ship permanently anchored in Patriot's Point Park, near Charleston, South Carolina, the thousands of visitors who came aboard her every year would like to buy a paperback edition of his book about her adventures.

Since I really liked and admired him—how many genuine American heroes does one meet in a lifetime?—I was glad to help Admiral Becton publish his own small edition of a paperback reprint of *The Ship that Would Not Die*.

I gave him names of printers and book manufacturers, and he republished the book himself, with permission of his coauthor. He sells it at Patriot's Point Park and elsewhere through Pictorial History Publishing Company, 713 South Third Street, West, Missoula, MT 59801, which gets a 10 percent commission for each $7.95 paperback sold.

The admiral told me when I called him that the first printing of 2,000 copies was almost exhausted. When I asked him if he was glad he republished the book, he said, "Certainly. And I'm looking forward to selling the second printing of two thousand more."

You can find a list of book manufacturers who do short runs in *Literary Market Place*, if you want to try the same thing.

4. *Editions in Other Countries.* If you can't keep your book alive in the United States maybe it should emigrate to another country where there is a better market. *Bread*, by Joan Wiener and Diana Collier, even though an award-winner when published in this country by Lippincott, is out of print in America, and Lippincott no longer publishes trade books. But it is alive and well in England with Robert Hale, its enduring British publisher, still selling. You may be able to sell your book in other countries, either through your agent or by submitting it directly to foreign publishers.

5. *Try Another Medium.* Even if your book is out of print in a never-ending contract, or scarcely available, it can live on in another medium. For example, *My Thirty Years Backstairs at the White House* was transformed into the miniseries, shown twice on NBC, *Backstairs at the White House*.

The miniseries version was then republished in hardcover and mass market editions—and the Bantam mass market edition became a best-seller all over again.

Stephen Shadegg's acclaimed biography, *Clare Boothe Luce*, was published in 1965 by Simon & Schuster, and achieved good sales and wide publicity. But Shadegg, in order to secure many hours of interviews with its subject—playwright, magazine editor, congresswoman, ambassador, and celebrity Clare Boothe Luce—had agreed not to sell the dramatic rights without her permission during her lifetime. Though producers often asked about it, as its agent I could never offer it, as she denied permission to do so.

Now that she has died, even as I write this, the West Coast co-agent who often handles dramatic rights for my agency, Harry Bloom of Harry Bloom Agency, has placed it under option with a producer for a TV film.

Such a film will not only give the book a new life in another medium, but might result in my getting a paperback publisher to bring it back into print.

Or you may be able to sell an audio or video version of your book—or it might remain available in electronic storage and transmission form, particularly if it has reference value.

Many books that are otherwise out of print can live on in microfilm form. For example, University Microfilms International of Ann Arbor, Michigan, has more than 100,000 out-of-print books available—and it can print out a photocopy, or several photocopies, of your book if it is part of their collection, for a fee—and share the fee with you.

6. *Breaking Out a Pamphlet.* Even though your whole book might be too expensive to meet a market for its information, or all those willing to pay full price have bought it already, there might still be a market for a section of it, published in pamphlet form. For example, Bantam Books published a Mini Book version of *The Illustrated Hassle-Free Make Your Own Clothes Book*, by Sharon Rosenberg and Joan Wiener that was only a few pages, and small enough to put in your purse.

7. *Textbook Use.* When bookstores and libraries stop ordering your book, it still might be worth keeping it in print with a scholarly or academic publisher, so it can be used as a textbook for college classes, or as "recommended supplementary reading." Some publishers specialize in this kind of book and may be worth contacting.

8. *Quotations and Excerpts.* As the agent of old as well as new books, I often get requests to grant permission to use in

new books long or short excerpts from books I represent, but that are out of print. For example, *Blue Collar Journal*, by John Coleman, described in Chapter 1, "Write a Nonfiction Book and Gain Satisfaction, Authority, and Cash," is now out of print—but lives on in many quotations in textbooks and in collections of extracts used by college and high school classes. I charge a fee, on the author's behalf, of course, for the right to quote from it.

9. *Large-Print Editions.* Though the regular edition is out of print, large-print publishers, who publish books for the sight-impaired, may still want to offer it to their readers. Several books I represent are now, long after their initial publication, available only in large-print editions.

10. *A Recognition-at-Last Edition.* The success of another book, related to your subject but published later, can bring recognition to your neglected but pioneer book. Agent Peter Fleming sold *The Food Sensitive Diet Book*, by Doug A. Kaufman and Raquel Skolnik to Larry Freundlich Books.

Even though authors and publishers thought this first work about a scientific breakthrough in cytotoxic nutrition would set the bookstores on fire, the sales were disappointing and the book was soon out of the stores. Then, the following year, Stuart Berger, M.D., wrote a book on the same subject, using much of the same basic research and statistics, and his book became a super best-seller—*Dr. Berger's Immune Power Diet.* Dr. Berger was thoughtful enough to agree to write an Introduction for a new edition of *The Food Sensitive Diet Book* and provide a cover quote: "This is the book that will tell you how to eat for your health."

Peter Fleming made a new sale of the book to Paperjacks, a mass market paperback publisher, which republished it in 1986—and when I spoke to him in the fall of 1988, it was still selling, he told me, "two or three hundred copies a month."

So there you have it—you have thought of a nonfiction book idea, presented it, sold it, written it, seen it published to publicity and acclaim, and managed to keep it alive!

18

Can This Be You Entering the World of the Writer?

Yes, it can. It's you, all right, stepping into what may become a whole new way of life.

Lots of writers lead the good life. Believe it. Fran says, "Though I moan and groan and bitch about how I suffer getting up with the chickens to start my writing stint every day, don't cry for me." And she gloats, "I still have better than banker's hours. I have my afternoons free. And when the manuscript is done, between books it's holiday and reward-yourself time.

"I guess my conscience starts to hurt because of all that lovely leisure, so I start thinking of the next book and again throw myself back into the dungeon every morning until *that* new book is done.

"And again I'm moaning and groaning and bitching."

"So why do I write?" Fran asks, and then answers her own question. "I admit it. Writing can be a bad habit—addictive. Once you are into it each day, you get high on power and the joy of self-expression. You're the captain conquering the stormy seas. You're the pilot—flying high."

How absorbing can writing be? It can make you more

absentminded than the most absentminded professor. Richard Goodwin, who traded away a life of speech writing for presidents, admitted that when he was writing a memoir of the 1960s, *Remembering America,* he once passed his own driveway five times because he was so absorbed in "writing sentences in my head."

That's how absorbing it can be.

If it's hobnobbing with people that you want, the writer's life is made for you.

As soon as you are a known writer, your social life will blossom. Writers are invited to numerous parties—and why? Because they are well informed, used to expressing themselves, and are generally interesting people. Also people are curious about writers, anxious to take a look at them, and proud to be in their company.

And another thing it can do is let you travel tax-free wherever the trail of your book research leads—to Hollywood, to the birthplaces of presidents and famous writers or inventors. It can lead you to the homes of the living rich and famous and powerful. It can take you from the Great Wall of China to archaeological digs in a Mexican desert.

I have known authors who previously had mundane jobs and were unhappy because they were scarcely noticed by their colleagues. But with a single published book, not only could they climb into a different lifestyle, but they suddenly found their voices and became quite vocal about their pet projects. And what is more, suddenly people gathered around and listened. The listeners savored the bright glow of authorship celebrity.

Yes, writers do rate and are a "must have" on many hostesses' lists. Peggy Wedon and John Kidner wrote a book about the food of Washington embassies, and now are frequent guests at embassy teas and luncheons.

A couple, Harvey and Marilyn Diamond, wrote a different kind of food book, and it, too, made them very much in demand—and changed their whole lifestyle. He was overweight. She was in poor health. In solving their own problems they learned enough to fill a book on learning how to shop for additive-free foods, how to cook, how to program exercise. The name of the book? *Fit for Life*.

Now the Diamonds enjoy speaking as a team at food conferences such as The International Natural Living Conference, an annual event at Lebanon Valley College, Annville, Pennsylvania. Naturally, at food conferences, the sale of their book is brisk. The book probably will be around for a long time.

Authors can become writers in residence at colleges and universities. By spending only as little as one day a week talking to students, the author gets a free residence and a small or not-so-small stipend—and is left with plenty of time to write.

Writers also become honored after-dinner speakers. Bryson Rash, a popular Washington based NBC-TV commentator, had for years made a hobby of collecting offbeat stories and myths about the nation's capital. When he retired, he put them all into a book—*Footnote Washington*—and is now enjoying new popularity as an after-dinner speaker. As he put it, "I'm having a ball."

And let's face it, the writing of books can spell M.O.N.E.Y. Your earning capacity may explode. But maybe it won't. Maybe you'll just earn a living turning out books—do you know how many people would give almost anything to work in a field that they enjoy? And don't forget, a field that could at any time and with any luck toss them into the ranks of those rich and famous folk we were talking about.

You are going through the looking glass into the magical world of the writer. Strange things will happen to you. I can almost guarantee it. Just the other day Fran called to tell me what had happened to her at a party she had attended at the home of church historian writer Mary Quigley.

A young, attractive woman came up to her and said, "You made me miss my plane!" and she wasn't smiling.

"What?" said Fran, sure the woman must mean someone else.

"You made me miss my plane and I had to call my friends

who were going to meet me at the other end. It was a mess."

"What did I do?" asked Fran, deciding she'd better placate this disturbed woman.

Still not smiling, the woman said, "I was reading your Nancy Reagan book at National Airport, and I got so involved I really thought I was in the White House."

Relieved, Fran laughed and grabbed the woman's arm. "Thank you, thank you," she said. "You've made my day. Tell me who you are."

"Well, I'm glad somebody's happy," the woman muttered as she walked away. "You sure didn't make mine." She turned back. "Oh, I live next door. I'm Lisa Mustakas. I read."

On the phone Fran told me, "As far as I'm concerned, that was the biggest compliment I ever had. That's the whole goal of writing—to transport someone into another world. And I did it, Oscar, how about that!"

"Congratulations," I said. "And it only took you thirty books to know it."

Let me tell you, new author, *that* is going to be *your* biggest thrill, too. *You will transport people into another world.* For a moment, for hours at a time.

But before that, I have to remind you, comes the work. The sitting down at the typewriter or keyboard day after day at the same time. Day after day. Even when you are not in the mood. And when nobody knows what you are doing or has said anything nice about your writing or encouraged you to keep going. So how do you do it? How do you get those sentences flowing day after day?

You do it by repeating and reminding yourself of those three mega-words we started the book with, the one in the title of the first chapter—Satisfaction, Authority, and Cash. So you have come full circle. I have taken you back to the beginning—that's the ending I chose from the list under "The Satisfying Ending." It's the one that just felt right to me.

And now, *adios,* until I meet you on the pages of your first book.

Checklist

What Makes a Good Nonfiction Book

Try to get as many of these elements into your first non-fiction book as possible, and it will assure that you will go on to write many other books as well.

1. *A New Angle.* Some new way of looking at something. A new approach or development.

2. *A Great Title.* Sometimes simplest is best. Sometimes a big long title is funnier. *If Life Is a Bowl of Cherries, What Am I Doing in the Pits?*—also good because of the pun. Sometimes a nickname—*Fishbait.* Sometimes a poetic allusion—*A Distant Mirror, the Calamitous 14th Century.*

3. *Organization.* It's divided into parts with labels. Or even though it's not divided, except by chapters, you can see that it's going somewhere.

4. *A Provocative Lead.* For some reason, when you

read that opening paragraph, you want to know more.

5. *Good Anecdotes.* The reader doesn't want to listen to your opinions endlessly. He wants a lively story, a little yarn.

6. *Lots of Quotes.* Don't say he talked about it. Tell what he said.

7. *Experts Speaking.* Even if *you* are the expert, the reader wants to know what *other* experts say. Give the other side of the argument, too. Nobody likes a know-it-all.

8. *Famous Names.* They add spice. Don't just drag them in. There has to be a story or reason they are mentioned. The more names the better, short of sounding like a name-dropper—and nobody likes those, either.

9. *The Unexpected Word.* Don't be afraid to use the vernacular and sprinkle in an unusual word here and there. Stuffy language leads to sleepy readers, so veer off occasionally to the less-traveled path.

10. *Appeal to the Senses.* Eye, ear . . . Why do you think poetry survives? It makes you hear things, feel things. It makes you see things—just by the choice of words. Once in a while use the elements of poetry to trigger emotion.

11. *Some Humor* if possible. Lots of humor if possible. Even gravediggers have their jokes.

12. *A Thought to Be Carried Away.* You leave the book inspired or charged up to do battle. Or just ready to build your own boat—or your own body to better health—because of your new know-how.

Acknowledgments

Oscar Collier and Frances Spatz Leighton would like to thank the following authors, editors, publishers, agents, and researcher who were kind enough to offer information, criticism, or material for this book: Adm. F. Julian Becton, Joan Bordow, Frank Brady, Maxine Brady, Harry Browne, Clyde Burleson, Suzy Burleson, Carol Cartaino, John R. Coleman, Lisa Collier Cool, Thomas DeTitta, Alan S. Donnahoe, Peter Fleming, Mary Barelli Gallagher, Shirley Gould, A. E. Hotchner Ken Hoyt, John Kidner, William Hoffman, Patricia Penton Leimbach, Steven Linakis, Milton Lomask, Charlotte Mayerson, Pamela McCorduck, Winzola McLendon, Thomas Miller, Lillan Rogers Parks, Nineta Rozen, Doris Schiff, Katherine Schowalter, James F. Seligmann, Charles Schuttleworth, Robert Stewart, George Sullivan, Helen Thomas, Marlie P. Wasserman, Peggy Wedon, Roy Winnick; and the book's editor, George Witte, for his patience, encouragement, criticism, and support.

Suggested Reading and Reference

HOW-TO, THEORY, EDITORS, AGENTS

The Autobiography, Giambattista Vice, Cornell University Press

A Beginner's Guide to Getting Published, Kirk Polking, Writer's Digest Books

The Biographer's Craft, Milton Lomask, Harper & Row

A Book of One's Own: People and Their Diaries, Ticknor & Fields

Books from Writers to Readers, Howard Greenfield, Crown

Comedy Writing Secrets, Melvin Helitzer, Writer's Digest Books

The Complete Handbook for Free-lance Writers, An Easy-to-Use Business Guide for Today's Writer, Kay Cassill, Writer's Digest Books

The Craft of Interviewing, John Brady, Writer's Digest Books

Effective Writing for Engineers, Managers and Scientists, H. J. Tichy, John Wiley & Sons

Getting the Words Right: How to Revise, Edit and Rewrite, Theodore A. Rees Cheney, Writer's Digest Books

Good Writing, Alan H. Vrooman, Atheneum

How to Be Your Own Literary Agent, The Business of Getting Your Book Published, Richard Curtis, Houghton Mifflin

How to Get Started in Writing, Peggy Teeters, Writer's Digest Books

How to Get Your Book Published, An Insider's Guide, Writer's Digest Books

How to Look It Up Online, Alfred Glossbrenner, St. Martin's Press

How to Write & Sell (Your Sense of) Humor, Gene Perret, Writer's Digest Books

How to Write the Story of Your Life, Frank P. Thomas, Writer's Digest Books

How to Write What You Sell, Jane Adams, G. P. Putnam's Sons

Into Print, A Practical Guide to Writing, Illustrating and Publishing (Includes self-publishing), Mary Hill and Wendell Cochran, William Kaufman, Inc.

Life Histories and Psychobiography: Explorations in Theory and Method, William McKinley Runyan, Oxford University Press

Literary Agents: How to Get & Work with the Right One for You, Michael Larsen, Writer's Digest Books

The Nature of Biography, John A. Garraty, Knopf and Random House

New Directions in Biography (Collection of essays), University Press of Hawaii (Published for the Biographical Research Center)

Nonfiction for Children: How to Write It, How to Sell It, Ellen E. M. Robert, Writer's Digest Books

On Writing, Editing and Publishing, Jacques Barzun, The University of Chicago Press

Pinckert's Practical Grammar, Robert C. Pinckert, Writer's Digest Books

267

Travel Writer's Handbook, Louise Zobel, Writer's Digest Books

The World's Great Letters—from Alexander the Great to Beethoven, Lincoln Schuster, Simon and Schuster

Words' Worth: A Handbook on Writing and Selling Nonfiction, Terri Brooks, St. Martin's Press

Writer's Guide to Research, Lois Horowitz, Writer's Digest Books

Writing Nonfiction that Sells, Samm Sinclair Baker, Writer's Digest Books

Writing and Selling a Nonfiction Book, Max Gunther, The Writer, Inc.

Writing and Selling Non-Fiction, Hayes B. Jacobs, Writer's Digest Books

Writing to Sell, Scott Meredith, Harper & Row

Authors' Previous Book

You might want to read our other book on writing: *How to Write and Sell Your First Novel*, Oscar Collier with Frances Spatz Leighton, Writer's Digest Books

STYLE GUIDES

A Manual of Style, University of Chicago Press

Dictionary of Modern English Usage, Henry W. Fowler, Edited by Ernest Gowers, Oxford University Press

The Elements of Style, William Strunk and E. B. White, Macmillan

It Was a Dark and Stormy Night: The Best (?) From the Bulwer-Lytton Contest, Compiled by Scott Rice, Penguin (a diverting how-not-to book on style)

The Standard Handbook of Style, Samuel Sillen, Grosset & Dunlap

Words into Type, Marjorie E. Skillin and Robert M. Gay, Prentice-Hall

REFERENCE

Dictionary of American Slang, Harold Wentworth and Stuart B. Flexner, T. Y. Crowell

Dictionary of Euphemisms and Other Doubletalk, Hugh
   Rawson, Crown
Dictionary of Slang and Unconventional English, Eric Partridge, Macmillan
*New American Roget's College Thesaurus in Dictionary
   Form,* New American Library
Oxford English Dictionary, 13 vols., 3 suppls., Oxford University Press
Roget's International Thesaurus, T. Y. Crowell
Webster's Third International Dictionary, Unabridged: The
   Great Library of the English Language, Merriam-Webster

DIRECTORIES

The Basic Guide to Research Sources, edited by Robert
   O'Brien and Joanne Soderman, New American Library
Contact Book, Celebrity Service, Inc., Biennial
*Directory: Historical Societies and Agencies in the United
   States and Canada,* Compiled and edited by Tracey Linton Craig, American Association for State and Local
   History
The Editor and Publisher International Yearbook, Editor and
   Publisher, published annually
Finding Facts Fast, Alden Todd, Ten Speed Press
Guide to American Directories, edited by Bernard Klein, B.
   Klein Publications
Guide to Reference Books, edited by Eugene P. Sheehy,
   American Library Association
How to Reach Anyone Who's Anyone, Michael Levine, Price,
   Stern, Sloan
*International Directory of Little Magazines and Small
   Presses,* Dustbooks, Annual
Literary Agents of North America Marketplace, Author
   Aid/Research International, Annual
Literary Market Place: The Directory of American Book Publishing, R. R. Bowker, Annual
Manhattan Consumer Yellow Pages, New York Telephone,

Annual (see listing, "Literary Agents," "Publishers," etc.)

Social Directory (of various cities, sometimes called Blue Book or Green Book)

Writer's Handbook, The Writer, Inc., Publisher, Annual

Writer's Market, Writer's Digest Books, Annual

CONTRACTS AND THE LAW

The Business of Being a Writer, Stephen Goldin and Kathleen Sky, Harper & Row

How to Understand and Negotiate a Book Contract or Magazine Agreement, Richard Balkin, Writer's Digest Books

Law & The Writer, edited by Polking & Meranus, Writer's Digest Books (reissued as *Writer's Friendly Legal Guide*)

The Rights of Authors and Artists, Kenneth P. Norwich and Jerry Chasen, Bantam Books

Writer's Legal Guide, Ted Crawford, E. P. Dutton

SELF-PUBLISHING AND VANITY PRESS

Complete Guide to Self-Publishing, Tom and Marilyn Ross, Writer's Digest Books

Consumer Alert—The Vanity Press, Federal Trade Commission, Press Release, dated January 14, 1970, write FTC Bureau of Consumer Protection, Washington, D.C. 20580

How to Get Happily Published, Judith Appelbaum and Nancy Evans, Harper & Row

The Publish-It-Yourself Handbook: Literary Tradition and How-To, edited by Bill Henderson, Harper & Row

How to Publish, Promote and Sell Your Book, Adams Press, 30 West Washington Street, Chicago, IL 60602

How to Publish Your Own Book, L. W. Mueller, Harlo Press, 1672 Hamilton, Detroit, MI 48203

Bookmaking: The Illustrated Guide to Design, Production, Editing, edited by Marshall Lee, R. R. Bowker

MAGAZINES

Publishers Weekly, 1180 Avenue of the Americas, New York 10036. Weekly

The Writer, 8 Arlington Street, Boston, MA 02116. Monthly

Writer's Digest, 1507 Dana Avenue, Cincinnati, OH 45207. Monthly

Index

Ackerley, J.R., 235
Advances, 6–7, 15–16, 35, 79, 97–
    109; and book contracts, 121, 122–
    23, 125–26, 133; negotiation of,
    122–23, 126; returning of, 217, 218.
    See also Royalties
Amundsen, Roald, 26
Animal House (film), 183–84
Asher, Martin, 235
Aslett, Don, 92
Auctions, 79, 100
Audiences, 45–52, 74–75, 78, 88,
    115
Author biographies, 74, 76, 77–79,
    80, 118; assembling of, 81–94; for
    the final book, 132; and photos of
    the author, 91
Authority, 4, 13–14, 16, 160–63, 249,
    262
Autobiographies, 23, 39, 54–66, 84,
    167–72; advances for, 97; research
    for, 155
Autobiography of Benjamin Franklin
    (Franklin), 170–71, 251

Bach, Richard, 236
Backstairs at the White House
    (miniseries), 36, 121, 256
Ballantine Books, 9, 32
Bantam, 16, 115, 257
Barnes & Noble, 19
Bartlett's Familiar Quotations, 162
Becton, F. Julian, 255–56
Belushi, John, 184
Bennett, Betty T., 173
Berger, Stuart, 258
Bernard Geis Associates, 6–7
Best-sellers, 5, 16–17, 23, 103, 130,
    252; defined, 244; My Life with
    Jacqueline Kennedy, 65, 141, 234–
    35; and negative reviews, 244;
    originally self-published, 221, 228;
    and publicity tours, 233, 234, 244;
    puzzle books, 224; The Closing of
    the American Mind, 21, 25
Betty, a Glad Awakening (Ford), 233
Biden, Joseph, 197
Biographies, 22, 23, 49–50, 51, 166–
    85; author. See Author biographies;

authorized, 177–78; editing of, 211–12; illustrations for, 153–54; interviewing for, 137, 146–47; legal problems with, 54; parts of, 179–85; unauthorized, 175–77
Bison Books, 86
Bloom, Allen, 21, 25
Bloom, Harry, 257
Blue Collar Journal (Coleman), 12–13, 258
Bombeck, Erma, 27
Book clubs, 98, 127, 235, 255,
Book contracts. *See* Contracts, book
Book doctors, 106, 189–90, 202–3
Book proposals, 5, 6, 19–30, 116, 212; and rejections, 111–12; and target audiences, 45–46; writing of, 53–80
Booksellers, 19, 47, 51, 108, 257; New Age, 28; and publication dates, 240; as sources of information, 113; and word-of-mouth recommendations, 236. *See also* specific booksellers
Books in Print, 48, 113, 250, 251
Book world, 16
Bordow, Joan Weiner, 8–9, 10, 32, 256, 257
Bowen, Elizabeth, 235
Brady, Maxine, 27
Branch, Taylor, 24
Brandeis (Paper), 255
Braue, John Rahn, 228
Bread (Collier and Weiner), 256
Brewin, Bob, 24
Brief History of Time, A (Hawking), 25
British American Publishing Ltd., 119, 223
Brod, Ruth, 54
Brodie, Fawn, 229
Brown, Helen Gurley, 17
Browne, Harry, 17
Bryan, William Jennings, 155
Bryant, Traphes, 184
Buchwald, Art, 27
Burleson, Clyde, 151
Burns, George, 234
Business of Being a Writer (Goldin and Sky), 109

Cady, Howard, 208–9
Carnegie, Dale, 23
Cartaino, Carol, 85, 92, 227
Catalog copy, 238–39
Catcher in the Rye (Salinger), 159
Catton, Bruce, 23
Cavin, Bram, 161
Charles Scribner's Sons, 209
Chase, Chris, 233
Chase, Edward T., 209
Cherokee Publishers, 107
Chicago Manual of Style, 210, 215
Chicago Tribune, 241
Clare Boothe Luce (Shadegg), 256–57
Closing of the American Mind (Bloom), 21, 25
Coauthors, 31–42, 104–5, 106, 146–47, 213; and letters of agreement, 37, 40–42, 105, 147
Coleman, John R., 11–13, 32, 258
Collier, Diana, 256
Collier Associates, 229
Commissions, 105, 108–9
Complete Guide to Self-Publishing (Ross and Ross), 227
Computer research, 139–40, 151–53
Confidential Secretary—Ann Whitman's Twenty Years with Eisenhower and Rockefeller (Donovan), 183
Congdon, Tom, 224
Congdon & Weed, 224
Conners, Bernard F., 224
Conscience of a Conservative (Goldwater), 16–17
Contract Bridge Complete (Kaplan), 27
Contracts, with agents, 108–9
Contracts, book, 53–54, 85, 120–33, 210; and advances, 121, 122–23, 125–26, 133; cancellation of, 218, 253–54; and illustrations, 153–54; legal dimension of, 100–101, 122–24, 131, 133; main elements of, 125–32; and serial rights, 100; termination of, 131; university press, 206. *See also* Rights

273

Cool, Lisa Collier, 229
Copyediting, 132, 210, 211, 214–19
Copyrights, 125, 131, 159, 197–98.
  See also Permissions
Crown, 90
Curtis, Richard, 121

Daily News, 90
David: Report on a Rockefeller
  (Hoffman), 191
Davis, Nancy, 181, 191
Deadlines, 7, 41, 106, 123, 129–30;
  failure to keep, 218; fear of, 186,
  187, 188–89; meeting, record of,
  213
Dell Books, 7
DeTitta, Thomas, 107
Diamond, Harvey, 260–61
Diamond, Marilyn, 260–61
Diaries, 169–70, 251
Dog Days at the White House
  (Leighton), 184
Donahue, Phil, 234
Donnahoe, Alan S., 84–85
Donovan, Robert J., 183
Doubleday, 19, 24, 90, 209
Doubler, Lavinia, 49
Dramatic rights. *See* Rights
Dr. Berger's Immune Power Diet
  (Berger), 258
Drunk Before Noon (Hoyt and
  Leighton), 24
Dr. Wildlife (Foster), 32
Dulles, Allen, 156
Dulles, Eleanor Lansing, 156
Dulles, John Foster, 156

Edison, Thomas, 172
Editors, 4, 46, 77, 87–89, 210; and
  agent referrals, 102; and contracts,
  53–54, 85. *See also* Contracts,
  book; copy, 132, 210, 211, 214–19;
  dealing with, recommendations for,
  207–19; manuscript, 210, 211; new,
  availability of, 223; production, 210;
  and rejections, 111–12; self-
  marketing nonfiction books, 110,
  114–19; and word-of-mouth
  recommendations, 236–37

Eisenhower, Dwight D., 16, 22,
  183
Elder, Joseph, 109
Ellen Levine Literary Agency, 103
Encyclopedia of Self-Publishing (Ross
  and Ross), 227
Etiquette (Post), 250–51
*Everything You Always Wanted to
  Know About Sex but Were Afraid to
  Ask* (Reuben), 16
Excerpts, 5, 13, 100, 257–58
Expenses, 41–42, 105, 107, 109, 121
Experts, 4, 35–36, 38, 49, 213–14,
  264; interviews with, 137, 138–39,
  140, 164; qualifications of,
  description of, 84–85

Farm Journal, 83–84
Fatal Vision (McGinniss), 148–49
Fiction, 4, 85, 86, 187
First-time authors, 5–6, 32
*Fishbait—the Memoirs of the
  Congressional Doorkeeper* (Miller),
  54–66, 141, 171, 179
Fisher, Jim, 226–27
Fit for Life (Diamond and Diamond),
  261
Fitting, Melvin, 114
Fleming, Peter, 258
Food Sensitive Diet Book (Kaufman
  and Skolnik), 258
Footnote Washington (Rash), 261
Ford, Betty, 233
Ford, Henry, 167
Foreign, editions, 5, 9, 14, 16, 115,
  256; rights, 40, 100, 101, 252; sales,
  and commissions, 105, 108–9. *See
  also* Rights
Forster, E.M., 235
Foster, Rory, 32
Frank, Anne, 251
Franklin, Benjamin, 170–71, 251
Franklin Watts, 32
Freedman, Marcia, 49
Freedom of Information Act (FOIA),
  157
Freud, Sigmund, 172
Freundlich, Larry, 224, 258
Freundlich Books, 224, 258

274

Friede, Eleanor, 236
Frost, Robert, 40, 177–78

Gable, Clark, 75
Gallagher, Mary, 65, 141, 171, 234–35, 246
Ghostwriters, 34, 36–37
Gladstone, Arthur, 86–87
Gleason, Jackie, 154
Glossbrenner, Alfred, 153
Goetz, Bernhard, 117–18
Goldin, Stephen, 109
Goldman, Albert, 183
Goldwater, Barry, 16–17, 243
Gonzales, Pancho, 18
Goodwin, Richard, 260
Grann, Phyllis, 209
Grove Press, 130
Gunther, Max, 144

Hamilton, Ian, 158–59
Harry Bloom Agency, 257
Hawking, Stephen M., 25
Hays, Wayne, 167
Heldman, Gladys, 18
Hemingway, Ernest, 169 70, 189
His Way: The Unauthorized
    Biography of Frank Sinatra
    (Kelley), 54, 171
Hoffman, William, 191
Holt, Rinehardt and Winston, 9, 130,
    178, 209, 243
Hotchner, A.E., 169–70
How to Be Your Own Literary Agent
    (Curtis), 121
How-to books, 18–19, 22–23, 40, 66–
    74, 127; editing of, 213–14;
    research for, 164; survival of, 250;
    writing of, 188. See also specific
    books
How to Look It Up Online
    (Glossbrenner), 153
How to Win Friends and Influence
    People (Carnegie), 23, 251
How to Write and Sell Your First
    Novel (Collier and Leighton), 85,
    187
How You Can Profit from a Monetary
    Crisis (Browne), 17

How You Can Profit from the Coming
    Devaluation (Browne), 17
Hoyt, Ken, 24, 155
Hudson, Rock, 148
Hughes, Howard, 151
Hull, Raymond, 28

Iacocca, Lee, 115
Ice House Gang (Sterling), 25
Illustrated Hassle-Free Make Your
    Own Clothes Book (Rosenberg and
    Wiener), 257
Illustrations, 49, 74, 79, 90, 221;
    agreements regarding, in book
    contracts, 153–54; cost of, 126;
    submission of, 91, 214
Independent Literary Agents
    Association, (ILAA), 103
In Search of J. D. Salinger
    (Hamilton), 159
Interviewing, 34, 137–39, 164, 256–
    57
Isherwood, Christopher, 235

Jackson, Michael, 168
Jefferson, Thomas, 229
Jenkins, Barbara, 86
Jenkins, Peter, 86
John Paul II, (pope), 168
John Wiley & Sons, 87
Jonathan Livingston Seagull (Bach),
    236
Joseph P. Kennedy, A Life and Times
    (Koskoff), 161
Joy of Cooking (Rombauer), 250–51
Jozak Company, 12–13

Kaplan, Edgar, 27, 131
Kaufman, Doug A., 258
Kelley, Kitty, 54, 166, 171
Kennedy, Jacqueline, 6–7, 9–10, 171,
    184; My Life with Jacqueline
    Kennedy, 65, 141, 234–35, 246; My
    Thirty Years Backstairs at the
    White House, 242–43
Kennedy, John, F., 130, 167, 184,
    242
Kennedy, Joseph P., 161
Kidner, John, 260

Kirk, John, 86
Kirkus Reviews, 119
Kleindienst, Richard, 84
Koskoff, David E., 161
Kristol, Irving, 235

Lane, Lisa, 89
Lane, Mark, 130
Lardner, Ring, Jr., 16
Lash, Joseph, 170
Legal advice, 15, 36, 40, 98; and book
  contracts, 100–01, 122–24, 131,
  133. *See also* Legal problems
Legal problems, 40, 54, 76, 100–101,
  142; libel, 157–58, 213; and serious
  errors, 215–16. *See also* Legal
  advice
Leimbach, Patricia P., 83–84
Lennon, John, 183
Lesly, Mark, 117–19, 223
Letters, collections of, 173–74
Letters of agreement, 37, 40–42, 105,
  147
Letters of recommendation, 93
Libel, 157–58, 213
Library Journal, 113
Liebling, A. J., 144
Linakis, Steven, 98
Lincoln, Abraham, 168
Lindberg Case (Fisher), 226–27
Lippincott, 12–13, 256
Literary agents, 4, 79, 92, 97–111;
  and agreements among coauthors,
  41; and book proposals, 5, 54; and
  campaigns to get books published,
  110–11; and commissions, 105,
  108–9; contracts with, 108–9;
  delivery of transcripts to, 213; and
  the editing process, 212–13, 214,
  217; finding a, 12, 15, 98–99,
  101–3; protection provided by, 34,
  124; and rights, 252–53;
  submissions made by, numbers of,
  221; tastes of, 208; trust in, 99,
  103–5; use of nonfiction book
  categories, 19
Literary Agents of North America, 20,
  103
Literary Guild, 65

Literary Market Place, 20, 103, 113,
  114, 153, 203, 256
Little, Brown, 209
Little, Josephine, 49
*Living in Sin: A Bishop Rethinks
  Sexuality* (Spong), 29
Loren, Sophia, 83
Love, Medicine & Miracles (Siegel),
  26
Luce, Clare Boothe, 256–57

McCorduck, Pamela, 13–14, 32
MacDonald, Jeffrey, 148–49
McDowell, Edwin, 238
McGinniss, Joe, 148–49
McGraw-Hill, 88, 118, 209
Machiavelli, Niccolò, 251
Machines Who Think (McCorduck),
  13
McKay, David, 209
McLendon, Winzola, 145
Macmillan, 49, 118, 163, 175, 209,
  236
Magazines, 78, 82, 88, 89, 90;
  excerpts, 5, 13, 100; writers, 13, 39.
  See also specific magazines
Mailer, Norman, 75
Marilyn (Mailer), 75
May, Elaine, 202
Mayerson, Charlotte, 87–88
Melville Herman, 17
Memoirs, 84, 167–72, 254, 260;
  *Fishbait—the Memoirs of the
  Congressional Doorkeeper*, 54–66,
  141, 171. 179. *See also*
  Autobiographies
Memoirs of an Attorney General
  (Kleindienst), 84
Miller, Arthur, 75
Miller, Tom, 88
Miller, William ("Fishbait"), 54–66,
  141, 171, 179
Miniseries, (television), 5, 36, 121,
  256
Mitchell, Burroughs, 209
Mitchell, Martha, 145
Money Panic (Weiss), 229
Monopoly Book (Brady), 27
Monroe, Marilyn, 75, 197

276

Morrow, 209
Morschauser, Joseph, 255
Mustakas, Lisa, 262
My Dog Tulip (Ackerley), 235
My Life with Jacqueline Kennedy
  (Gallagher), 65, 141, 234–35
My Thirty Years Backstairs at the
  White House (Parks), 36, 121, 242,
  256

National Geographic, 152
New American Library, 93, 209
Newspapers, 5, 13, 22–23, 100, 102.
  See also specific newspapers
Newsweek, 13, 238
New Yorker, 144
New York *Post*, 118
New York Times, 12, 16, 177, 178,
  238, 241–42; *Almanac*, 162; *Book*
  Review, 113, 235; editor moves
  reported in, 223; *Index*, 139, 162
Nonfiction books, 9–10, 18–30; art,
  architecture, communication and
  criticism, 25, 51; autobiographies,
  See Autobiographies; biographies.
  See Biographies; business, money
  and finance, 17, 28; contemporary
  scene, reportage, 24, 31; games and
  puzzles, 26–27, 89, 114, 131, 224;
  health, medicine, fitness, nutrition,
  9, 10, 26, 31, 91, 258, 260–61;
  history, 23–24, 102, 156–57, 225–
  26, 256; hobbies, collectibles, 29–
  30, 51; how-to. *See* How-to books;
  humor, 27; introductions for, 87;
  nature, 25; occult and paranormal
  ("New Age"), 27–28; reference, 29,
  47, 103, 162–63; science and
  technical, 13, 24–25, 39, 127, 225;
  self-help, 22–23, 251; sex and
  relationships, 17, 29, 164; social
  science, issues, social history, 25;
  sports, 18, 20, 25, 34, 49–50;
  travel, exploration, and geography,
  26, 31
Novels, 4, 85, 86, 187

Onassis, Aristotle, 6–7, 9–10, 171
O'Neill, Thomas P. ("Tip"), 97

Options, 121, 132
Oral histories, 156–57
Oswald, Lee Harvey, 130

Painter's Handbook (Sandreuter),
  22
Papa Hemingway, (Hotchner), 170
Paper, Lewis, 255
Paperbacks, 5, 9, 16, 47, 124;
  Ballantine, 32; Citadel, 255;
  earnings from, 40, 98, 126;
  originally published by vanity
  presses, 228
Paris Review, 224
Parks, Lillian Rogers, 36, 161, 242,
  256
Parting the Waters (Branch), 24
Patty, Ann, 235
Pepys, Samuel, 169
Permissions, 214, 254, 257–58. *See*
  also Copyrights
Peter, Laurence, J., 28
Peter Principle (Peter), 28
Picasso, Pablo, 182–83
Picasso: Creator and Destroyer
  (Strassinopoulos), 182–83
Pickens, T. Boone, 97
Plagiarism, 157–58
Plimpton, George, 224
Polo, Marco, 26
Poseidon Press, 235
Post, Emily, 250–51
Prentice–Hall, 114, 209, 216, 224,
  255
Presley, Elvis, 148, 166
Prince (Machiavelli), 251
Privacy, invasion of, 157–58, 213
Publication dates, 129, 240–41
Publishers Weekly, 113, 119, 223
Pulitzer, Roxanne, 234
Putman's, 209
Pyramid Books, 228

Queries, 114–19, 223; letters, 114–16;
  telephone, 116–19, 226
Questionnaires, 165, 238
Quigley, Mary, 261
Quotations, 158–59, 182, 196–98,
  257–58, 264; cover, 235, 237, 239

Radio, 13, 46, 82, 90–91, 234, 244–45
Random House, 87, 159
Rash, Bryson, 261
Ray, Elizabeth, 17, 167
Reader's Digest, 32, 162
Reader's Guide to Periodicals, 139,
159–60
Reagan, Nancy, 97, 166, 175–77,
181–82, 191, 262
Reagan, Ronald, 176, 181–82, 191,
240, 242; memoir by, 254
Rejection, 106, 110–12, 189–90
Remembering America (Goodwin),
260
Research, 9–10, 33, 79, 85, 149–65; of
the competition, 48–50, 73, 78;
computer, 139–40, 151–53;
enjoyment of, 34; financing of, 14–
16; importance of, 36; for
interviews, 139–40; photo, 153–54;
responsibility for, among
collaborators, 37–38
Reuben, David, 16
Reviews, 13, 16, 50, 77, 78, 102; of
books from vanity presses, 228; and
diligence in research, 150; and
errors, 215–16; of My Dog
Ackerley, 235; negative, 243–44; vs.
the power of word-of-mouth
recommendations, 236; and
publication dates, 240–41; as
sources of information about
publishers, 113; of Subway
Gunman, 119; of The Lindbergh
Case, 226–27; in The New York
Times, 113, 177, 178
Rights, 5, 16, 108–9, 234, 257;
agreements regarding, in book
contracts, 121, 125, 127–29;
foreign, 40, 100, 101, 252. See also
Foreign editions; reclaiming of,
252, 253, 254, 255; serial, 100, 239–
40
Rinzler, Alan, 9
Robert Frost: The Later Years, 1938–
1963 (Winnick), 178
Rockefeller, John, D., 154–55
Rodale Press, 22
Rogers, Lillian, 121

Rombauer, Irma S., 250–51
Roosevelt, Eleanor, 161, 170, 242
Roosevelt, Franklin D., 30, 161, 170
Rose, Charlie, 234
Rosenberg, Sharon, 257
Ross, Marilyn, 227
Ross, Tom, 227
Royalties, 6–7, 16, 40, 98; agreements
regarding, in book contracts, 126–
27, 133; and foreign sales, 101;
handling of, by agents, 104, 109,
111; new publishers and, 224; "on-
acceptance," 214; from paperback
sales, 40, 98, 126; statements, 129
R. R. Bowker Company, 20
Rutgers University Press, 225–27

St. Martin's Press, 87, 138, 212
Salinger, J. D., 158–59
Sample chapters, 65, 74–76, 79–80,
85–88, 106, 116
Samuelson, Paul A., 11
Sandreuter, Gregg, 22
Schowalter, Katherine, 87
Schultz, George P., 11
Science Digest, 13
Scientific American, 138–39
Scott, Robert Falcon, 26
Search for the Real Nancy Reagan
(Leighton), 175–77, 181–82, 191,
262
Secret Life of John Chapman (film),
13
Segal, David, 208
Self-marketing, 107–8, 110–19, 121.
See also Publicity
Self-publishing, 220–29
Seligmann, James, 15, 102
Sex and the Single Woman (Brown),
17
Shadegg, Stephen, 243, 256–57
Shaw, Sydney, 24
Shelley, Mary Wollstonecraft, 173–74
Shelley, Percy, 173
Ship that Would Not Die (Becton and
Morschauser), 255–56
Shuttleworth, Charles, 117–19, 223
Siegel, Bernie S., 26
Simon, Henry, 224

Simon & Schuster, 21, 74, 77, 119, 209, 224
Sinatra, Frank, 54, 171
Skimin, Robert, 98
Skolnik, Raquel, 258
Sky, Kathleen, 109
Smullyan, Raymond, A., 114
Sparks, Fred, 6–7, 9–10, 32, 186–87, 193
Speakes, Larry, 242
Spong, John S., 29
Sports, books, 18, 20, 25, 34, 49–50
Stasssinopoulos, Arianna, 182–83
Sterling, Chandler, 25
Stewart, Robert, 175, 209
Stillness at Appomatox (Catton), 24
Stockman, David, 240
Stranger in My Bed (Slater), 147
Subject Guide to Books in Print, 48, 113
Subway Gunman (Lesly and Shuttleworth), 119, 223
Sullivan, George, 66–74
Swan, Robert, 26

Taylor, Elizabeth, 47, 97, 166
Tchelichew, Pavel, 187
Television, 25, 46, 78; miniseries, 5, 36, 121, 256; rights, 40, 101; viewers, 51. *See also* Television appearances
Television appearances, 13, 16, 83, 90–92, 118; and publicity tours, 234–35, 244, 245; talk shows, 234, 241
Tennis (Gonzales), 18
Textbooks, 5, 12, 34, 127, 257
Thompson, Lawrence, 177–78
Thurber, James, 27
Time, 13, 238
Titles, 77, 78, 263
Treasury of White House Cooking, A, (Leighton), 22–23
Triumph of Politics (Stockman), 240
Truman, Bess, 242
Truman, Harry, 183
Trump, Donald, 47, 166
Tyler, Parker, 187

Uncle John's Original Bread Book (Braue), 228
University Microfilms International, 257
University of Nebraska Press, 226
University presses, 225–27

Vanity presses, 227–29
Victory Through Vegetables (Wiener), 9, 10
Videotext, 152
Vietnam on Trial, Westmoreland vs. CBS (Brewin and Shaw), 24
View, 187

Wallace, Thomas, 178
Warren Commission, 130
Washington Fringe Benefit (Ray), 17
Washington Post, 162, 241
Wasserman, Marlie, 225–26
Wedon, Peggy, 260
Weiss, Martin, 229
What Happened to Goldwater? (Shadegg), 243
W. H. Freeman, 13
White House Chef (Leighton), 22–23, 34
Whitman, Ann, 183
Who's Who, 77, 84, 90, 139, 163
Who Was Who, 163
Whole Earth Catalogue, 221
Wind Power for Your Home (Sullivan), 66–74
Winfrey, Ophra, 234
Winnick, R. H., 177–78
Witte, George, 87, 212
Woodson, Minnie, 229
World Almanac, 162
Word-of-mouth recommendations, 235–37
Writer's conferences, 106–7, 114
Writer's Digest Books, 20, 85, 227
Writer's Handbook, 113
Writer's Market, 20, 103, 113
Wyman, Jane, 191

Young, Gene, 12

Zebra Books, 27

279